ROL

G

TOTALLY
TRUE TALES
FROM THE TRACK

ROLLERGIRL

Melissa "Melicious" Joulwan

A TOUCHSTONE BOOK
Published by Simon & Schuster
NEW YORK   LONDON   TORONTO   SYDNEY

TOUCHSTONE
Rockefeller Center
1230 Avenue of the Americas
New York, NY 10020

This work is a memoir. It reflects the author's present recollections of her experiences over a period of years. Certain names have been changed. Dialogue and events have been re-created in part from memory and in some cases have been compressed to convey the substance of what was said or what occurred. The trading cards contained in the book depict fictitious personas and are not intended to portray actual facts or events.

For information regarding special discounts for bulk purchases, please contact Simon & Schuster Special Sales at 1-800-456-6798 or business@simonandschuster.com.

Designed by Joy O'Meara

Manufactured in the United States of America

10 9 8 7 6 5 4 3 2 1

Library of Congress Cataloging-in-Publication Data is available.

ISBN-13: 978-0-7432-9715-8
ISBN-10:   0-7432-9715-6

BY THE SKATERS, FOR THE SKATERS

To all the Rollergirls
with love and bruises

CONTENTS

Flat Track Derby is a dazzling carnival on wheels.

Hosted by sideshow barkers, it's a sport of speed-skating pinup girls and brutal body checks, played out against a backdrop of head-banging rock. The spectacle drives fans into a hormone-and-beer-induced frenzy.

Flat Track Derby is loosely based on the banked track Roller Derby that aired on late-night TV in the seventies. But we took the way the old game was played—both on the track and behind the scenes—and cut it up like a concert T-shirt.

We play on a Flat Track—an oval, outlined in lights, on a standard skating rink floor. No rail separates us from our fans, and no barrier keeps us from playing anytime, anywhere.

Forget the league owners and promoters of the past who traded skaters like collectible dolls. The new leagues are DIY—do-it-yourself—and skater-owned. We answer to ourselves, and skate or die by the credo "By the skaters, for the skaters." All the jobs required to manage our leagues—from athletic training to event production, finance to marketing—are done by the skaters. We work and skate for the fun and the glory, not a profit. In 2005, leagues across the U.S. formed the Women's Flat Track Derby Association (WFTDA) to govern our sport.

The game isn't the only thing we've reinvented. When we lace up our skates, we take on new names—like Rice Rocket, Misty Meaner, Raquel Welts, and Triptease—and alter egos. All the better to kick an opponent's ass and not feel guilty in the morning. Our personas are fictitious—we make ourselves into the girls of our dreams—but the confidence and fun of playing at being someone else on the track is 100 percent real.

There are thousands of Rollergirls across the country. In New York. Chicago. Huntsville. Detroit. Albuquerque. Seattle. Las Vegas. Denver. Raleigh. Kansas City. Dallas. Madison, and more. The Flat Track revolution started with my league, the Texas Rollergirls, in Austin in 2003. Just a year later, there were more than forty leagues up and rolling all across the country. In February 2006, the first National Flat Track Derby Championship was held in Tucson, Arizona; since then, the tally of grassroots leagues has grown to more than one hundred. Suddenly, we're all over TV and magazines and newspapers.

But behind the hype and the hysteria, the shiners and the smeared lipstick, the fishnets and the fury, are the girls. Beautiful, athletic, strong, smart, relentless Rollergirls. I'm going to introduce you to them, and tell you how it all started, deep in the heart of Texas.

STARTING WHISTLE

01

Hellions on Wheels

Jo's Coffee on Congress Avenue in south Austin is the kind of place where you instantly feel comfortable, even if you're a new transplant to Texas, like I was in 2001. The latte drinkers are good-looking in their own I-know-who-I-am way. The staff is bright and friendly and prone to cracking wise. The soundtrack is retro-hipster: the Cure, Elvis Costello, Hank Williams, Frank Sinatra.

I'd moved to town with the love of my life, Dave, nine months before, and we were still living in an anonymous, dreamlike state. We could never quite remember which freeway exit led to the Target, but somehow we always found it. Occasionally, we'd run across a celebrity at Jo's—ZZ Top guitarist Billy Gibbons or my 1986 heart-throb, singer-songwriter Charlie Sexton. We had no family in Texas, and our "friends" were a variety of waiters, waitresses, bartenders, and other drinkers, diners, and musicians that we ran into again and again in our attempts to get out of the house and "meet some people."

I was in love with Austin—the live music, the comfort food, the feeling that I was in one of those music videos from the eighties where tromping down a dusty road in vintage cowboy boots seemed like the best idea ever. But I was also growing weary of knowing only the people who served things to me and required a tip. Although Austin was my first choice for a new home, I was blue.

Dave and I had moved to Austin so we could have a do-over on our lives. We'd both been following what I think of as the "grown-up path." We had director-level jobs at a corporate Web development agency—and the fat salaries that went along with the positions. It was what I'd always thought I wanted: the title "creative director" on my business cards and an assistant who brought me salads during lunch meetings because my schedule was so hectic I couldn't possibly take a break. It was the go-go life that I had dreamed of in college. And I hated it.

There were minor annoyances, like pitch meetings with straightlaced white guys (and their tight little ponytails and striped ties). Or the fact that the executives had gotten rich from our IPO while the rest of us were left with big tax bills for the "privilege" of our stock options. Or the fact that the phrase "maximize billable hours" was meant to be my mantra.

The last straw came during a vacation. I was visiting my family in Pennsylvania, baking cookies with my four-year-old niece Pepper. We were up to our elbows in chocolate-chip cookie dough when the phone rang. It was my boss; she needed to discuss a second round of layoffs with me: "I know you're on vacation, but I thought you'd want to be involved in the decision making, since it affects one-third of your staff."

I put my hand over the mouthpiece of the phone and told Pepper to leave the kitchen. As I watched her toddle away, I realized I had just become the kind of person who sends her cookie-making niece out of the room to take a call about layoffs during a vacation.

So I quit.

Not too long after I submitted my resignation letter, I went to

Temple Tattoo—to Mr. Scott Silvia, the best old-school tattoo artist in the land—and I had my left forearm permanently inked as a reminder to never "take a meeting" again. My tattoo is a black panther surrounded by yellow, pink, and red roses. She wears a crown, and she's ferocious and beautiful and sleek and powerful—all the things I wanted to be in my postcorporate life.

Austin seemed like a great place for Dave and me to reinvent ourselves. I once read a passage in a tour book that theorized that the reason Austin has such great nightlife is because during the day, it's too damn hot to move around. In San Francisco, even summers are gray and chilly most of the time—black turtlenecks and big black boots were my standard uniform before we relocated. But I was now in the land of flip-flops, tank tops, shorts, and the mad dash from one air-conditioned building to another.

The draw of a caffeine buzz trumps the climate at Jo's. Dave and I were parked on stools at the counter—sweating—watching the traffic slide by and idly talking about what to do with our day.

The back wall of Jo's is the DIY equivalent of a town crier: posters, handbills, flyers, postcards, and hand-drawn notes are tacked, stapled, and taped floor-to-ceiling. Notices about rock shows, yard sales, lost puppies, a sofa for sale, belly dancing classes, political speeches, houses for rent, and volunteer gigs overlapped, creating a paper patchwork quilt, a snapshot of the crazy-good stuff Austin has to offer. I regularly used Jo's wall as a to-do list: "Tuesday night, we should go to the Alamo Drafthouse . . . Jesse Dayton's playing at the Continental Club on Friday!"

In the upper-right-hand corner of the wall on that particular Sunday was a poster for "All-Girl's Roller Derby." The punk-rock girl in the illustration wore old-fashioned roller skates, knee pads over fishnet stockings, and a helmet. There was a skull and crossbones on her ripped tank top, a "fuck you" expression on her face. "With live music from the Flametrick Subs. Playland Skate Center. Tickets $5."

Roller skating and punk-rock chicks . . . irresistible! We decided to check it out, and I started to obsess about what to wear.

When Dave and I pulled into the parking lot of Playland Skate Center to watch our first-ever Roller Derby bout, the scene was already jumping off. Cars were parked bumper-to-bumper on the residential streets around the rink, filling every legal spot between the perfectly landscaped driveways. People streamed toward the building in packs, like the Jets and the Sharks headed to a showdown.

The boys wore the standard punk-a-billy uniform: cuffed jeans or Dickies work pants with pristine wife beaters, black boots, chains on their wallets, and chips on their shoulders. Tattoos snaked up their arms and the sides of their necks; their hair glistened in the sun, pomade melting to an extra-shiny lacquer in the Texas heat. And the ladies! Short skirts or fit-like-skin capri pants, fishnet stockings, ruby red lips, and jet black eyeliner that flicked up—just so—at the outer corners of their eyes. They vamped and flirted and giggled and chatted as they made their way across the shimmering asphalt to the front door, vintage handbags dangling off their wrists.

Playland is in north Austin, a neighborhood so different from mine in south Austin's 78704, it could be another city entirely. We southies decorate our yards with shrines to the Virgin of Guadalupe and pink flamingos; every corner has a fly-by-night taco stand. Up north, it's a kitsch-free zone of SUV dealers and sprawling ranch-style houses with arrow-straight rows of daffodils. Dropped right in the middle of the suburban sprawl, like Oz landing in Dorothy's backyard, is Playland.

The skating floor is huge: 27,500 square feet, or about half a football field. The acrylic surface is a putrid shade of lavender, scraped and dented in some spots to reveal a pale yellow underfloor. Suspended over the rink are multicolored lights and a six-foot roller skate covered in disco-ball mirrors. Just inside the entry door, racks display rows of rental skates: dun-colored with orange wheels and dark brown laces.

The hipster crowd sat on the floor, or stood in clusters around the track and on the carpet-covered benches for a better view. Electric fans the size of airplane jet exhausts fought a valiant crusade against the heat being generated by the thousand bodies packed into the rink. A thick layer of cigarette smoke hovered in the air, and music thudded in the cavernous space. In the center of the floor, an oval track was outlined in white Christmas lights. On that track, the reason we were all there. The main event. The most amazing thing we'd ever seen: Rollergirls.

The Flat Track at Playland Skate Center

At the time, beyond recognizing that they were skating very fast, it was impossible to make sense of what they were doing. But I didn't care. They seemed taller than regular girls. Certainly tougher. And so much sexier. More fit than the honey-blond-and-manicured girls on the elliptical trainer at the gym. I was riveted.

The only Roller Derby I'd seen prior to that night at Playland was on a *Charlie's Angels* episode. The great mystery of the show was not so much the insurance scam the Angels investigated, but how Farrah Fawcett fit her helmet over her gigantic blond waves. But these women blew Farrah away! They were a blur skating around that oval track. They bashed into each other. They tripped themselves, then jumped up to race back into the fray. They slid on their knees. They crashed together, tumbling to the floor in a tangle of arms and legs and flailing skates. They skidded and glided and leapt and twisted. They were graceful and awkward and altogether amazing.

"I had a horrible case of the Sunday blues, just moping around the house. After watching me all day, my beau Blake said he was taking me out . . . to the Roller Derby. 'Nothing like girls in short skirts and torn fishnets knocking the shit out of each other to make you feel better,' he said. I thought to myself, Yeah . . . that'll make *you* feel better. But I went. I was mesmerized. I turned to Blake and said 'I *must* do this.' And he asked, 'Do you skate?' I answered, 'I do now!'"

—APOCALIPPZ, HELL MARYS/TEXAS ROLLERGIRLS

The group of girls putting on the show was known as Bad Girl Good Woman Productions, and the bout that I saw that night in August 2002 was their first time performing for the public. They'd been at it for a year or so, learning to skate and holding fund-raisers to get their four teams up and rolling.

The Rhinestone Cowgirls wore red Western shirts—with spangles, fringes, rhinestones, and rivets—and Daisy Duke shorts or up-to-there miniskirts. With fishnets on their legs and their boobies strapped into bustiers and push-up bras, they were what Lori Petty would have been if *Tank Girl* had been set in a turn-of-the-century Western. That night, they played the Putas del Fuego. Literally translated, their name means "whores of fire," and they dressed the part in black skirts painted with red and gold glitter flames. Even to my untrained eye, the Putas were definitely the Bad girls among the naughty girls. There was something particularly menacing and feral about the way they taunted the other players and the audience.

The team called the Holy Rollers got the biggest reaction from the crowd. They were a male fantasy come to life on wheels: parochial school girls in plaid miniskirts that would never have passed muster at my parents' Catholic school. But the Holy Rollers didn't look shameful. They were brazen in skimpy tank tops, knee socks, the de rigueur skirts, and mock-pious cross pendants and rosary beads. They might have been my favorite team, were it not for the Hellcats and their logo: a black panther wreathed in roses, just like my tattoo.

AC/DC's "Highway to Hell" reverberated off the walls and the house lights dimmed. Red, yellow, blue, and white lights flashed over the track and, one by one, the Holy Rollers skated onto the rink as the announcer called their names. Strawberry. Helen Fury. Holli Graffic. Mean Streak. Miss Conduct. The crowd whooped and stomped and generally lost its mind in a frenzy of excitement.

The faux Catholic school girls looked unbeatable. They reminded me of some of the girls who went to my high school—the girls with feathered hair and parents who worked nights. They smoked at the bus stop, talked during assembly, organized pencil drops in class, and regularly threatened to beat me up in the locker room. The Holy Rollers appeared to be that kind of tough crowd. But then the Hellcats took the floor, led by Pris.

Pris is probably only a little taller than average height, but she looked like a pink-and-black-clad amazon. Her dark hair was cut in a chin-length bob, tucked behind her ears under her black helmet. Her face was striped with war paint—a thick black horizontal band across her eyes—and she skated like a banshee. She was the Hellcats' primary jammer, which I learned later meant that she was a sprinter and the player on the team responsible for scoring points.

But watching the first time, I didn't know that. All I knew was that she looked otherworldly. Like a superhero. She seemed to will herself through the pack of girls, her legs bent at steep angles. She deflected body checks and went down on one knee, then popped back up before anyone could register that she was down. She balanced on one skate around the corners, turned and skated backward to taunt the other team, pumped up the audience by pointing and waving at them, and cheered for herself like she, too, was overcome by her performance.

★□★

Celesta Danger/celestadanger.com

Pris #86
HOTROD HONEYS/TEXAS ROLLERGIRLS
POSITIONS: *Jammer, Blocker, Pivot, Replicant*
LIKES: *Loud guitars; Marshall stacks; fastbacks;* Blade Runner; *comic books; thunderstorms and neon lights*
DISLIKES: *Hell Marys; Honky Tonk Heartbreakers; Hustlers*

Pris's world was turned upside down when she crashed her Mercury Cougar and was pulled from the wreckage by Tomcat. Pris escaped with only a few burns, but the loss of her Cougar forced her to find a new set of wheels. Broke and desperate for transportation, she strapped on a pair of black speed skates. They not only got her around town, she realized she had otherworldly agility, extraordinary stamina, and superhuman strength on the track. The replicant Rollergirl was born!

PRIS FACTOID: *Her paternal grandmother's great-aunts were Czech trapeze artists known as the Flying Silhouns.*

□★

At halftime, the score was so close, it was still anybody's game: Holy Rollers 18 to the Hellcats 17, but the audience didn't seem to give a damn about the score. It was about the girls.

Across the rink, the Flametrick Subs set had started. They're a psychobilly band, which means they amp up the raw ingredients of hillbilly music—lyrics about drinkin' and gamblin' and women, sung with a twang—with an extra dose of rock 'n' roll danger. In front of the band, a combination dance floor–mosh pit was taking shape, with the fancy rockabilly girls in high heels swinging around the circle with their partners. But because it's Austin, there were also gray-haired hippies in tie-dyed shirts doing the happy-twirly dance, and a cloud of little girls, maybe five or six years old, skipping around everyone else's feet.

At the other end of the rink, the beer line snaked across the floor, intersecting the scenesters waiting for nachos, and the chattering, smoking queue outside the ladies' room. Everywhere I looked, I saw beaming faces. Dour, "I'm too cool to let you know I'm having a good time" expressions were nowhere to be found. Roller Derby was pure, unadulterated fun—and no one was afraid to show it.

During halftime I picked up a program that helped me understand what the devil was happening on the rink. Despite the on-track skirmishes and girls flying—ass-over-teacups—into the crowd, the game of Flat Track Derby is a real sport, with rules and penalties for breaking them. When it's played well, it brings together strategy, skill, teamwork, determination, and psychological warfare.

There are three positions: jammer (aka, the speed), blocker (aka, the brawn), and pivot (aka, the brain).

Each team gets one jammer on the track at a time. She starts at the back of the pack and wears a star on her helmet. Her mission is to haul ass and get through the pack—by being sneaky, fast, brazen, daring, and slippery.

Then there are the blockers—each team gets three on the track at a time. They play defense and offense, bullying the other team's blockers, making holes for their jammers to skate through, and trying to stop the other team's jammer by *almost* any means necessary.

The pivots—one from each team—wear a stripe on their helmets and skate at the front of the pack. They control the pack's speed and act as the last line of defense in demolishing the other team's jammer.

The basics of a Flat Track Derby game are fairly simple: during a period of play called a "jam," one jammer from each team sprints through the pack of eight skaters, while the opposing players try to stop her. The pack starts with pivots in front, blockers in the middle, and jammers at the back. When the pack is in formation, the ref blows the whistle and all the skaters except the jammers start rolling. Then the ref blows two short whistle-blasts to signal the jammers to take off. The first jammer to fight her way through the pack becomes lead jammer.

The first time through the pack, if the jammers go out of bounds, there is no lead jammer and the jam will continue for the full

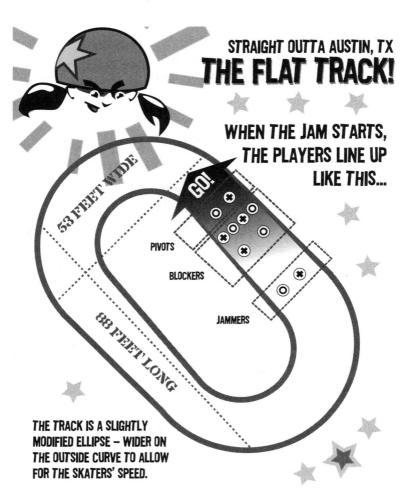

STRAIGHT OUTTA AUSTIN, TX
THE FLAT TRACK!

WHEN THE JAM STARTS,
THE PLAYERS LINE UP
LIKE THIS...

53 FEET WIDE

88 FEET LONG

GO!

PIVOTS

BLOCKERS

JAMMERS

THE TRACK IS A SLIGHTLY MODIFIED ELLIPSE – WIDER ON THE OUTSIDE CURVE TO ALLOW FOR THE SKATERS' SPEED.

two minutes. The jammer doesn't earn points if one or both of her skates is out of bounds while she's passing other skaters.

For the next two minutes—or until the lead jammer calls off the jam—mayhem ensues. Jammers run on their toe stoppers, sprint, duck, bob, and weave to pass the opposing team and earn points. The blockers and pivots do everything they can to put the brakes (and breaks) on her. When tempers flare, the game can take on the blood lust of combat. Like ice hockey, there are times when a fight is a smart strategic move, a weapon in a skater's handbag of tricks to prevent the other team from scoring.

The "game" itself consists of two skating periods. Each period is thirty minutes of adrenaline-fueled fury, and there's a halftime (beer-time, music-time, primp-time) between periods. At our Texas Roller-girls' home games, we usually have doubleheaders.

At all times, the pivots are required to stay within twenty feet of the front of the pack—and the blockers must stay within twenty feet of the back of the pack. That means there's no chasing down the jam-mer until you finally catch her, and no hanging out behind the pack to clobber the jammer when she's defenseless.

Like the mythical natural-looking tan-in-a-can, tie games in Roller Derby do not exist. If the score is tied at the end of the second period, the game will roll into the high drama of Sudden Death—a bat-tle for a final two-minute jam. The team with the most points at the end of the overtime jam is the bout winner.

If Rollergirls are the queens of the rink, the referees are the gods. In lots of leagues, the refs are also league coaches—friends of the family, husbands, fans—so the refs have to work extra hard to be impar-tial. And their word is law; zebra shirts have the final say in all decisions. Woe to the Rollergirl who dares mess with a ref, even if it is her boyfriend: touching, pushing, harassing, and trying to sweet talk a ref in any way may be grounds for getting booted right out of the game.

Just as I was getting a grasp of the mechanics of the sport, the

Rhinestone Cowgirls and Putas del Fuego skated out to AC/DC's "Hell's Bells" for the second half of the bout. The halftime break hadn't improved their behavior. Unlike traditional sports where breaking the rules means time in the penalty box, the penalties at that first Roller Derby bout were strictly for laughs. Girls were sentenced to spinning a hula hoop for two minutes or to a trip down "Spank Alley," a row of eager audience members armed with paddles to swat the derrière of the offending skater as she rolled past.

Trying to recall the specifics of those first games is like trying too hard to grab the shreds of a dream before they dissipate in the morning light. In my memory, it's a blur of fishnets, cleavage, catfights, warrior girls, chain-smoking tough guys, crushed beer cans, piercing whistle blows, and a continuously rocking soundtrack. Our conversations *during* the game went something like this:

"Did you see *that*?"

"Holy shit! Oh my God!"

"Ow! Holy crap!"

"Get her! Kill her! Stop her! Get her . . . yeah! Fuck, yeah! Holy shit!"

I was entranced, and entertaining a life-changing thought: I wanted to be a Rollergirl. With each lap the girls skated around the track, I became more convinced that I *must* become a Rollergirl. The move to Austin, my panther tattoo . . . they were just the first steps to what was beginning to look like my destiny: Roller Derby.

Sometime during the second half we ran into a musician friend, Clay. He's "a guy who knows a guy." You need some muscle to back you up, or a good mechanic, or a locksmith, or the best way to smoke a rack of baby-back ribs, Clay may not be your man—but he knows who is. So I shouldn't have been surprised when, right in the middle of me gushing about Pris and how I wanted to be a Rollergirl, he said he knew her.

"You wanna meet her? Come on, I'll introduce you," he said.

"Right now?" I said in the voice that I usually squeak out when faced with meeting one of my heroes. (I made the same ridiculous sound when I met John Taylor from Duran Duran and Brian Setzer from Stray Cats.)

Clay took my hand and pulled me through the crowd to where Pris stood among the mortals. She was even more incredible up close: close to six feet tall in her skates, sweaty, and muscular. She looked like a hired assassin when she skated, but off the track, her smile was friendly and so wide, it threatened to slice her face in half, just below the intimidating black stripe painted across her eyes.

Clay introduced me to Pris, and I had an out-of-body, babbling experience. Clay acted as translator, explaining that I wanted to try out to be a skater. Then something incredible happened. Pris wrote her home phone number with a Sharpie on the corner of my program, looked down at me, and said, "Cool! We need girls who can skate. We have practice tomorrow night. Call me."

The Hellcats ultimately beat the Holy Rollers, 39 to 31, but I was distracted by the thought that I might be going to a Roller Derby practice the next day. I was *thisclose* to becoming the new me, a tougher-than-waterproof-black-mascara roller babe.

Dave and I rode the tide of exhilarated fans that swarmed out into the parking lot. The greasers revved their engines, trying to burn off the extra testosterone that had been riled up during the games, and the girls—in twos and threes—alternately mused aloud about maybe trying out for Roller Derby themselves, or talked smack about what we'd just seen.

I was spinning, alternating between two strongly held convictions: Of course I would call Pris the next day and go to practice.

There was absolutely no way that I would call Pris the next day and go to practice.

About halfway home, I turned to Dave: "Aw, shit. I don't have roller skates."

CHAPTER

CHAPTER

02

Roller Rookie

I adore people who are brave enough to make asses of themselves for my amusement. Will Ferrell's cheerleader on *Saturday Night Live;* the pretty girl who'll imitate Ronnie James Dio in front of a couple hundred people at karaoke. My helmet is off to the people who eagerly raise their hands when performers ask for a volunteer from the audience or ask the "stupid questions" at a seminar.

I'm not one of those people.

I'm a fan of dress rehearsals. I make notes to prep before important phone calls, and like some crazed homemaker from the fifties, I label serving dishes with Post-it notes before parties to make sure I have a place to put the Nacho Cheese Doritos and the Sour Cream & Onion Lays. So on the Monday morning after the Roller Derby bout, I went on the hunt for roller skates and a place to practice before I went to Playland for the real practice with the Roller Derby queens.

It should come as no surprise that on the tail end of the inline skating boom—and long before the Roller Derby revival and the movie *Roll Bounce*—there weren't a lot of options for old-school skates (called "quads" because each skate has four wheels) in sporting goods stores. In fact, on my journey to all of the Academy Sports & Outdoor stores in the greater Austin metropolitan area, I found just one style of quad skates. They were blindingly white ankle boots ("constructed of 100% man-made materials") with white laces, electric blue wheels, and white stoppers. My high school colors. Definitely not cool. The $29.95 price tag didn't inspire confidence in their Roller Derby readiness, either, but I was desperate to see if skating was like riding a bike ("It comes right back!"), so I took them home, along with a black skateboarding helmet and a set of Rollerblade pads.

"During my eighth birthday party I fell flat on my ass and was so traumatized that until last year, I hadn't skated since. Now here I am, twenty years later, going as fast as possible and knocking down bitches."

—MALICYN WONDERLAND, THE SLAUGHTERERS/DALLAS DERBY DEVILS

A few hours later, I was skating in circles at Skateworld, another rink in north Austin. Each lap around the floor took me a year back in time, until I was fourteen again. Is there some roller rink owners' regulatory board that dictates that Dazz Band be played a requisite number of times per day and that all rinks must smell like stale popcorn and bubblegum-scented disinfectant? I bopped to the beat of "Funky Town" and "Let It Whip," doing the wacka-wacka with my feet, crossing my ankles and scissoring them apart. I almost expected to see my old skating crush Vince Morgan and his roller posse showing off in the center of the rink.

When I was a kid, I was the poster child for skating-rink nerds. In 1981, when I was in seventh grade, my friends and I started skating at Willow Lake. The floor was the original hardwood from the fifties—warped in some places, not-so-shiny in others—and the sound system was tinny, like a bad MP3 funneled through an old tape recorder. But it was neato, because we got to hang out with the high school kids: tough girls with wide-toothed combs in the back pockets of their Sergio Valenti jeans, and couples who skated to the slow songs with their hands in each other's back pockets before making out in the shadowy corners.

When I was in eighth grade, the Roller Roost opened in Pottsville, and it was a Big Deal. It had a state-of-the-art pale yellow acrylic floor—smoother and slicker than the old-fashioned wooden floor at Willow Lake. Instead of us skating in the afternoon sunlight that filtered through dirty old windows, we circled the warehouse rink under colored lights and strobes that pulsed to the beat of the music. Roller Roost had a snack bar where the older kids threw popcorn at each other and smoked cigarettes, and an arcade section with Defender, Asteroids, and pinball machines. In the middle of the action, a DJ booth. It was Xanadu come to life.

But it wasn't just the skating that drew me there. It was Vince Morgan.

He was a senior at my high school when I was a freshman, the heart-throb of four school districts. Every girl I knew—and every girl I didn't know—had a crush on Vince Morgan. They made prank calls to his house on school nights and hung up when he answered. They slipped notes for him to his sister Wendy to deliver on the school bus.

He was tall, blond, cocky, and

Vincent Morgan

unattainable. In faded Levi's and a pressed white cotton shirt, Vince was our Marlon Brando. He was everything a preteen girl could want. Dangerous: he went to Vo-Tech school instead of college prep. A rock star: he was arguably the best skater at the Roller Roost, which, at the time, made him a Schuylkill County celebrity. He didn't have a car, but he did have friends who drove, so he held out the promise that, if the stars aligned appropriately, he might whisk you away for the perfect kiss at the hilltop pagoda in Reading.

He was mellow cool personified—street-smart and clever enough to hold up his end of a flirty conversation, but no teacher's pet. He held court in the cafeteria, making the lunch ladies blush on his way through the line. He loitered in the high school lobby. He never rushed, languidly getting wherever he was going in his own good time. His responses to the gym coaches, who seemed to always be riding his ass about something, were laconic, if he answered at all.

He was everything I wasn't, and I was smitten.

He worked as a dishwasher at my dad's restaurant, and I prayed I'd be scheduled for his shift, while I just as desperately hoped I wouldn't. The idea of talking to him was just too wonderful and too terrifying. But fate intervened in the form of my parents wanting me to have the character-building experience of a weekend job, and I landed the plum Sunday morning dishwashing shift with Mr. Vince Morgan.

In my imagination, we shared intimate, truth-baring conversations. In reality, our interactions probably didn't rise above, "Man! It's sure busy today" and "Can you hand me that towel?" But I loved it anyway. I was momentarily elevated to a level of social status I would never have enjoyed on my own when, at the Roller Roost on a Friday night, Vince said hi to me in front of a gaggle of the popular girls.

Never mind that he and I never shared a couples' skate. Or that when the announcers called for triple whips, I was never the one to hold Vince's hand, but took the end spot with some sweet young thing between me and the Prince. He was my imaginary boyfriend, my partner in pretend kisses and romantic interludes under the disco ball to the sounds of Journey's "Open Arms."

I had spent so much time at the Roller Roost mooning over Vince, I accidentally got pretty good at skating. Now, as I lapped the Skateworld rink, it was all coming back to me. I remembered how to cross my legs on the corners to pick up speed. I even did a few laps backward. I was wobbly, and the thought of crashing was terrifying. As adults we just don't fall very often; we're out of practice. But I felt as ready as I could be for my first Roller Derby practice.

> "I was what they called a 'rink rat' at the Bellevue Skate King (which is funny, 'cause that's where we practice now). In other words, I went there mostly to make out with boys."
>
> —HURRICANE LILLY, THROTTLE ROCKETS/RAT CITY ROLLERGIRLS

It sounds like a silly thing to be hung up on, but the white skates I'd bought were a problem. I have an aversion to white shoes. I retired my last pair of white pumps in 1986, right after my graduation party at which I was unceremoniously dumped by my boyfriend ("Sorry. I just don't want to go out with you anymore."). I usually replace the white laces in my Converses with colored ones. I refuse to wear white sneakers, even though I work out at home and no one else sees them. My new skates were so white they glowed; so bright, they made my eyes twitch. My confidence about going to practice was telescoped directly into those skates. I told Dave I couldn't go.

"I can't wear those skates. And if I don't have skates, I can't go. So I'm staying home."

He let me sulk for a while. Then he grabbed a black Sharpie, laid the ridiculous skates on the kitchen table, and carefully drew an anarchy symbol on each side of the boot—giving me instant punk-rock cred, and eliminating my excuse for bailing on practice.

We didn't talk about it, but he knew, and I knew: I was scared to go. And I was terrified not to go. Because then I'd have to live with the knowledge I'd missed an opportunity to be like Pris and the other Playland gladiators.

Opening the door to walk into the rink that night, my stomach did the Twist and my palms were slick. My feet propelled me forward, but I felt like the rest of me was flying backward through a tunnel.

The energy inside Playland was dramatically different than the night before. Gone were the adoring crowds, the dramatic lighting, the booming music, the palpable excitement. The smell of smoke lingered, but it reeked of the party being over. Around the lobby area, about a dozen skaters pulled on knee and elbow pads, laced on their skates, halfheartedly stretched. Without their costumes and larger-than-life personas they seemed both more familiar and more intimidating. Because they seemed just like the Mean girls from junior high.

I had the wrong kind of notoriety when I was a teenager. My straight-A report card—and the strict manners my parents drilled into my brother and me—meant I was a favorite of the teachers. Our chorus director, in particular, adored me. With my long blond hair, pastel-colored Fair Isle sweaters, and trusting nature, I was a northeastern Pennsylvania Sandra Dee. It made me an easy target. I never remembered to be cautious when the Mean girls took an unusual interest in me. Sometimes, I even handed them the weapons they needed to skewer me.

As I watched the girls at Playland put on their skates, I realized my Marshmallow Creme skates were worse than I thought. The other girls wore black, low-cut speed skates—the equivalent of a '54 Chevrolet that's painted primer black, chopped, and lowered. I'd just pulled up to the light in my 1996 Buick Skylark rental, singing with Neil Diamond on the radio.

I looked for Pris—the only skater I sort of knew—but didn't find her. Aside from a "Put on your stuff and warm up!" shouted across the lobby, no one had spoken to me yet, so I imitated everyone else. Geared up, I joined the girls skating in lazy circles around the rink. We crisscrossed our feet without lifting them from the floor—right over left, left over right. We took the corners on one foot, holding out the opposite leg for balance. We squatted and sprinted and then everyone convened in the center of the floor for stretching.

"Hey! I like your skates."

I turned to the girl next to me. She looked nice enough, but I'd been fooled before.

"I'm The Wrench," she said. "Your skates are cute."

"Thanks. My boyfriend Dave made 'em for me."

I braced for the mocking. "They look cool. Too bad we can't do something like that with these," she said, pointing at the red and white stripes on the sides of her skate boots.

We watched a tough-looking skater roll into the middle of our stretching circle. "Get up, bitches," she said. "We're gonna see what you can do."

It was Cherry Chainsaw. Like many of the people I would meet in my early derby days, details on her were sketchy. People were reluctant to talk about her too much and when they did, they were so vehement, so heated in their opinions, I was skeptical of their veracity. So she remains something of a mystery. Here's what I can tell you: she was an art skater. That means she did spins and jumps and other fancy moves while wearing spangled dresses and those thick, fake-flesh-colored pantyhose that are worn over their skates.

Cherry had the weathered crinkle of a newspaper left in the driveway too long. Given the way she cultivated her crazier-than-you vibe—I'm pretty sure she thought "crazy bitch" was a compliment—I don't think she would mind my saying she had the air of the dotty old lady down the street who keeps a sawed-off shotgun behind the rocking chair on her front porch.

She scared the crap out of me. But all those leaps and twirls had made Cherry a strong skater, and when she wasn't cackling with mirthless laughter, she was generous about sharing what she knew. We just had to wade through the four-letter words and batty tangents to get to the good stuff.

I was trying my best to skate fast, pushing hard with my feet, pretending to be confident.

"Are you a chicken? You're scratching like a chicken!" she yelled at me, making a snickering noise that, ironically enough, sounded a lot like a Rhode Island Red. That night I learned that the proper way to skate is not to kick your feet back—like a chicken—but to push out with each foot directly to the side.

I was taught a lot of lessons that evening. The best news was that to be placed on a team, all I had to do was show up. If I was tough enough (or foolish enough) to take the hits and the practice schedule, I'd eventually be assigned to one of the four teams.

It turns out that worrying about falling and trying to prevent a fall are far more torturous than actually taking the spill. But there are correct and incorrect ways to fall. Right or wrong method, I woke up the next morning with bruises on my knees, elbows, shoulders, thighs, forearms, butt cheeks, and the palms of my hands.

While falling came naturally, I found that a better way to stop while rolling was also the one that looked the best. The fancy stop begins with a half-spin, then progresses to an impersonation of "Billie Jean"-era Michael Jackson: a pop onto both tiptoes, toe stoppers pressed to the floor. Wrist guards, required; one glove, optional.

While I basked in the glow of learning the turnaround stop, Cherry Chainsaw announced that we were going to work on jumping; I thought for sure that I'd heard her wrong. But as I discovered that first night, despite what I thought I knew about gravity and my relationship to it, I *could* jump while wearing eight wheels on my feet. We also did some fighting drills; the "heave-ho" (faking an elbow to the other girl's ribs) and the "football tackle" were my two favorites.

The numero uno role of Roller Derby that I learned that night: never, ever skate without a mouthguard.

Like the hitchhiker-with-a-hook-for-a-hand story, Roller Derby has its own cautionary rite-of-passage tales, and I was told the mother of all of them that night. When the Roller Derby girls began practicing together, they didn't wear safety gear. Their knobby knees and elbows, their slender wrists, their tender noggins were left unprotected. One night while scrimmaging, someone's leg got tangled up in someone else's skate or elbow or some such—not an unusual occurrence—and one of the girls careened face-first to the floor. When she sat up, she was missing her front tooth.

The kicker of the story? When another girl asked if she was going to stick with Roller Derby, she smiled a bloody, toothless smile, and said, "Fuck, yeah."

A few days after my first practice, I bought a pair of black Pacer RTX 429 Pro Sunlite speed skates recommended to me by The Wrench, and as the weeks passed, I dutifully attended practices at Playland. Soon, I stopped scratching like a chicken. I could reliably jump a few inches off the floor—just enough to clear a leg or arm. I could take a direct hit without a) yelping in fear and b) crashing to the floor. And I learned to give as good as I was getting.

03

Pack Mentality

It quickly became clear that there were definitely two camps within the league: the Nice girls and the Mean girls. The Nice girls were smart, friendly, accomplished. They knew how to have a good time, but they also had functioning telephones, permanent residences, jobs with paychecks at regular intervals. They were adults, but not so grown-up they'd forgotten how to have a good time.

The Wrench, whom I'd met at my first practice, was a Nice girl personified. At 5' 10", she was a commanding physical presence on the track, but she was playful. Sometimes it was like everyone but her had forgotten that Roller Derby was a game. So she reminded us by laughing maniacally with every block or pulling a girl's shirt up over her head—a much-needed injection of goofiness when things got too intense.

She and I bonded over triathlon war stories; The Wrench had started a successful triathlon training camp for cancer survivors. She became my preferred partner for fighting drills. We'd tackle each other at full speed, then roll on the floor, giggling too hard to bother with fake punches. As far as I could tell, she'd always been one of the cool kids—an authentic punk rocker who followed her gut instead of trends—but she accepted my nerd credentials without bias. The Wrench was one of the people who made the bruises of Roller Derby—both to my ego and to my body—worthwhile.

★□

Celesta Danger/celestadanger.com

The Wrench #67
HELL MARYS/TEXAS ROLLERGIRLS
POSITIONS: *Blocker, Pivot (retired)*
CARS RESTORED: *8* ⚙ **CARS DESTROYED:** *257* ⚙ **CARS "BORROWED":** *Unconfirmed*

The Wrench was born deep in southern Illinois, the product of her devout Catholic mother's love for a greasy pit crew captain from the wrong side of town. She was an angelic child, happy to read her daily catechism and send novenas to the Blessed Holy Mother, but chicken pox kept her out of a coveted seat in Home Ec class, and she landed instead in the much-maligned Auto Mechanics Shop. Seven years later, The Wrench wrapped rosary beads around the rearview mirror of a stolen Hemi 'Cuda and burned rubber on her way out of town to the Street Machine Nationals in Oklahoma. By the time she'd pried her foot off the accelerator, she was in the parking lot of the Horseshoe Lounge in Austin, Texas, where she made fast friends with roller queen Holli Graffic. Too many Lone Star tallboys later, the bleary pair sat in the steaming wreckage of The Wrench's Barracuda after a booze-fueled joyride round the Longhorn Speedway. "Don't worry," Holli told the sobbing young Wrench, "I'll get you a whole new set of wheels!"

RIVALS: *Eight Track & Melicious, Hotrod Honeys/Texas Rollergirls; Bettie Rage, Honky Tonk Heartbreakers/Texas Rollergirls*

□★

But the Mean girls . . . I'd never hung out with girls like them before. One night at practice, they taught us the pack drill.

The idea was that one skater would act as the jammer while the rest of us—twenty-five or thirty other skaters—formed a pack. Keep in mind that during a game, there are only ten players on the track—and half of them are trying to *help* their jammer. In the pack drill, the number of blockers was tripled, and the jammer was left to defend herself.

"Send the new girls through," a Mean girl named La Coneja said with her characteristic cackle.

Among the Mean girls, La Coneja, one of the Putas, was the worst of the lot. She had the physique of a day laborer: sinewy, tanned arms and legs, with a slight hint of a beer belly. Her face looked like she'd run into the business side of a cast-iron skillet. Everything about her was hard; the equivalent of the hooker that no one makes a movie about—the one *without* the heart of gold.

"No Roller Derby track could be worse than a mosh pit."

—SUZY HOTROD, QUEENS OF PAIN/GOTHAM GIRLS ROLLER DERBY

I smiled a lot at practices. Despite how difficult it was, I loved skating and feeling myself getting stronger—and I think my interminable cheerfulness was an offense to La Coneja. The more I avoided her, the more she tried to interact with me. My taste in music, workout wear, socks, and hairstyles were fair game. She mocked the stickers I put on my skate case, mimicked my skating posture, ridiculed the way I blocked.

When I complained that it was dangerous to sprint with metal chairs stacked at the edge of the track, she imitated me in a childish voice and called me a baby. When I suggested the coaches call penalties during the pack drill, she elbowed me in the ribs and blindsided me with a body block.

The pack drill became my personal nightmare. It seemed more like an opportunity to beat up on unpopular or slow girls than a skill-enhancing activity. It was the adult version of playground dodge ball, the bullies egged on by La Coneja's assertion that newbies should go first. Like a pack of hyenas coordinating an attack on a wounded zebra, the Mean girls could smell fear and as Mean girls do, they worked together:

"She's coming up on your inside . . . take her out! Stop her!"

"She's cutting. . . . Outside! Outside!"

As I struggled to get through the writhing pack, every blocker tried to nail me with full force. But hitting me wasn't only their goal when I was the *jammer;* they amused themselves by using me for target practice when I was blocking with them, too. For my first two months of Roller Derby, my arms and shoulders were covered in quarter-sized bruises, marks left by other skaters' bony shoulders, their elbow pads, their wrist guards, and, occasionally, their helmets.

Number two on my list of Mean girls was Iron Maiden. The captain of my dream team Hellcats, she was a follower who fancied herself a leader simply because she was bossy. She always traveled in a pack with her friends Hot Lips Dolly and Miss Information; the three of them seemed as likely to attack each other as someone outside their cabal.

My dislike for Iron Maiden was so powerful, the sight of her made my mouth taste like a filthy penny. She expertly played the role of the dirty skater. She'd purposely fall, then reach out with both hands in an attempt to grab the wheels of approaching skaters. Like a gangbanger, Iron Maiden had made her "bones" at the league's first public bout. Sidelined by an injury, she was unable to play in the game, but during a scuffle on the track, she'd run into the fray—in her shoes—and soundly clocked an opposing player with her fist.

She expressed opinions like undisputed facts, and she often seemed to be in the ladies' room when it was her turn to get the next round of drinks. I found her offensive on every level. But I did my damnedest to make her like me because my fate was in her hands. It was up to the captains of each team to choose their new team members from the pool of rookies, and more than anything, I wanted to wear the pink and black of the Hellcats.

I hid my distaste when she condescended to speak to me, and I must have been convincing. After about four weeks of practice, Iron

Maiden officially invited me to join the Hellcats. I named myself "Melicious" and took the number 11 in homage to my favorite lucky number in craps.

Like most deals with the devil, getting my heart's desire didn't work out as I'd planned. One of the attractions of the Hellcats, beyond the flattering uniforms and the panther logo, was that the girls seemed more like a gang than a team. I'd never played team sports, and I was suspicious of too much girl-bonding. I found comfort in the independence of the members of the Hellcats.

But our team was too literally like a bunch of cats. Autonomous. Prima donnas. Finicky. Overly sensitive, with hidden claws. I had several teammates whom I liked a lot: Hydra, who mixed her killer instinct to win with a matter-of-factness about sports that left all the drama on the track where it belonged . . . Riff Scandell, devastatingly stylish and a true rock 'n' roller . . . Honey Hotrod (who would later become Lucille Brawl), always ready with an insightful and bitingly funny aside . . . Tomcat, the sweetest mean-looking skater to hit the track.

None of them could compensate for Iron Maiden's influence. Gutter-punk skinny and the palest shade of goth, Iron Maiden seemed to believe she was the physical prototype for the definitive Hellcat. Though she preached girl power and the "third wave of feminism" gospel, she led us like a dictator. Among other things, she appeared to have clear ideas about how a Roller Derby skater should look. Iron Maiden's uniform set the standard for the team: black short-shorts with fishnet hose and a pink blouse tied seductively just above her ribcage, all the better to display her sleek abdominal muscles.

If the Hellcats were meant to be fashioned in Iron Maiden's likeness, she also demanded that we worship at the altar of Pris. It wasn't Pris's fault. For all her bravado on the track, the *real* Pris was humble and silly. She had an easy laugh, took her skating skills for granted—which also meant she had very little ego—and hated team politics. It was as if one day she'd put on skates and discovered she could do amazing things. She accepted it the way other people accept that they're 5' 3" or can do long division in their heads.

In Iron Maiden's eyes, however, the jammers were the divas of the show, and the rest of us were the supporting chorus, best kept in the back row. She put Pris on a pedestal and reminded us often that none of the rest of us could reach it. The pressure on Pris to carry the team must have been enormous, but it was impossible to get her to talk about it. Why stand around and relate, when you can shut up and skate?

As much as I admired Pris, I envied her, too. She was a star and a phenomenal skater, and I wanted to be both.

☠ ♥ ☠

The prevailing philosophy when I joined the league was that being a blocker was easy. Roller Derby rookies usually started out in the pack; our only instruction was to hit the other girls. I heard "Take her out!" a lot. It took some time to get used to the idea that not only was I given the permission to barrel into an opposing player on a whim, I was expected to do it, and that I would be applauded for doing it.

It's just not normal, using one's body as a battering ram. The derby mantra—"Hit, or be hit"—was completely foreign to me. Before I joined Roller Derby, I'd never been in a fight (although I'd dodged plenty of them). I specialize in being polite and making others feel comfortable. I don't even like to beat Dave at backgammon. I'm not innately aggressive or competitive—I had to get tough, and having my ass knocked to the floor by chicks who never hesitated to hit first was a strong motivator.

Eventually, I liked being a blocker; it was fun, in a twisted definition of fun that included taking whatever La Coneja served up. But I dreamed of being a jammer.

When we scrimmaged at practice, I desperately hoped that Iron Maiden would put me in as the jammer. I was convinced I was ready, sure that the only thing holding me back was Iron Maiden's obvious bias against me because I wasn't a size 4 Hellcat.

I was a chubby little kid, an overweight teenager, and an adult who flirted with obesity before deciding in my early twenties to do something about it. I researched nutrition and started a healthy eating plan. Too embarrassed to go to a gym, I worked out with videotapes in my living room every day for two years. Then I became a certified aerobics instructor and personal trainer. When I got bored with indoor workouts, I started to swim, bike, and run so I could compete in a triathlon.

All of that activity made me strong and fit, but it didn't make me skinny. Sometimes I'm resentful: of my metabolism, of my love of comfort food, of my buxom build. But mostly, my body and I are on the same side now.

It's a complex love-hate relationship, and it colors just about everything in my life. Roller Derby was the first time ever that being referred to as a "big girl" was a compliment. As a blocker, broad shoulders and hips can be an advantage, and it was pretty awesome when a tiny fellow rookie looked at me and said, "You're a big girl. Lucky!"

"Roller Derby has really increased my acceptance of my own body. I can use my size to my advantage in my position as a blocker and pivot—and I'm no longer worried about someone seeing up my skirt . . . although it does help to wear special underwear!"

—BAD SISTER HEIDI, VAUDEVILLE VIXENS/MAD ROLLIN' DOLLS

I didn't feel lucky. When Iron Maiden didn't put me in as a jammer, I was convinced it was because she had a fat-girl bias: If I had washboard abs, I thought, I bet I'd be in there jamming.

Each time Iron Maiden called a lineup, I stared at the floor—not wanting anyone to see how eager I was to be given a shot. I chanted in my head, "Mel, jammer. Mel, jammer," willing her to say my name.

One night, finally, she did.

We were scrimmaging against the Putas del Fuego and my archrival, La Coneja, was in the lineup. This was it—the showdown I'd been waiting for.

Members of the Holy Rollers and Rhinestone Cowgirls sat in the center of the rink, chitchatting and only peripherally paying attention to the track. I took my place at the line with the other jammer and waited for the whistle. When it blew, I took off as fast as I could, trying to control my breathing and to remember to cross on the corners. I hit the back of the pack and dodged around the back blocker. I cut left to the inside of the track and snuck by the middle blocker. Focus, I told myself. Breathe, as I slid by the front blocker and, finally, the pivot. I was lead jammer, and I was free of the pack.

I skated down the straightaway and then rounded the curve, the pack just ahead of me again. If it had been a real game, I'd have been on the brink of starting to score. As it was, I felt like I was earning points vital to my confidence and my reputation in the league. As I picked up speed before reaching the back of the pack, I heard Strawberry say from the center of the track, "Look at Melicious!" and for the first time, I understood why athletes strive to be number one. It was so seductive. So electrifying. The sound of my name said in a slightly breathless tone.

I put my head down, pushed my feet as far to the sides as I could to make the most of each stroke, and plowed through the blockers at the back of the pack.

I wish I could brag about how many points I earned on that jam, or share details about the artful strategy I used to sneak past the pivot at the last second. The truth is, it was luck or the blockers not paying attention, or the other jammer being tired, or some combination of all of those things that made me the lead jammer that night. But I didn't know that then. I was convinced that, not only was I ready to play in the next bout, I was ready to jam. I wasn't going to rest until Iron Maiden put me in the game lineup as a jammer.

☠ ♥ ☠

I'd been practicing for about a month and, according to what loosely served as regulations in the early days of the league, I wasn't yet eligible to skate in the upcoming bout. But the captains had a top-secret meeting and decided that a few of us rookies were ready to play. On September 29, 2002, I would make my debut as Melicious when the Hellcats played the Putas del Fuego.

That week established an odd and unfortunate tradition. Even though we set a new schedule for our bouts every year, my cycle has adapted so that I'm guaranteed to have PMS during bout week. I'm irritable, klutzy, bloated, and insecure when I most need to be focused, coordinated, strong, and confident.

Our last practice before my first game was a dress rehearsal. I stood on the track, pouting, in a full face of makeup and my freshly pressed pink uniform shirt. When the Hellcats and Putas took the track for our last scrimmage—"Let's take it easy on each other, ladies. No injuries before the game, right?"—I felt murderous. Fueled by hormones, I was like the mother who miraculously lifts the car off her trapped kid. I was a woman on a mission to knock some bitches down.

Unfortunately, Iron Maiden wasn't in synch with my estrogen and progesterone levels; my name appeared less in the lineup than I thought I deserved. According to her notes, I wasn't going to play the jammer position at all, and I was only in a few times as a blocker. Forget that I should have been grateful to be playing at all; I was incensed. Outraged. So I threw a temper tantrum that started in my head: Why wasn't I jamming? What did I have to do to get these girls to like me?

We joke that Roller Derby means never having to say you're sorry and—like the movie *A League of Their Own*—there's no crying in Roller Derby. But I can tell you, that's a stinkin' lie. In no time flat, I went from powerful derby girl to thirteen-year-old misfit. Tears stung my eyes. Somewhere in my reptilian brain, my subconscious decided it would be better if I came off as a psycho bitch than a crybaby. I snapped something obnoxious at Iron Maiden and the rest of the team and sprinted off the floor.

The problem with forty-some girls in a skating rink is that there isn't a lot of room for privacy. I went to the water fountain . . . girls! To the bathroom . . . girls! To the lobby . . . girls! I finally found a dark corner behind a bank of lockers and the Fun Crane machine, and let the tears flow. I had a pink, sweaty, snotty Roller Derby breakdown. When I stopped crying and only pathetic sniffles remained, I realized I was now trapped behind the lockers with mascara running down my face.

I pulled myself together and went back to the scrimmage, my cheeks burning with embarrassment.

"Hey, Melicious," Iron Maiden said, barely glancing up from her lineup sheet. "We were just wondering where you were. Wanna go in as jammer on the next one?"

On game day, I was like a rubber band stretched to almost-breaking. I cleaned my skate wheels and packed my gear, then checked and rechecked my bags. So much stuff! Skates, pads, helmet, mouthguard, energy bars, water bottle, comb, powder compact, Sharpie, black eyeliner, blush and brush, lip liner, lipstick, glitter, camera, leather newsboy cap, flat shoes in case the high heels I was wearing hurt my feet, sandwich, apple, cell phone, hand mirror.

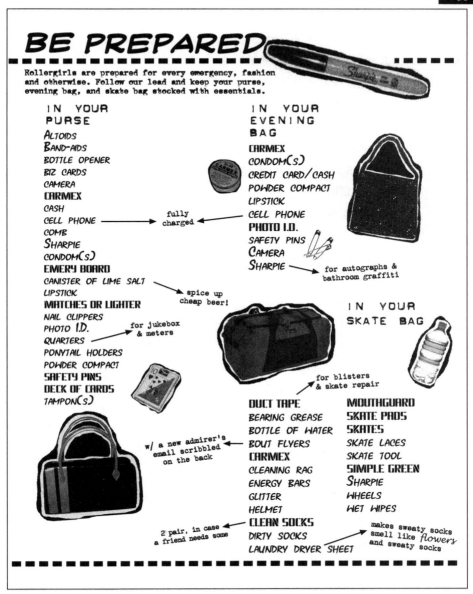

BE PREPARED

Rollergirls are prepared for every emergency, fashion and otherwise. Follow our lead and keep your purse, evening bag, and skate bag stocked with essentials.

IN YOUR PURSE

ALTOIDS
BAND-AIDS
BOTTLE OPENER
BIZ CARDS
CAMERA
CARMEX
CASH
CELL PHONE ──→ fully charged
COMB
SHARPIE
CONDOM(S)
EMERY BOARD
CANISTER OF LIME SALT ──→ spice up cheap beer!
LIPSTICK
MATCHES OR LIGHTER
NAIL CLIPPERS
PHOTO I.D. ──→ for jukebox & meters
QUARTERS
PONYTAIL HOLDERS
POWDER COMPACT
SAFETY PINS
DECK OF CARDS
TAMPON(S)

IN YOUR EVENING BAG

CARMEX
CONDOM(S)
CREDIT CARD / CASH
POWDER COMPACT
LIPSTICK
CELL PHONE
PHOTO I.D.
SAFETY PINS
CAMERA
SHARPIE ──→ for autographs & bathroom graffiti

IN YOUR SKATE BAG

for blisters & skate repair

DUCT TAPE
BEARING GREASE
BOTTLE OF WATER
BOUT FLYERS ──→ w/ a new admirer's email scribbled on the back
CARMEX
CLEANING RAG
ENERGY BARS
GLITTER
HELMET
CLEAN SOCKS ──→ 2 pair, in case a friend needs some
DIRTY SOCKS
LAUNDRY DRYER SHEET ──→ makes sweaty socks smell like flowers and sweaty socks

MOUTHGUARD
SKATE PADS
SKATES
SKATE LACES
SKATE TOOL
SIMPLE GREEN
SHARPIE
WHEELS
WET WIPES

On the way to Playland, I was being impossible: snapping driving instructions at Dave and fiddling with the radio, exaggerated sighs punctuating every turn of the dial. About halfway to the rink, I realized I'd forgotten the bag with my energy bars and water bottle in our driveway. It was 90-something degrees in our un-air-conditioned car, and we were trapped in a bumper-to-bumper snarl. Dave yelled that he couldn't wait till the bout was over. I told him he was a selfish jerk—despite his unwavering support and encouragement—and refused to speak for the rest of the ride.

I'd been in chorus and plays and musicals throughout most of my life, and the nervousness before those performances usually gave me energy. I was terrified the first time I did a triathlon, but my nerves dissipated as soon as I dove into the water for the swim. But this was completely different. The combination of performing for an audience and playing a new sport was freaking me out. Anxiety had me by the throat.

For your amusement, here are some of the irrational fears I had about my first bout:

> *What if my laces break?*
> *What if I didn't eat the right stuff today, and I bonk in the middle of the bout?*
> *What if my wheel falls off?*
> *What if my boobs bounce out of my bra?* (maybe not so irrational)
> *What if I get weird fat tummy rolls when I'm skating?*
> *What if the audience thinks I look lame instead of cool?*
> *What if I break my ankle/neck/jaw/tailbone/wrist/spirit?*
> *What if no one applauds for me during my intro?*
> *What if I trip and fall on my intro?*
> And the worst: *What if we lose?*

My fears were unfounded. When the announcer belted "Ladies and gentlemen . . . Hellcats number eleven . . . she's vicious and delicious . . . she's Meeeeellllliiiiiccccciiiiooooouuuuusssss!" I skated smoothly onto the track, waving to my mom and Dave and my pals Jesse and Emily sitting trackside. The Hellcats lost the game that night, but my most vivid sense impression of that first bout was the pain.

The Putas del Fuego were notorious for hitting hard, but I hadn't realized they'd been holding back in practice. Their team was made of elbows—a writhing, pointy, flinty pile of jagged bones. I think my ass was on the floor more often than I was upright. I got in some hits of my own, but the game was a no-holds-barred demolition derby. I did land a particularly hard body block to one of my least favorite Putas, and felt immense satisfaction when her tiny flame-encased butt slammed to the floor. But La Coneja got me good in defense of her teammate. I was her personal punching bag. As I clattered to the floor again, she bared her teeth at me in a semblance of a smile, like an orangutan that's just thrown a pile of poop at zoo visitors.

Whatever minimal strategy my team had discussed—"Hit hard! Get Pris through!"—any hope of organization, coordinated effort, or focus was gone. It was a free-for-all. And the crowd, bless their mercenary hearts, ate it up. My skating sucked, but the crowd was oblivious. They roared like we were champs. The Putas won that game, but afterward, my friends were all compliments and praise. Watching pinup girls fumble around on skates is wildly entertaining, and it was obvious that our fans loved it. But I wanted to do more. I wanted to be tough and proud. An athlete.

In a quiet moment with my mom, I asked, "So . . . did I look mean and scary out there?"

She said, to my chagrin, "Oh, no, sweetie," her voice warm with that special honey-mom tone, "you looked beautiful."

A month later, it was time for our championship bout; we were playing the Rhinestone Cowgirls for first-place bragging rights. In honor of Halloween, we added fake fur ears, paws, and tails to our Hellcats uniforms. The costume brainstorm and resulting arts-and-crafts projects pulled our team together in a way that strategy discussions never had;

we didn't agree on much, but we rallied around those damn cat ears.

When I got to the rink to warm up before the bout, the Sunday afternoon kiddy skate was still in full swing. As I passed parents on the way to their cars, they pulled their kids closer, eyeing my cleavage and torn stockings. The Playland regulars and surrounding neighborhood weren't yet accustomed to roller queens in their midst.

As I put on my skates in the rink, a three-foot-tall girl in brown rentals approached me. Her knuckles turned white as she gripped the railing in front of her, her feet threatening to slide out from beneath her.

"Why are you wearing those ears?" she asked, tilting her head to the side and looking at me through narrowed eyes, like she wasn't sure what to make of me. I explained that I was in the Roller Derby and tried to talk about my team without saying the word "hell." I didn't want to be accused of ruining quality family time and corrupting innocent children. She told me her name was Hannah and that she was there for her sister's birthday party. "We ate pizza and played the Hokey Pokey," she said.

One by one, other five- and six-year-olds joined her at the railing, their eyes big and round and lit up.

Their breathy voices tumbled over each other: "Can you go fast?" "Is that girl on your team?" "How many teams are there?" "Can you go backward?" "When is your birthday?" "Can I have your autograph?"

Then one of them asked the question adults rarely dare: "How old are you?"

When I answered, Hannah said with authority, "Thirty-four! I would have put you in your early twenties."

Our capacity card for Playland, courtesy of Austin's friendly neighborhood fire marshal, allows for 1,100 people, including all of our crew and skaters; we had so many people in the house that night, it was almost impossible to get from one end of the rink to the other unless you were a skater with access to the derby track.

The first half of the game with the Rhinestone Cowgirls was much like my previous game—an uncoordinated but valiant effort on the part of the Hellcats to beat the crap out of our rivals. At halftime, we were ahead—a first for me. My other first that night was a trip to the Penalty Wheel and AmberDiva, the Penalty Mistress.

During our warm-up laps, I'd knocked LadyHawke to the floor, and throughout the first few jams of our bout, she was a nuisance: heckling me, poking me with her elbows, slapping my helmet with her wrist guard, pretending to pull off my tail. By the fifth jam, I'd had enough. But when I launched my attack, she saw me coming; all I could manage was a good shoulder hit before she took me down in a football tackle. We landed in a tangle, and LadyHawke gripped my helmet, repeatedly banging my head against the floor. When the refs pulled us apart, she took off with one of my kitty ears.

I chased her around the track and the audience roared. For a split second, it registered that the audience was responding to what I was doing—I made them cheer! When I finally caught LadyHawke, I tackled her—to louder whoops—and was about to sit on her when Quicksilver, our ref, arrived. She'd had enough of our crap and sent both of us to the Penalty Wheel for punishment. LadyHawke and I jostled each other all the way around the track, cursing and mugging for the audience to rally them to our cause. I gave the wheel a spin and watched it land on "Catch a Kiss." My punishment was to toss a ball into the audience and then plant a kiss on the lucky fan who caught the ball.

Of course it was scooped up by . . . not the handsome roller fan of my dreams, but a dumpy dude in a burnt orange Longhorns T-shirt, jeans, sandals (sandals! with socks!), and a baseball cap (backward, of course). When I leaned in to give him a quick peck on the cheek, he jerked his head to the left—sneaky bastard—sliding his lips onto mine. I think he even tried to slip me a little tongue. Punishment indeed.

☠ ♥ ☠

The Hellcats kept a six-point lead on the Rhinestone Cowgirls during most of the second half and, I have to admit, it felt great to be ahead. But then, in the fourth jam of the half, the Rhinestone Cowgirls kicked it up a notch and tied the score. With only thirty seconds left in the game, we started a fifth jam with Pris as the jammer. At the end of the two minutes, the score hadn't changed; it was a tie. We went to Sudden Death. Our two teams would skate a jam for a maximum of one minute; the first team to score a point would be declared the champs.

Pris and Electra Blu lined up against each other at the line. The crowd was on its feet, making an unholy noise. The whistle blew. Pris and Electra sprinted toward the pack in a blur of red and pink. Pris got there first. Sudden Death was over. The score was 46 to 45, and the Hellcats were the first-season champions.

My parents gave me flowers and made a fuss. My teammates grabbed each other in an uncharacteristic group hug. Fans snapped photos and asked for autographs and yelled "Hellcats! Hellcats!" whenever they saw a skater in pink. I should have been happy and excited, but the whole experience left me hollow, like an outsider again. I'd had zero experience with team sports prior to joining the league. I'd never won any athletic competition. I had no context for sports, but I was disappointed by the emptiness of our win.

Even though the scoreboard objectively said we'd triumphed, the numbers didn't erase the fact that, in my mind, we weren't a team. We were a bunch of girls, wearing matching shirts, sniping at each other at practices and vying for attention. There were no words of support or shared vision. Just competition—with each other and everyone else. Although there were definitely a few Nice girls I genuinely liked, we had an underlying level of distrust that I found unsettling. If this was team sports, I wasn't sorry I'd missed out.

I probably expected too much. Maybe movies like *The Bad*

News Bears had ruined me. But I felt then—and now—that our sport should give us more than bruises. We should play with a sense of honor and a sense of humor. Respect our teammates and our competition. Be more than girls in short skirts on wheels. We should be the heroes I saw the first time I watched the Roller Derby.

THE OLD
BRAWL GAME

04

Bank on It

It makes me flush with pride to say that Flat Track Derby started in Austin, Texas, and that the Texas Rollergirls were the first league to totally commit to the Flat Track. But I've got to give props to where the sport started.

The legend of Roller Derby's beginnings has all the makings of a popcorn-and-Jujubes big-screen matinee: memorable characters, intrigue, sex, violence, and lawsuits, all set against the backdrop of the Great Depression. I'm madly in love with the story, and I don't really care if it was exaggerated for dramatic effect by an imaginative shyster. The tale is romantic and melodramatic, with all the built-in pageantry of an Esther Williams movie and the adventure of running away with the circus.

Allow me to introduce you to Mr. Leo Seltzer, an entertainment and sports promoter extraordinaire and the inventor of the original Roller Derby. I've only casually glanced at photos of the real Leo Seltzer because I like to imagine him as an Edward G. Robinson character, chomping on a big fat cigar, with a tumbler of whiskey in one hand and a pen in the other, cajoling and charming some rube into signing on the dotted line.

Papa Leo's sport rolled onto the scene when Americans desperately needed the distraction of live entertainment. After the stock market crash of 1929, the world—led by the U.S.—plunged into the Great Depression. Banks and businesses collapsed, and 25 percent of the able-bodied American workforce was unemployed. Hoovervilles sprang up in cities large and small, and the heartland turned into the Dust Bowl.

Just like reality show contestants who chase their fifteen minutes of fame today, Americans in the twenties and thirties were eager to make themselves famous and maybe earn a little extra scratch in the process. What better way to make a buck than flagpole sitting? Or walking in endless circles on a track? Or dancing till you drop? It was the era of the kooky marathon, and all over the country, new endurance records were being set. It wasn't long until promoters realized that exploiting this new entertainment might be a good way to make a buck.

That's when Leo Seltzer entered the picture.

As the owner of three movie theaters in Portland, Oregon, Leo was doing all right for himself. The only industry to thrive during the Depression was the Hollywood film machine. For three or four hours, families could forget their troubles by watching Shirley Temple dance across the Good Ship Lollipop. But Leo was a savvy promoter and realized the marathon craze really had legs.

At first, he specialized in walkathons. Pause for a moment and imagine how starved for entertainment you'd need to be before you'd pay to sit in an arena and watch competitors walk in circles until they collapsed.

But Leo was no dummy. He said, "They'll buy it once, twice maybe—but a third time is pressing your luck." So he spiced up the monotony of walkathons with other curiosities, like ice-sitting contests, vaudeville comedians, and even unusual public wedding ceremonies, including Sally and Cecil's cellophane wedding in which the bride wore a head-to-hemline clear plastic wedding gown.

In 1933, Papa Leo relocated his business to Chicago, and the Windy City inspired him to try something new. After reading that 97 percent of all Americans had roller-skated at some time in their lives, he doodled some ideas on a tablecloth in a booth at the fabled Johnny Ricketts restaurant. That was when the Transcontinental Derby was born.

WHAT IT TAKES TO BE A "GIRL ROLLER RACER"

Honey Thomas, one of the original Roller Derby queens, outlined for a reporter the traits a girl needed to make it in Roller Derby:

1. Nerve and spunk
2. Ability to take bumps and bruises
3. Natural athletic ability
4. A fighting heart that will not quit
5. Some natural endurance
6. Some skating ability

[From *Roller Derby to Rollerjam: The Authorized Story of an Unauthorized Sport* by Keith Coppage (Squarebooks, 1999)]

It was like a G-rated dance marathon on wheels. Twenty-five squeaky-clean, fresh-faced boy-girl couples vied to outlast each other while skating laps on an oval track. With eighteen laps to a mile, the teams skated the approximate distance from New York City to San Diego, and their progress was tracked with tiny lights on a giant map of Route 66. To help put it in perspective, I give you the Transcontinental Derby Index:

4,000   *miles skated in a Transcontinental Derby competition*

57,000 *total laps equal to 4,000 miles*

110 *average miles a fast skater could complete in one day*

36 *days needed to complete Transcontinental Derby*

25 *dollars a Transcontinental Derby skater earned each week*

14 *hours per day that Transcontinental Derby skaters were on the track*

Every day, for approximately seven weeks, from noon until 2:00 a.m., the skaters circled the track. And spectators watched! When the skating marathon debuted on August 13, 1935, it attracted 20,000 spectators. (Today, the capacity for a basketball game—America's second most popular sport—at Madison Square Garden is 19,763.)

Although the teams were made up of pairs, the men and women skated separately. Leo was paternal, providing food, shelter, clothing, medical care, and a strict code of conduct for the skaters. Alcohol and hanky-panky among the skaters were prohibited. But it wasn't long before sex and violence entered the picture.

The story of the sexification of Roller Derby goes like this: during a 1937 marathon in Miami, one of the bigger, more lumbering skaters jostled and elbowed the smaller, faster skaters during a men's race. When the refs stopped the action to penalize the offender, the audience booed. At the ref.

The writer Damon Runyon was in the audience that night. Well-known for his short stories about gamblers, thieves, winos, pimps, and whores—and his sharp eye for catching significant details others missed—Runyon recommended to Papa Leo that he make bickering, brawls, and bad blood a permanent addition to the sport. According to legend, the two put their heads together and wrote the new rules of the game that very night.

Good-bye multiday marathon. Feuds, fistfights, and a point system became standard parts of the action, and fans weren't the only ones who noticed. Soon the skaters' hijinks were the stuff of the sports pages and the gossip columns. Reporters gave nicknames to the most infamous and popular skaters, like Wes "Casanova" Aronson and Josephine "Ma" Bogash.

Fast-forward about a decade, and Roller Derby was still going strong. In 1949, the five-day world series of the National Roller Derby League was played in Madison Square Garden for an audience of 55,000. But fans are fickle, and eventually we shove our pop culture royalty off their pedestals—just ask Britney Spears. By 1953, the Roller Derby wave was mostly over, replaced by the next-generation cool of college campus panty raids, drive-in movies, the hula hoop, and the seduction of the devil-box: TV.

A few games were still played by die-hard skaters for devotees, but the sport definitely went underground, and not in the alternative, counterculture way. In the sixties and seventies, Roller Derby resurfaced on television with a new team of stars. The quasi-classy elements were gone—forget the fedoras, big-band music, and code of conduct of the early days. The ready-for-TV Roller Derby was an unabashed celebration of the lowbrow. The skaters were tough, brash, and foul-mouthed. When the cameras panned the crowd, the home-viewing audience saw a mélange of Aqua Net hairdos, turquoise blue eye shadow, plaid sport coats, bushy sideburns, and billowing clouds of cigarette smoke.

Sure, they look cheesy now, with their B-movie sci-fi-flick uniforms and obviously fake stunts—smashing each other with chairs? really?—but those seventies skater chicks were our role models when we were just starting out.

My two favorites are Joanie Weston and Ann Calvello. By all accounts, they were like the best of a Vegas showgirl and Olympic athlete, blended together and served up in a frosty glass on eight wheels. They were among the first derby queens to prove that by displaying flash and style—without compromising a smidgen of their athleticism and competitive drive—they could win over the audience, taking fans for a ride.

The two women were opposites. Good cop/bad cop. Hero and antihero. Each the ideal foil for the other. The crowd was enthralled when they went helmet-to-helmet with each other in games. Though they were opposites, together they made sense. You couldn't really enjoy one without the other.

Ann, a proud Leo, decked herself out with lions—on the rings she always wore, her eyeglasses, her eight tattoos—and called herself Lioness. But the audience dubbed her "Banana Nose." And "Demon of the Derby." And "Meanest Mama on Skates." She was the derby queen that fans loved to hate, and she wouldn't have had it any other way. She was once overheard telling a fan who'd promised to root for her in a game, "You're gonna root for me? You better not, honey, I'm the bad guy."

She joined the Roller Derby in 1948. As my roller sisters and I would do more than half a century later, Ann watched one Roller Derby bout and knew it was something she had to do. She continued to play the game until 2000—the only professional athlete in any sport to compete in seven decades.

Ann was a scrapper, both the initiator and the finisher of most of her fights. Her fans had their own nicknames for her, but the refs called her "Queen of the Penalty Box." During her notorious career with the San Francisco Bay Bombers, she spent the equivalent of an entire week cooling her heels, and her temper, in the box.

All of that banked track combat took its toll. Ann endured the agony of breaking her nose twelve times, busting her elbow four times, splitting her collarbone, snapping her tailbone, and cracking her ribs so many times that it was futile to try to keep a tally. When Indianapolis honored her with Ann Calvello Day on April 15, 1972, an injury prevented her from attending. That's pretty punk rock.

So was Ann's attitude toward authority, her uniform, and her appearance. She did what she liked and apologized to no one. A consummate performer, Ann knew that it was more than the wheels on her feet that put the fans' asses in the seats. She referred to her bustline as "tickets," instructing her teammates to "Get your tickets up, ladies!" on the way onto the track.

When the management gave her a new jersey, she'd attack the sleeves and neckline with scissors, all the better to show off her assets. Should her jersey accidentally slip during a fight, it revealed a lacy, racy bra and darkly tanned tummy. Her hair was a rainbow of colors: Wendy O. Williams platinum blond, green for St. Patrick's Day, lavender, fire engine red, blue, hot pink, and even polka dots. She wore a scarf knotted around her slender neck, and it fluttered in the wind she generated as she sped around the track, her black pivot's helmet tipped at a rakish angle on her head.

It ain't bragging if it's true, and Ann got away with all of her escapades because her skating was the substance behind her style. Extremely competitive and driven by pride, Ann loved the derby world, but had a single-minded determination to be a winner: "They're all my friends, but not when I'm skating."

In one of her last interviews before she died in March 2006, Ann said she thought there was a little bit of her in each of us modern Rollergirls. She was right. Every time I readjust my push-up bra after a hard-fought jam, or change the color of my bangs from pink to purple to green, I wink up at Ann and thank her for clearing the way through the pack for the rest of us.

If Ann was the black hat, Joanie Weston was the Goody Two-shoes heroine in white. The press and fans lovingly called her the "Blond Bomber" and "Golden Girl." Sportswriter Frank Deford described her as a "brave Viking queen." To the fans who packed the Roller Derby arenas, she looked like a Hollywood starlet who'd dropped into their midst: statuesque, buxom, athletic, and oh-so-blond. But she was also tenacious and muscular, like the corn-fed girls of America's heartland. The combination of brawn and beauty was riveting. Joanie was a vision that rolled out of blue-collar dreams and onto the track.

A true California girl, Joanie was born in Huntington Beach in 1935, and was the prototype for the fifties surfer girl. But she was no bikini-clad, boy-crazy Gidget—Joanie also excelled at horseback riding and softball. While she was a student at Mount St. Mary's College, she once walloped eight home runs in a single game. In 1962, she won Hawaii's outrigger canoe championship. She could have played any number of sports, but Roller Derby captured her heart.

Joanie claimed in interviews that when she tried out for Roller Derby in 1954, she was "the least awful of a very bad bunch of people, and they needed someone desperately." She liked to tell the story of how during one of her first laps around the track, she stumbled in front of a pack of skaters and all of them fell on top of her. But that was just a sweet girl being modest. Joanie was a star pivot, known for her powerful stride and sense of fair play. She was voted "Roller Derby Queen" four times and was the longtime captain of the Oakland Bombers.

Before joining the tawdry, rowdy world of Roller Derby, Joanie had considered a career as a nun. A thoughtful, intelligent woman who read voraciously when she was off the track, she never grew comfortable with the rougher aspects of the game. "I've had my share of fights—even won most of them. But in the winning, I've always felt like a loser. . . . I don't think hostility is in my bag."

Her kindness made her a fan favorite. If an admirer brought her a hat as a gift, she'd wear it during her warm-up laps, and she was always willing to pose for photos and sign autographs. Her composure and grace made her a hit with the media. She was their first choice for interviews and insight; radio, television, and newspaper reporters were as charmed by her authenticity as her fans.

When Joanie died on May 10, 1977, of Creutzfeldt-Jakob disease, her obituary in *The New York Times* celebrated her athleticism and strapping size: "[M]iss Weston was as pretty as they come, her hair was longer and bleached blonder than anybody else's, and, at five feet ten inches and 165 pounds, she had the perfect Roller Derby build." I think she would have loved the *Times* summary of her—a nice, pretty girl who could kick your ass. When I find myself cursing my broad shoulders and less-than-lithe body as I look in the mirror—or worry that I lack the killer instinct to excel as a player—I remind myself that Joanie was a big ol' girl, and there was no one lovelier.

Although women like Ann and Joanie were superstars in the derby world, they weren't enough to sustain the popularity of the sport, and Roller Derby again fell off the radar in the eighties. Video killed the radio star, and the overexposure of TV, coupled with the grind and expense of constant touring, eventually assassinated Roller Derby.

Through the twists and turns, the Seltzer family kept one toe stop on the track, and when inline skating became a national sensation, Roller Derby was transformed into "Rollerjam," which premiered on The Nashville Network (TNN) in December 1998. Played in a beautifully tricked-out studio in Orlando, Florida—with a banked track and rock-show lighting—Rollerjam was played on inline skates by athletes culled from roller hockey and speed skating. The skaters were an attractive bunch, but the inherent drama of the sport was overshadowed by storylines borrowed from pro wrestling. After an initial burst of popularity, the ratings dropped and the final whistle blew.

Once again, Roller Derby faded away—until the turn of the millennium in Austin, Texas.

CHAPTER

05

An Awfully Good Idea

Roller Derby has always had a slightly shady reputation. Tawdry. Raunchy. Seedy. The phrase "lowest common denominator" is usually mentioned, too.

Which brings me to Devil Dan.

Picture Austin, Texas, the "live music capital of the world." Free thinkers. Musicians. Artists. Hippies. Activists. The place to be—if you're a tattooed, punk-rocker type— is Red River Street, a troublemaker's paradise where an adventure seeker can knock back a drink, then wander next door for fresh ink at the tattoo shop. The kitschy boutiques and smoke shops are rife with hometown and visiting musicians, off-duty cocktail waitresses, gutter punks, suburbanites slumming it for the night, and college students with freshly minted IDs.

Into this den of opportunity—and plenty of idle hands to do Satan's work—sauntered a sketchy character from Oklahoma known to me only as Devil Dan. Sometime in 2000, he took up residence on bar stools along Red River and insinuated himself into the cocktail waitress-bartender-bouncer community. He became a fixture on the scene, hanging out, knocking back Jack D, talking shit.

One night, Devil Dan overheard an idea . . . an awfully good idea.

Like an impresario, he co-opted the brainstorm and ran with it. With flyers posted on telephone poles and bulletin boards, he lured a bunch of Austin's alterna-girls to a recruiting meeting.

"The girls in this town are really angry," Devil Dan told them, squinting through cigarette smoke. "I want to start a Roller Derby, like a sideshow, with hot girls and fire twirlers." He talked about midgets and the Jim Rose Circus and a derby—played in "the Thunderdome"— for theater, not sport.

"Don't worry about knowing how to skate," he told them. "The sound effects and light show will make up for it."

Devil Dan may as well have been standing at the crossroads at midnight with a contract in his hand. Everybody went for it—from girls willing to strap on skates to a bar owner willing to pony up cash to finance the venture and bands willing to perform for free at fund-raising parties. Devil Dan was in business, one step closer to being a postmodern P. T. Barnum, the Big Man, running the show for the little ladies.

He set up four teams—names, themes, uniforms, and all— then appointed a Red River scenester to head up each one:

Rhinestone Cowgirls—captain, Hot Lips Dolly
Holy Rollers—captain, Miss Information
Putas del Fuego—captain, La Muerta
Hellcats—captain, Iron Maiden

By February 2001, the fledgling Roller Derby had about twenty members assigned to teams, and they'd held coming-out parties and fund-raisers. But the girls had yet to start skating. They met with Devil Dan and hung out in bars and talked about skating—a lot—but the Roller Derby was beginning to seem like "all talk, no action."

According to derby lore, Devil Dan suddenly blew out of town.

It could have been the end of Roller Derby in Austin, but the girls had committed to the idea. They weren't going to be stopped.

The vacuum left by Devil Dan's departure opened up an opportunity for the team captains. Iron Maiden, Miss Information, and Hot Lips Dolly adopted a collective nickname they'd been given in a local magazine article—the SheEOs—and grabbed the reins of the start-up league. They named the organization Bad Girl Good Woman Productions. (La Muerta was one of the original SheEOs but she left the league soon after I joined.)

With Devil Dan out of the picture, the girls were optimistic. But there was still the issue of learning the game and, for some of them—like Sparkle Plenty and Bettie Rage—learning to skate.

In the early days, the league held practices at Skateworld. They hired a skating instructor to teach the inexperienced girls the basics—rolling forward, stopping, crossing on the corners, and going backward—while some of the more athletic girls took the lead in hammering out the details of the sport. Roller Derby had effectively been extinct for decades, so there was no training manual or rulebook. The Wrench, an accomplished personal trainer, set up a training program that would help prevent injuries while increasing the girls' strength. Strawberry, a former soccer player, and Hydra, a ranked amateur handball player, shared what they knew about team dynamics to rally the troops.

The skaters formed a Rules Committee, headed up by Sparkle Plenty, to adapt the old-school regulations to create a twenty-first-century sport. Together, they drafted the first set of Flat Track rules.

The old-school Roller Derby was played on a portable track with angled curves that kept a crew busy for hours setting it up. The new Rollergirls knew that acquiring one of the old-school banked tracks was an impossibility for the short-term—tracks cost upward of $20,000—so they devised a way to play the game on the floor of

Skateworld. Electra Blu found the dimensions of an old banked track online, then used a CAD program to calculate what the measurements would be if the banked track was smashed flat. Annie Social came up with the bright idea to outline the Flat Track oval with ropes of Christmas lights.

By spring of 2002, the league had forty-five players. They'd internalized the rules and they held practice scrimmages regularly. Their uniforms were ready to go. They were eager to hold their first bout and show Austin they really were playing Roller Derby. A game—just for invited family and friends—was scheduled for June 23.

The skaters brainstormed all the tasks that needed to be done to make the bout a reality—building a scoreboard, renting light and sound equipment, laying down the track, booking bands, and hundreds of other details. When the list was complete, they each volunteered for the jobs and started the tradition of the skaters, literally, running the show.

The first friends-and-family bout in June went as smoothly as it could. The girls enjoyed their first taste of the limelight, and Austinites saw their first glimpse of their hometown Rollergirls. One of the skating stars to emerge that night was Miss Conduct.

The first time I ever saw her, Miss Conduct was scurrying into the Playland restroom with a bundle of assorted crap in her arms. I'd been a member of the league for about two months, but we'd yet to meet. She's tiny, maybe five feet tall, and she was almost overwhelmed by the bundle she carried. With a grunt, she plopped it all on the counter by the sink: balled-up T-shirts, a gauzy skirt, skate pads, socks, a canvas bookbag bulging with who knows what, a helmet, a tangled bundle of keys, and keychains. She looked like a Gypsy who had been turned into a pixie by a witch with a twisted sense of humor. Her long red dreadlocks were decorated with rags and bows, and her face was meticulously made up with perfect—I mean, perfect—cat's-eye liquid eyeliner and Clara Bow lips.

She saw me watching her, then did something startling. She threw her arms around me in a hug, pressed the top of her head to my chest, and, muffled against me, said, "You must be one of the new girls. It's so good to meet you."

Over time, I learned more—but not much more—about her. She was a part-time DJ, part-time dancer, and full-time flower child. She dressed like a whacked-out magician's assistant—black tutu, ripped-just-so T-shirt, spiked collar, and black lace-up knee boots on a Saturday afternoon—but lived like a hippie. Stories circulated about her that were slightly fantastic: that she lived on a dry-docked boat, that it took her four hours to get ready to go anywhere.

She was the consummate example of the dichotomy between derby persona and real-life personality. The "real" girl was groovy and laid back and energetic and sweet and flip, all at the same time. She loved skating and music, and, more than anything, I think, she wanted to be a star. The Rollergirl was a wily, nimble jammer with a punk attitude. She specialized in sneaking through the pack by finding the tiny holes that blockers didn't even realize they left open, and she regularly threw her helmet in frustration. Miss Conduct knew how to work the spotlight better than anyone. She waved at the crowd. She flipped them off. She lifted her skirt to show her ruffled panties, then coquettishly glanced over her shoulder in mock horror as if to say, "What? Me?"

At that first friends-and-family bout, while the audience was watching skaters like Miss Conduct, the SheEOs were observing the audience—and they saw dollar signs.

According to the veteran skaters, management of the league was quickly becoming an issue. Skaters were each coughing up $25 per month in dues and donating their time to make the league a success.

None of them wanted or expected to be paid, but they felt they deserved a voice in how the league was managed.

By now, you might be asking yourself: If the forty-five skaters in the league were so smart, why were they letting the SheEOs run the show? To understand the answer to that question, you have to think back to junior high . . . to the popular girls who ruled the school. Surely you knew a girl when you were thirteen or fourteen who—if you really thought about it—you didn't like at all. But you desperately wanted *her* to like *you.* If she invited you to her table in the cafeteria, or she wanted to copy answers from your Social Studies test, you felt a flush of belonging, a thrill of acceptance.

That's how the SheEOs were. They had an impressive mastery of junior high politics. They were charming and mesmerizing and adept at talking their way out of corners. It was a reenactment of the middle school pecking order, and even twenty- and thirty-something Roller-girls aren't immune to it.

But the SheEOs, for all their preteen power, underestimated the girls that were attracted to Roller Derby's combination of athleticism and aggression. Most of the skaters were number-one-best-quality people. They weren't always on the brink of a catfight. They had day jobs and families, and they were surprisingly committed to the league. Roller Derby sparked something in them that made them haul their asses out of bed on Saturdays—after making it to last call the night before—to practice and to meet for league business.

About midway through their first season, the SheEOs "retired" from skating. They claimed that the stress of running the league and trying to skate, too, was an unmanageable amount of work.

After their retirement, we rarely saw them. When they did show up for practices, they laid down rules about skater behavior. We were instructed that we would show up for appearances when they told us to. We were admonished to keep our opinions about league business to ourselves. They informed us that they owned our names, our images, our uniforms: "You'll only wear your uniforms in public when we tell you it's OK to wear them in public." It riled the skaters. We'd created our own names and personas, and we paid for our own equipment, our own USA Roller Sports insurance, and every stitch of our uniforms out of our personal bank accounts.

Most of the time, however, the SheEOs ignored us, sitting at a table in the corner of the rink, heads together, smoking cigarettes and whispering. Eventually, they stopped coming to practice completely, and the only time we saw them was at monthly league meetings.

One Saturday a month, we'd all straggle into a Tex-Mex restaurant in south Austin and settle in for the SheEO show. The three of them would sit at the head table in the front of the room, like the bridal party at a wedding reception. The meetings were ostensibly so they could give us updates on the latest league news, but since they didn't attend practices or do the majority of the league jobs, they didn't have much to share. It reminded me of the staff meetings we'd had at my dot-com job in San Francisco, in the bleak days of layoffs and the voluntary mass exodus of good people.

From the skaters' perspective, the league belonged to all of us. Tinkerhell was in charge of merch sales. The Wrench did training and production. All of us earned bruises and sore muscles at practice, performed at the bouts, and ran around town with flyers to promote the games.

But the SheEOs continued to believe the league belonged only to them.

Information was disseminated in our organization through an unreliable grapevine. News eventually got around to everyone, but it was so bastardized and had passed through so many layers of innuendo, prior relationships, accidental misunderstandings, and blatant misdirection, it was hard to know what to believe. But I had my own reliable information network—my carpool.

Twice a week, during the thirty-minute drive to and from skating practice, The Wrench, Lucille Brawl, Bloody Mary, and I shared what we knew. The SheEOs seemingly didn't realize that all of the skaters talked to each other. Nor did they know that each time they invited one of us to a "special meeting," we reported back to the rest of the skaters.

When I was invited to meet with them at a coffeehouse to talk about a marketing project—"Don't tell anyone, Mel . . . we don't want to make any of the other girls feel bad that we chose you"—I was initially flattered. But it wasn't long before I realized their modus operandi was to separate us from the pack, suck whatever information they could out of us, then throw us back.

The south Austin carpool became a safe place to compare notes. That's how my friends and I learned what the SheEOs were up to.

Sometime in the previous year, the SheEOs had formed an LLC with each other. They'd started acting like they owned the organization, because on paper, they did.

For Christmas in 2002, the SheEOs made a big gesture of giving each of us a gift: a glossy calendar featuring photos of every skater in the league. I distinctly remember the air-kiss and hug I got from Iron Maiden as she bestowed my present upon me. Two months later, we found out the calendars weren't gifts at all. They'd been printed by the SheEOs to be sold as merch. Finished too late for calendar season and ugly to boot, the calendars didn't sell well.

Meanwhile, our bouts were selling out, and we were attracting national attention.

Remember the Comedy Central show *Insomniac with Dave Attell*? The comedian would go to a town with a camera crew, find the local freaks, get nuts with the yokels, and show the rest of America why <*insert-town-name-here*> would be a wild place to stay up all night.

In January 2003, he came to Austin, and we put on a bout just for him.

The shoot was a huge success. Dave Attell was an instant

fan—mostly, I think, because Scarlot Harlot kicked his ass during the bout. In true Rollergirl fashion, we all tripped over each other to throw ourselves in front of the camera and to pose for photos with the comedian. Later, Attell wrote an article for *Playboy* magazine about his adventures around the country and dubbed us "Best Hottie Wheels."

It should have been a happy time—we were on national TV! Our wacky start-up hobby was becoming a sensation that was going to be seen in living rooms from Portland to Tallahassee and even my hometown of Orwigsburg, Pennsylvania.

But the SheEOs were becoming more blatant about wearing their greedy hearts on their sleeves. Hanging out at a Red River bar after the taping, the SheEOs blabbed and cackled among themselves and their hangers-on about how well things were going for the league. They stood on their bar stools and boasted that they owned Roller Derby.

I often thought of quitting—we all did. But I was hooked. I was getting fit and strong. I had a large circle of incredible women friends. When the SheEOs left us to our own devices—which they did most of the time—we had a blast together. It seemed crazy to let these women take away something that the rest of us treasured.

So we rolled our eyes. We called them horrendous names behind their backs. We hoped that we could work with them—or around them—to make things better. At one point, we elected skater reps to take our concerns to the SheEOs and negotiate on our behalf. Though the SheEOs allowed the skater reps to attend their private SheEO meetings, the reps were powerless to effect any change. The SheEOs thought they could do whatever they wanted, and for a time, they were right.

☠ ♥ ☠

In 2002, seeming eager to enhance their status as derby moguls, the SheEOs decided to expand the league with a fifth team.

They invited proposals for a new team theme and eventually selected Electra Blu's idea for the Hustlers: a troupe of seventies divas in purple and silver—part Ziggy Stardust, part Donna Summer, and 100 percent funky. The plan was to hold tryouts to find a dozen new girls, and then to train them with the help of Electra Blu, their captain and the only veteran on the team. The Hustlers would then make their skating debut when the new season kicked off in early 2003.

"At tryouts, I was worried that I wouldn't be perceived as 'tough enough' because I didn't have any tattoos, didn't curse, drink, smoke, or party or wear fishnets. During the three-lap sprint, I was lined up with five other girls behind White Lightnin', our pacer. I pulled ahead of her after the first lap, but as we were rounding a corner, she tried to cut in ahead of me and tripped over a cone. She laid right out in front of me. I flew over her and crashed helmet-first into the judges' table. I got up, my lip bleeding profusely, and finished the race."

—RICE ROCKET, HOTROD HONEYS/TEXAS ROLLERGIRLS

The talent at the tryouts was incredible. We watched the girls skate and gauged their willingness to try new moves. The captains conducted mini-interviews to see what kind of personality the girls might bring to their skating. That night, we had a pretty good idea who our rookies would be, and a few days later, the Hustlers were a reality.

A lot of the veteran skaters hoped that the influx of new girls—and their unrestrained enthusiasm for Roller Derby—would reverse the downward spiral of the league atmosphere. But as Eight Track said later, that's like a married couple on the brink of divorce thinking a child will save their union. The rookies—their fresh eyes, their inquisitiveness, and the way they were treated by the SheEOs—magnified the flaws in our skater-SheEO relationship.

Meant to be the saviors of our marriage, the Hustlers—and a handful of new girls recruited for the existing teams—were treated like poor second cousins. At practice, they were isolated from the rest of us, forced to skate at the edges of the rink—working on remedial skills—while the rest of us trained. The excuse offered by the SheEOs for the newbie quarantine was "lack of practice space for everyone," but I think the real reason is that the SheEOs and some of the other Mean girl veterans simply enjoyed lording their status over the new girls. The rest of us had already toughened up to their bullshit; rookies gave them an opportunity to be the Mean girls they thrived on being. Although most of us were kind and welcoming to the newbies, the sting of criticism and exclusion are what lingered in the Hustlers' minds.

One of the central figures of the league—its heart—was AmberDiva. By the time I came along, she was the Penalty Mistress, in charge of the carnival wheel of punishment that skaters were forced to spin when they broke the rules of the game. She'd started out as a skater herself, but was sidelined by a broken ankle. She often spoke wistfully about the skater she might have been if she hadn't been injured, but she so embodied the Penalty Mistress role—in and out of the game—that I couldn't imagine her doing anything else.

Her domain during the game was Spank Alley, a line of spectators with paddles in hand, ready to deliver a swat to rule-breaking skaters. There were times the fans were more unruly than the derby girls, and AmberDiva kept the biggest testosterone-fueled macho men in line with a sure smile, a sharp word, and a flick of her hip.

At league meetings, when conversations became heated, AmberDiva was the one to stand up and remind us all how much we meant to each other. She had a graceful way of shaming us into treating each other with respect—especially when we were angry. If you crossed her in some way, she let you know it. But when she did, it was with genuine affection and empathy, like she wanted to make you feel better for pissing her off.

The only thing that rivaled her affection for the skaters of Bad Girl Good Woman (BGGW) was her devotion to her son, Tulsa. She was one of those fun moms, letting him get dirty, run around, be a kid. She helped organize a babysitting circle with the other skater-moms so they could attend practices and special events. She stayed up late on weeknights after putting Tulsa to bed to devise new penalties, make props covered in glitter and feathers, and to plan her goth-princess costume for the next bout.

She wooed skaters into forgetting team boundaries by inviting mismatched groups of girls for beers after practice. Spunky and oh-so-stylish, she had a true heart and she laughed like she knew a secret and would share it if you asked her nicely. AmberDiva was one of those people that immediately made a lasting impression.

That's why it was such a blow when we learned on February 2, 2003, that she'd died suddenly of tragic causes.

I don't remember who called to give me the news, probably The Wrench or Strawberry, but I have a distinct sense memory of standing in my kitchen and feeling sucker-punched. Like I'd forgotten how to speak English.

The rest of the day was a flurry of phone calls—crying, laughing, reminiscing, fretting, and, mostly, shared silence. We were young-ish girls, not many of us had experience with funerals and death, and the ones who did had painful memories of friends' car crashes or grandparents' illnesses. All of those memories flooded back and tangled around the new ones, wrapping my friends into emotional knots.

That awful day, the league gave us a sense of family and togetherness. I believe that feeling of community is the one thing that helped us put up with all the rest of it—the tension, the constant bruises and soreness that are inevitable in our sport, the emotional turmoil of being around sixty women almost every day. All of those negatives somehow became one giant positive. Like family, we would stick it out, in good and in bad.

Driving to the funeral home, it was as if the sky knew the sun shouldn't shine. The wind was bitterly cold and all around us was flat gray—no clouds, no light, no depth at the horizon. But even in mourning, the derby girls were a colorful bunch. Inside the chapel, the pews were packed with skaters, fans, AmberDiva's family, and other friends. Breaking up the sea of black was a leopard print coat or a vibrant red scarf, tattoos, Easter-egg-colored hair. It was a solemn occasion, but like AmberDiva, it had just the right touch of flash.

Whatever lines had been drawn among the teams or skaters or SheEOs had been erased by the tragedy. Without exception, every member of the league had been touched by AmberDiva. After the service, we huddled together in the parking lot and released balloons that floated away on the wind.

A few weeks later, we held a memorial celebration at one of AmberDiva's favorite Red River bars. Audience members paid $5 each to spin the Penalty Wheel for a chance to win one of her signature feather boas or a kiss from a skater. All of the proceeds were donated to a college fund for her son, Tulsa, and at the end of the night, the Penalty Wheel was retired.

AmberDiva left her mark on me. She told me once that I had "mad style," and asked to borrow a black Lolita dress to wear to a bout. As thanks for the loan, she had the dress dry-cleaned and gave me a gift of black sheer stockings with a tiger printed on the ankle, surrounded by rhinestones. The dress is still in my closet. I can't bear to get rid of it, but I'll never wear it. I've never taken the stockings out of the package, but I see them in my drawer every time I dress for a bout.

After much debate and soul-searching, we decided to hold our scheduled February bout at Playland just a short time after Amber-Diva's passing. Called the Valentine's Day Massacre, it was dedicated to her memory, and all of us wore pink armbands with our uniforms.

The compassion that bridged the chasm between the skaters and the SheEOs in the aftermath of her funeral should have remained. It didn't. The SheEOs were up to their old, divisive tricks. Dressed as 1920s gangsters in fedoras and ties, topped by feather boas, they carried toy machine guns and fake-fired at us as they paraded around the rink. Later, when captions were applied to the photos from that night, someone playfully labeled their picture with these words: "The SheEOs of BGGW ain't nothing but a buncha gangsters," and described how they "pitted" the girls against one another.

But AmberDiva's death had irrevocably drawn the skaters together, and the power the SheEOs had over all of us was about to be challenged.

CHAPTER

CHAPTER

06

Bonfire of Vanity

South By Southwest is the biggest music festival in the
country. When it hits Austin in mid-March, it hijacks every
bar, club, concert hall, and restaurant with a stage. For
people who don't want to spend $175 on a wristband for
admission into official SXSW shows, there are dozens of
free showcases, house parties, and impromptu jam sessions on street corners, in front yards, on the blacktop in
front of a pawnshop. The city vibrates with live music of
all genres, and country fans mingle with the punk rockers
who bang their heads right next to hip-hoppers.

    If you're a music fan, you want to go to SXSW. If
you're a musician, you want to play at SXSW. If you're a
wannabe rock star, learning you're going to be part of
SXSW feels like winning the lottery. So when the SheEOs
announced that our league was playing a bout at the
Austin Music Hall on the Saturday afternoon of SXSW—the
biggest day of the festival—I was thrilled. It was like an
unsigned band landing a gig on the main stage of Warped
Tour.

    Headlining our bout was Nashville Pussy, a good
ol' Southern trash hillbilly band that sounds like it stayed

up listening to AC/DC all night. The Hellcats were playing the Holy Rollers. The Rhinestone Cowgirls were facing the Putas del Fuego. We were all playing SXSW!

But it wasn't long before the rumbling started. Again. Like every other edict handed down by the SheEOs, the veteran skaters had questions. The team captains—whose first priority was the health and happiness of their skaters—had concerns about the SXSW gig that the SheEOs seemed unable, or reluctant, to answer.

The Austin Music Hall is a general admission venue, an enormous concrete rectangle. A bar sits along the back of the hall, and directly above it is a balcony that provides a straight-line view to the stage at the opposite end of the room. In between the bar and stage is a glassy-smooth cement floor that's crisscrossed with small grooves, like the seams in a sidewalk. The ceiling is supported by square concrete pillars that divide the main floor into three sections. The idea was to put a slightly reduced version of our track in the center section, directly in front of the stage, so we'd be skating in the area between the concrete ceiling supports.

Worries buzzed. How would we keep skaters from crashing into the cement pillars? Is the floor safe for skating? Does our insurance cover the Austin Music Hall? Will the show attract enough fans to make it financially feasible? Will enough skaters be sober—in the middle of SXSW—to put on a good show and be safe?

The SheEOs hand-waved and equivocated. They talked about our backstage access and the three dressing rooms we could claim as ours. They gushed about how excited Nashville Pussy was to headline our show. They had stars in their eyes. The high profile of SXSW was just too alluring to turn down.

As March 15 approached, the veteran skaters did everything they could to make it OK for the rest of us. The Wrench pulled some strings so we could get into the Music Hall early to do a test-run on the floor. Skaters donated mattresses and futons to wrap around the cement poles. Volunteers were recruited to be skater-catchers—big-muscled, big-hearted boys to stand guard at the pillars and catch a skater if she seemed headed for a collision with the concrete.

The perimeter of the skating area was lined with yellow emergency tape to keep fans out of danger. We were assured that our insurance coverage was in effect at the Music Hall. It began to look like everything was falling into place. We could stop worrying about the logistics and start planning our strategy—and outfits—for our debut on our largest stage yet.

I may have been foolish or naive or in deep denial, but I wasn't worried about skating at the Music Hall. Safety isn't something I worry about when I'm skating. If it was, I don't know how I would ever get back on my skates and into a jam. Once my gear is on, I stop thinking about what could happen and give myself over to our sport. So I figured I'd go to the Music Hall, get a feel for the floor, and trust that if Holli Graffic or Devil Grrl knocked me out of bounds, the skater-catchers would nab me.

It was only my second SXSW as an Austinite, and I was looking forward to a week full of live music. My best friend Rich was coming to visit from L.A. with his girlfriend, Alex, and we were gonna live it up. Shows all day and night. Breakfast at 2:00 a.m. Plus, they were finally going to see me skate, live and in person.

The day of the bout, it seemed like everything would unfold just as I hoped. The street in front of the Music Hall was crowded with people meandering around in the early afternoon sun. They looked a little rough around the edges—SXSW had been going on for four days, so sleep deprivation and beer consumption had taken hold. I felt like a rock star walking past them into the Music Hall. Dolled up, we attracted a lot of attention, and it was still a new thrill to see a stranger elbow his buddy and point.

Inside, it was the usual hubbub, with crew, skaters, friends, band members, VIPs, and Music Hall employees scurrying like ants to set up for the show. One of the things I like about our league is that our shared prebout ritual is a barrage of affection and compliments. Mixed into the hugs, air kisses, high fives, and handshakes are murmurs of: "Ooooh, you're lookin' hot today." "Hello, pretty mama." "Hiya, gorgeous." We're all each other's biggest fans and the gushing is a necessary precursor to the ass kicking that comes later.

But at the Music Hall that day, there was a strain under the smiles and the sweet talk. On the surface, everything looked just the way it should, but the energy was off. The team captains were jittery. The SheEOs were more frenzied than usual. The Hustlers were pissed off because they weren't skating in the bout. The SheEOs had decided the Hustlers would do a disco-skate dance number instead. Dressed in their uniforms, they'd each be introduced to the crowd and skate a lap around the track, but they weren't going to be playing the game. It was the third time their debut had been postponed.

I didn't have a specific production job to do, and there was still an hour until the doors opened, so I wandered the building, soaking it all in and trying to shake the unease that was beginning to settle in my gut.

As promised, we were assigned three dressing rooms backstage. They were less glamorous than I'd imagined: cinder block walls; bare bulbs that cast a harsh, jaundiced light; ratty thrift-store furniture harboring a forensic bounty of DNA. The wall opposite the dressing rooms had been autographed by all the musicians who'd cooled their heels in the hallway before us. Dave Grohl! Willie Nelson! I abandoned the search for Mike Ness's name—lead singer of Social Distortion and my number one musical hero—and joined the rest of the girls on the loading dock.

Iron Maiden and Hot Lips Dolly huddled together, whispering violently about something, stabbing the air with their hands and scowling, like cats just beginning to arch. The bravura of the SheEOs reached higher heights than ever that day. They'd been fielding phone calls from promoter-types who promised them all-expenses-paid Roller

Derby tours to Japan and TV deals with price tags a girl could retire on.

When Jarrod, Lucille Brawl's beau, met Hot Lips Dolly that afternoon, he said, "Hi, I'm Jarrod. I'm a skater-catcher today."

She replied, "Hi, I'm Hot Lips Dolly . . ." She waved her arm around the Music Hall at the skaters in an expansive gesture, " . . . and this is mine."

☠ ♥ ☠

Our SXSW bout officially started when the SheEOs took the stage to kick off the action. They preened and made self-congratulatory comments to the audience. Then the announcers called the Holy Rollers and Hellcats to the track.

I don't remember any specific plays from our game, and the score has long since disappeared from everyone's memory. I do know that the crowd reaction was energizing. Most of the audience had never seen anything like it. Their faces lit up with every hit, every crash, every speeding jammer. The fights were greeted with the loudest roars. Once the starting whistle blew, it became like any other game for me. Skate, hit, duck, smile. The skater-catchers did their job. The announcers called the action. The refs blew their whistles.

Fifteen seconds into the bout between the Putas del Fuego and the Rhinestone Cowgirls, the world went cockeyed. Whiskey L'Amour, a rookie for the Cowgirls, was skating in her first game. A slight push from behind sent her into a spiral, and she did a pirouette on her toe stops, the gold fringe on her Western shirt flying on the breeze as she spun. She clattered to the floor like a windup doll running out of steam, and the crowd erupted in cheers.

But then Whiskey didn't get up.

There's a photo of her skating before the game. She looks proud and lovely in her denim miniskirt and tube socks. Her cheeks are flushed. Her eyes are bright. She is the picture of happy opportunity. All potential.

But in less than a blink, she was a crumple on the concrete floor.

The rest of us kept our distance. It's a rule of derby to give a downed skater room to breathe and to maintain her dignity. No gawking. Each of us knows whether or not our face would be welcome hovering over an injured friend, so only Whiskey's closest pals gathered around her on the track. The story they brought back to the rest of us made our stomachs clench. Her foot seemed to be detached from the rest of her leg. Her skate dangled at a sickening angle, held in place only by her sock.

She says now that she didn't feel any pain until almost half an hour later, when she was in the ambulance. In the moments following her fall, there was a scramble. The SheEOs had lined up an EMT to be on-call at the bout, but he didn't have a full array of equipment. He splinted Whiskey's leg with duct tape and a stack of *Austin Chronicle* newspapers. When the ambulance arrived, an EMT shot her in the arm with morphine and whisked her off to the hospital.

The crowd went back to their beers, the volume on the music cranked, and the rest of the game was played. By the time Nashville Pussy was demolishing the crowd's eardrums, everyone seemed to have forgotten about Whiskey.

It was the Saturday of SXSW, and Whiskey wasn't the only one to come out on the losing end of an accident, so she was left on a stretcher in the hall of the emergency room. For seven hours, she waited in a painkiller fog. Then she went under the knife. She emerged from the operating room to find her mom waiting after a frantic four-hundred-mile drive from Louisiana.

The doctors reported that Whiskey had suffered a clean break of both her tibia and fibula. Her foot was separated from the rest of her leg. The pirouette that so entertained the audience was a result of her toe stop getting stuck to the floor. Her upper body went for a spin, her leg did not.

Whiskey spent three days in the hospital and was visited by her team, a few other derby friends, and an administrator who was eager to discuss her plans to pay her rapidly mounting hospital bills.

When Whiskey tried to file a claim for her injury, she found that the league's insurance coverage hadn't extended to the Austin Music Hall. None of us had been covered during that game. We thought we would be safe, that we had insurance coverage. We didn't.

When we learned that Whiskey's personal medical insurance only covered a portion of her hospital stay and treatment, we demanded that the SheEOs use league money to help pay her bills. They reluctantly agreed to reimburse her—Hot Lips Dolly and Iron Maiden even said they'd visited her in the hospital to give her the good news. When we finally talked to Whiskey, she told us that the SheEOs had never phoned or stopped by to check on her and she hadn't heard anything from them about paying her medical expenses.

Eventually, Whiskey says, they gave her a few hundred dollars.

☠ ♥ ☠

A few weeks later, I walked up the driveway to Cha Cha's house. Though Bettie Rage and Strawberry were at my side—and the Hustlers and most of the other skaters surrounded us—I felt vulnerable and small. Anxious. We were advancing into the enemy territory of the Putas del Fuego and the SheEOs.

We'd all been at team meetings that night when we heard— many of us for the first time—about the covert machinations that had been transpiring within the league. A group of skaters—led by The Wrench, Strawberry, Electra Blu, and the team captains—was ready to give the SheEOs an ultimatum: they either agreed to grant every skater in the league voting rights and allow rank-and-file skaters to elect a management team to work with the SheEOs, or we would all secede to form our own league.

When our rebel leaders approached the SheEOs with their request the first time, the discussion came to an irreversible halt. The SheEOs seemed to suggest, in colorful language, that we were all replaceable. The meeting at Cha Cha's house was a final attempt to make peace.

Cha Cha lived on the east side, in a large house with a wrap-around porch. We passed some of the members of the Putas del Fuego, lounging on deck chairs and smoking cigarettes in the dark of the porch, as we walked down the driveway to the backyard. Inexplicably, a bonfire crackled in the fire pit in the center of the yard; it was like walking into *Lord of the Flies.* Iron Maiden, Hot Lips Dolly, and Miss Information were positioned across the yard, the flames flicking into the sky between us. All around the perimeter of the fire, clusters of girls from the Holy Rollers, Hustlers, Hellcats, and Rhinestone Cowgirls waited. They stood with their hands on their hips, or arms folded across their chests. The Hustlers were particularly impatient. Some raised their chins in defiance. Others whispered to the girl next to them, or kept their eyes trained on the ground, avoiding contact with the SheEOs.

Across the yard, Miss Information spoke.

"So, we hear that some of you have, um . . . concerns about the league. We wanted to give you this opportunity to ask us questions."

I'd promised my team I wasn't going to say anything. I pleaded with them to help me: "Don't let me talk. Seriously. I'm just going to listen. I have nothing to say to those girls."

But when the moment came, I thrust my right hand up over-head: "I have a question."

My voice sounded like someone else. Tight. Like something that could deliver blunt-force trauma. "Why do you three think you have the right to own us? To do whatever you want? To keep information from us? When all along, we've been the ones skating and doing the work?"

I felt a hand on my arm; Bettie Rage's fingers were cool on my skin. I stopped talking and waited. The flames crackled and sparks popped into the dark. On the other side of the fire pit, Iron Maiden sat on a crate, peering into the near distance, like a cat staring down a phantom only it can see. She repeatedly twisted a lock of her hair, first one way, then the other. Hot Lips Dolly stood off to the side, looking perturbed, like she wondered when the annoyance would be over so she could get back to . . . whatever. Only Miss Information faced the group, her face cloudy.

The Hustlers stood together, nearer to the SheEOs than I was, and their resentment was palpable. Their commitment to breaking away and starting our own league was unquestionable and brave. I only hoped that the other girls weren't faltering in their conviction. The SheEOs were master manipulators. They had a way of explaining things that could lull the listener into maybe not completely buying their story, but believing the story *could* be true. Once that door was open a crack, the SheEOs slithered in.

The meeting lasted about forty-five minutes and one thousand years. In that time, we made zero progress. The conclusion seemed foregone. The SheEOs continued to reject the notion that all of the skaters deserved to be equal owners of the league, and the rest of us refused to accept that we were not.

At one point, I remember asking Strawberry how long we had to stay. The circular arguments were making another lap, and my skin was crawling. It reminded me of getting tattooed. I'm fine. I'm fine. I'm fine, and then suddenly, I want to choke the life out of the tattoo artist.

Strawberry took my hand and gave it a squeeze. "It's OK," she said. "Bettie Rage will know when it's time. She's got a good internal clock. She'll know."

I admired her patience.

It seemed that almost everyone was talking at once. Iron Maiden continued to silently twist her hair, Hot Lips Dolly and Miss Information were red-faced, their voices raised, their bodies tense. Around the circle of skaters, groups muttered to each other, and individuals yelled in frustration, stabbing the air with their fingers or closed fists.

Then Strawberry's voice, clear and resolute, cut through the chatter.

"If you want a say in what happens to you, if you want to be treated with respect, if you want to be part of a league that's by the skaters and for the skaters, where every skater gets a vote, then you know what to do."

She turned her back on the fire, on Hot Lips Dolly and Iron Maiden and Miss Information, and walked toward the driveway that led back out to the street.

I went after her and matched my stride to hers, walking by her side.

Quietly, she said to me, "Please tell me they're following." I peeked over my shoulder.

The skaters—all the members of the Rhinestone Cowgirls, the Hellcats, the Hustlers, and the Holy Rollers—had turned their backs on the fire and the SheEOs. They marched down the driveway behind us.

"They're all following you," I said. "They're coming."

ROLLERGIRL RIOT

CHAPTER

07

By the Skaters, For the Skaters

TCB

by Christopher Gray, *Austin Chronicle*
April 25, 2003

ROLLER DRAMA

Neither side is saying much because attorneys are involved, but there's been a coup d'état in Austin's roller derby ranks. Several skaters have broken away from Bad Girl Good Woman Productions to form their own federation, the Texas Rollergirls. One rollergirl, Melicious, says the split came due to "growing pains" and a desire to be more "community-based." Meanwhile, BGGW issued a succinct press release Monday, stating in part, "Bad Girl, Good Woman Productions, All-Girl Roller Derby Entertainment wants to make it clear that we are not affiliated with this group."

"This is no fun at all!" added BGGW "She-EO" Heather Burdick via e-mail. Small wonder: Four of the five squads—all but the Putas del Fuego—have joined the Rollergirls, but since BGGW owns the team names, they now go by "Gun-Totin', Rough-Ridin' Rodeo Sweethearts," "Engine-Revvin' Frisky Felines," "Groove Thing Shakin' Disco Divas," and "Sexy Schoolyard Scrappers." The upstart league has its first bout 7 pm, Sunday, at Playland Skate Center (8822 McCann), with refreshments by Beerland and music by the Sexy Finger Champs and DJ Shiv. Tickets are $10.

Our rebel management had expanded to include me and a few others who felt strongly about what our league could be, if the skaters called the shots. We called ourselves "transitional management" to convey to the rest of the skaters that we were going to help get things set up, then step aside; ultimately, the skaters would vote on who should manage the league and how.

The members of the transitional management were each other's lifeline—on our cell phones and e-mail to each other almost constantly. By "almost constantly," I mean from 7:00 a.m. until midnight or 1:00 a.m. most nights. If we weren't making plans or sharing information about progress, we were crying in panic or frustration. Almost every conversation eventually circled around to the crucial question: How many of the skaters do we have for sure?

We'd run down the team rosters, doing a status check, tallying names and numbers. Eventually, 80 percent of BGGW—almost every skater except the members of the Putas del Fuego—joined our revolt, and we named our new league Texas Rollergirls. But for a few weeks, it wasn't clear that we'd be successful. Many of the resolute women who'd stalked away from the bonfire had soon reverted into questioning, worried, waffling girls who weren't sure what do to. The transitional management had announced our desire to hold a bout in April, and we believed we could all pull it off. Some of the skaters' e-mails to our Yahoo! group asked valid questions, laced with anxiety: How would we pay for Playland rental? Where were we going to hold practices?

When? Was BGGW going to sue us? Did the SheEOs, as they'd threatened in e-mails and phone calls, really own our skater names and uniforms?

Their fear was understandable. I was scared to death that we'd made a grave mistake. But I was equally as sure that we couldn't continue the way we had been.

We planned a league meeting to discuss their concerns, plan for our bout, and hear from an attorney who would demystify our situation and help us get our own LLC established. It was the first time—since Roller Derby in Austin had started in 2000—that a real, live lawyer was on hand to answer questions and make sure all the T's were crossed.

The morning of our league meeting, the transitional management team met at my house. While I made coffee, Dave got bags of breakfast tacos at the corner Tex-Mex joint, and all of us practiced our speeches, made notes, and prepared to face the girls who were our staunchest allies and also our harshest critics. On the agenda that day: determining who was really with us, defining our league structure, and holding a vote that would decide if the April 27 bout would happen.

It was a four-hour marathon on the deck of Mother Egan's Pub. We argued. We cajoled. We negotiated. We brainstormed. We cried. Oh, boy, was there crying. But at the end of it, we had a management structure, had voted in managers for every leadership role, had signed our LLC paperwork, and were officially 100 percent, no doubt about it, the Texas Rollergirls.

And we were holding our first bout in three weeks.

At the time, it was like being run back and forth over an emotional cheese grater. But when I look back on it now, I'm so proud it makes me blush, for real. We committed to each other that we would cherish our relationships with local businesses, since they're the ones who keep us rolling. We unanimously voted to donate time and money to local charities, including a trust fund for AmberDiva's son, Tulsa. Our management structure mirrored a corporate org chart—Advertising & Sponsorship Director, Art Director, Events Director, Finance Director, Charity Liaison, Marketing Director, Merchandise Manager, Production Director, Secretary, Training Coordinator—with one major difference: no CEO. Along with the team captains, the managers formed our governing body and negotiated with each other to run the league.

We've tweaked our structure a bit since then, but the underlying principle is the same: by the skaters, for the skaters. The decisions and agreements we made that day have gone on to influence our sport and leagues all over the country.

☠ ♥ ☠

After that meeting, we knew we had the skaters and the know-how to pull off a great bout, but we didn't know if we'd have an audience. It was my job to make sure we did. I'd been elected the Marketing Director.

My job had two primary components: 1) blabbing on the phone, sending e-mails, and meeting face-to-face with everyone I could to differentiate ourselves from the BGGW league; and 2) dissuading the skaters of the Texas Rollergirls from talking shit in public about BGGW and the split.

The few women who remained with BGGW didn't make it easy. They took Sharpies to the walls of every restroom of every bar on Red River and left graffiti accusing us of being "thiefs." (The incorrect spelling was delicious.) They proclaimed, "Texas Rollergirls are fat and ugly." For about a week, we considered adopting that as our official tagline.

I'm only a tiny bit ashamed to say we retaliated with Sharpies of our own—some of the graffiti may even have been in my handwriting. BGGW made it so easy to mock them and so difficult to resist the temptation. While we were busy planning our first bout, they were

organizing an afternoon of public Jell-O wrestling. We declared ourselves "Jell-O Free in 2003" all over downtown—and smug never felt
as good as it did when we saw the photos from their romp in the gela-
tin. Muddy, pale, with a green cast from the lime Jell-O, and dotted
with flies, they didn't look like Roller Derby skaters.

Meanwhile, our promotion of the upcoming game was attracting media attention. The local public broadcasting station planned to
send cameras to our first bout, and magazines wanted to talk to us.

OLD-SCHOOL   VS.   FLAT TRACK DERBY

Banked Track	vs.	Flat Track
Owned by one white guy	vs.	Owned by a gang of chick skaters
Clean-livin'	vs.	Hard-livin'
Athletic uniforms	vs.	Pinup girl uniforms
Traditional teams	vs.	Badass gangs
Uniformity	vs.	Individuality
Underpaid employees	vs.	Unpaid DIY owners
For profit	vs.	For fun and charity
Corporate	vs.	Grassroots
National league	vs.	Local leagues with national co-op
Traditional penalty box	vs.	Penalty box + playful penalties
Girl next door	vs.	Femme fatale
Soda pop	vs.	Beer! Beer! Beer!
G-rated	vs.	PG-13
Big band	vs.	Rock 'n' roll

Those were some of the first interviews that our skaters got to do. In BGGW, any conversation with the press was handled by the SheEOs. In Texas Rollergirls, I tried to make sure that there was an opportunity for every skater to get her moment in the spotlight. The enthusiasm for our league, and passion for our game, is evident in those interviews. One of the TV pieces includes a shot of Sparkle Plenty explaining that she didn't know how to skate when she joined the league. As she talks, the footage under her voice-over cuts to her speeding around the track as a lead jammer in a bout. When Strawberry confessed on camera that she found the crowd reaction intoxicating—"It's like being in a band, with people screaming my name"—the scene jumps to her celebrating a great play with a hip swivel and a pumping fist in the air. It's impossible not to cheer along with her.

As we set up for our first bout as the Texas Rollergirls, I reminded myself that we'd done everything we could to make the game a success. We had print and radio press coverage, and we'd fly-ered all over town. We'd talked of nothing else to friends and family. All that remained was to put on a good show. Audience or no, we were making our debut. As the opening band began their set, the news was passed from the lobby of Playland to the center of the rink, to the dressing room in the back corner: the line of people outside waiting to buy tickets stretched from the front door of Playland to the street, a queue of spectators half a football field long.

We skated that night as the Purple, Plaid, Black, and Red teams, a precautionary measure in response to the SheEOs insistence that they owned our team names. There were also a few tense hours while we sorted out whether any of us really could be arrested—as the SheEOs alleged—for theft of BGGW merch that was still stored in a Texas Rollergirl's garage. (In a show of solidarity, we swore that if one of us was dragged off in handcuffs, we'd go together—on skates.)

Beyond a handful of BGGW skaters getting drunk and kicked out of our bout for disorderly conduct, nothing untoward happened that night. In fact, we were a smashing success. The Hustlers made a stunning debut and crushed the Honky Tonk Heartbreakers. It was the first time anyone outside the Hustlers team had seen Dinah-Mite jam, and it was astonishing. All of us—the audience, the skaters, the announcers—knew that we were watching the woman who would change our game. Her athleticism and sex appeal was undeniable; her skill was going to push the rest of us to improve.

There would be no stopping the Texas Rollergirls.

CHAPTER

CHAPTER

08

The Four-H Club

Our first season as the Texas Rollergirls was a cyclone of bouts, special events, media ops, and building trust among each other and with our community. We promoted our new team names: the parochial school girls became the Hell Marys, the rodeo sweethearts became the Honky Tonk Heartbreakers, the car gang became the Hotrod Honeys, and the Hustlers got to keep their name because BGGW had never embraced them as part of the old league. We announced a full season schedule and signed a contract with Playland for six games, from April right through to the October championship.

While we were getting our feet under us as the Texas Rollergirls, the remnants of BGGW began to organize, too. They recruited new skaters and acquired a banked track, setting a new direction for their league. In a move I believe was designed to confuse our Austin fans—and ride the Texas Rollergirls' media-friendly coattails—Bad Girl Good Woman changed its name to Texas Roller Derby Lonestar Rollergirls. It was an annoying ploy, and it worked. People often confuse our two leagues. Since then, our two organizations have (mostly) been in a state of détente.

They're committed to their old-school banked track, and the Texas Rollergirls helped foster the Flat Track revolution across the nation.

During our first season, we established badass relationships with sponsors and partners that still support us. We started a tradition of skating in AIDS Walk Austin and collecting food for the Capital Area Food Bank. We partnered with Keep Austin Beautiful, and are the proud adoptive parents of a section of Cesar Chavez Avenue, where we hold cleanups several times a year. I think one of the most moving experiences of that first year was presenting a $1,500 donation to the Children's Advocacy Centers of Texas. When Electra Blu and I handed over the giant check—it was six feet long and took both of us to manage— I got shivers. We were actually making a tangible difference in our town. In addition to the showgirl makeup and torn fishnets and catfights that sent our audience members into spastic gyrations of happiness, we were giving back to the community. We were doing exactly what we intended to do, and it felt good.

But we had a lot of silly fun, too. To meet our fans and raise our profile, we held a Punk Rock BBQ and Watermelon Seed Spittin' Contest, Big Glove Boxing, Derby-style Twister, and the pièce de résistance created by our Event Director, Riff Scandell: full-contact musical chairs (played with slightly tipsy Rollergirls and live music from an old-timey jazz-hokum-blues-hillbilly band called the White Ghost Shivers, featuring a seven-foot-two ukulele player named Shorty).

Our mix of show-womanship, good manners, loyalty, business savvy, and generosity earned us a reputation for being easy to work with and reliable. Incredible opportunities landed in our laps, like Rollergirls knocked out of bounds. One of the biggest was the Republic of Texas (ROT) Biker Rally. Held annually the weekend after Memorial Day, it's the largest gathering of bikers in Texas. In 2003, we were booked as one of the Rally's afternoon headliners on the main floor of the Travis County Expo Center.

DOLLA DOLLA BILL, Y'ALL

Our tongue-in-chic bad behavior and sintastic uniforms garner us a lot of attention on the track, but we're accomplished in our everyday lives, too. We even have real jobs!

Bicycle wheel builder—Anesthesia, Minnesota Rollergirls

Corporate event planner—Apocalippz, Texas Rollergirls

HIV prevention & counseling—Bad Sister Heidi, Mad Rollin' Dolls

Matchmaker for a dating site—Barbie Brawl, Minnesota Rollergirls

Bookbinder—Boston Strangler, Minnesota Rollergirls

Biotech quality control analyst—Cheap Trixie, Texas Rollergirls

Tattoo artist and shop owner—Devil Dog, Minnesota Rollergirls

Middle-school language arts teacher—Helen Wheels, Tucson Roller Derby

Special investigator (with top-secret clearance)—Honey Ryder 007, Dallas Derby Devils

Photography assistant—Hurricane Lilly, Rat City Rollergirls

Elementary school teacher—Lucky Strike, Texas Rollergirls

Limo driver—Mandelicious, Minnesota Rollergirls

Massage therapist—Misty Meaner, Texas Rollergirls

Product usability consultant—Smash Hit, Texas Rollergirls

Theatrical costume seamstress—Speedy Marie, Texas Rollergirls

Dog trainer—Vanna Whitetrash, Mad Rollin' Dolls

School librarian—Vendetta Von Dutch, Texas Rollergirls

Synagogue bookkeeper—Muffin Tumble, Texas Rollergirls

The Expo Center—home of Austin's ice hockey team—is a humongous arena plopped right in the middle of 150 acres of a whole lot of nothing. Until the 33,000 bikers arrive. They come in packs and gangs of men in leather do-rags and women in skimpy bikini tops (or no tops at all). With tans that show the wear of countless hours in the sun, their skin and their attitudes are weathered and hard-bitten. They arrive in RVs and pickup trucks with their motorcycles on trailers, or make the trek in caravans of bikes. In one afternoon, they transform the area around the Expo Center from barren, dusty fields into Sodom and Gomorrah. It's fantastic!

Landing that gig at the ROT Rally was a big deal for us. We'd be playing for our largest audience ever—the arena holds 6,000 people—and it was a chance to see what folks outside our Austin safety zone really thought of our crazy sport.

For Derringer .44, a rookie in 2003, it was a dream come true. The only wheels she loves more than the Sure Grip Power Plus wheels on her skates are the ones on her 1976 Swiss Army motorcycle. She'd been instrumental in helping us land the ROT Rally gig, and the collision of her two worlds had her frolicking around the Expo Center like a St. Bernard puppy—unstoppable, excitable, and endearing.

Six feet tall in her bare feet, she's a Valkyrie in skates, leather chaps, and a cowboy hat. An eclectic conglomeration of brains, beauty, and brawn, Derringer is a cyclone under normal circumstances. She's a Harvard Ph.D. and is on the staff of the Department of Integrative Biology at the University of Texas (with Biology research interests in "Evolution of sodium channel genes and tetrodotoxin resistance in vertebrates," among other things).

She can also pimp your hot rod with Von Dutch–style pinstriping and sing her original country-Gypsy songs for you while playing the accordion, guitar, banjo, harmonica, or piano. Every year, she throws a Hungarian Rhapsody party, complete with goulash, traditional music and dancing, and vats of red wine. (No, she's not Hungarian.)

And yeah, she can skate like nobody's business, with the speed of a jammer and the heft of a blocker. She is formidable.

Punk Rock Phil was the Honky Tonk Heartbreakers mascot, number one fan, quasi coach, and official historian. He's as much a member of our league as a human can be without a) being a woman, and

b) wearing eight wheels. He's immediately identifiable by two things: his punk-n-proud mohawk and the enormous Texas flag he waves at every bout.

Picture the scene. It was Saturday afternoon. Ninety-plus degrees outside and painfully sunny. Day three of the ROT Rally hedonism tour. The arena was packed with about five thousand boozy bikers who had maybe come into the arena specifically to watch our bout, but, more likely, had been drawn in by the air conditioner cranked to frigid, the ample seating, and the refreshing darkness.

The announcers did their thing and the spotlights bobbed around our track on the arena floor, as all of us waited on the loading dock/dressing room—amped up like we were plugged into a wall socket—to hear our names boom through the P.A. system.

When the announcers intoned, "Ladies and gentlemen . . . the Honky. Tonk. HEARTBREAKERS!" the arena filled with the whoops and stomps of the crowd, and Punk Rock Phil led the team procession onto the track. He galloped ahead of them, waving the flag, as Derringer later described him, "like Davy Crockett on methamphetamine." No one can recall if Punk Rock Phil was too exuberant or if Derringer was too distracted, but about halfway around the track, flagpole met dazzling smile in an improbable confluence of variables that put the flagpole directly at mouth-height. Before the first whistle had blown, we'd suffered our first four ROT Rally casualties: Derringer's front teeth.

Still in her wristguards, she spit four white Chiclets into her hand, wrapped them in a piece of gauze, popped in her mouthguard, and skated her first bout ever as a Texas Rollergirl.

Just as we'd hoped, the bikers loved our hijinks. The crowd's cheers bounced around the arena, filling our ears and encouraging us to skate fast and hit harder. I don't know if it was the drama of the venue or the "We did it!" feeling that got the best of us, but we had more than our fair share of injuries that day. Barbarella broke her wrist and had to have her wristguard cut off by the EMTs. Pris screwed up

Roller Derby Sisters & Rivals

★□★

RJB Photo

Bonnie Collide #32

SOCKIT WENCHES/RAT CITY ROLLERGIRLS

POSITIONS: *Blocker*

LIKES: *the fast lane; open roads; music turned up loud; Stuckey's; the smell of high-octane fuel and pine-scented air fresheners*

DISLIKES: *gridlock; cops with radar; Yugos; counting to ten; gas prices*

BONNIE COLLIDE FACTOID: She's engaged to Cooter the Grease Monkey, the Sockit Wenches' mascot. In a rockabilly monkey-mechanic jumpsuit—with ears, tail, and tall pompadour—he throws faux-feces (Tootsie Rolls) at the crowd and the refs in protest.

Diagnosed with extreme, debilitating road rage, Bonnie Collide was sentenced to an anger management program. When her instructor recommended a change of scenery, she hit the road to Seattle and, on the advice of an equally enraged friend, joined the Rat City Rollergirls. Her road rage is in remission—but if you take the track with her in the pack, make sure your insurance policy is current. You do not want to be on the receiving end of a fender-bender from Ms. Collide.

Celesta Danger/celestadanger.com

Derringer #.44

HONKY TONK HEARTBREAKERS/TEXAS ROLLERGIRLS

AUSTIN TEXECUTIONERS, 2006 DUST DEVIL NATIONAL FLAT TRACK CHAMPIONS

THEME SONG: *"It's Alright, Ma (I'm Only Bleeding)," by Bob Dylan*

Derringer was born in an Airstream trailer on Lake Mojo Swamp near Angleton, Texas. She inherited her mother's alligator wrangling talents and her father's stature, so Derringer spent her early childhood catching snakes and sending the neighborhood boys into the hospital. She spent her twenties learning swordfighting and the samurai arts, traveling the world in search of intrigue and danger. Her tortured lovers (may they rest in peace) have included a Latino soccer champ, an aerobatic test pilot, a bike racer, a convicted hijacker, a dinosaur bonedigger, a racecar driver, and several rock stars. Though she's a Texan, her heart longs for New Mexico, "the place all Texans and aliens end up when they both need a little more kickin' room."

RIVALS: *Ivanna S. Pankin, Neander Dolls, Sin City Rollergirls*

□★

her knee during warm-ups. Pinky dislocated her shoulder (and was taken to the hospital by Sparkle Plenty, already in an arm cast from a skatepark mishap.) Lucy Furr wrenched her shoulder. Many beers lost their lives in the stands—all in the name of derby action. In an illegal use of "tickets," I was almost suffocated by Eight Track's cleavage when she knocked me on my ass, straddled me, and rode me like a Harley while the announcer shouted to the crowd, "Come on, ya pussies . . . make some noise!"

As for Derringer, her smile—thanks to the artistry of a cosmetic dentist—has been restored to pre-ROT Rally brilliance, and she and Punk Rock Phil are still thick as thieves.

Derringer's parents' reactions to the news of her injury were diametrically opposed and both amusing and infuriating. The first thing her mom said on the phone: "Oh! That's so sad . . . you always had such a pretty smile!"

Yes, Mom. I'm fine. Thanks for asking.

But her dad, in an instant, recognized Derringer as a hero. A former college basketball star, he'd had his teeth knocked out during games back in the day. Derringer said he almost seemed proud of her, like her teeth were war casualties. Ah, Roller Derby. Bringing families together.

While the league as a whole was enjoying the boost of our success, the Hustlers were showing us what they'd been working on during their banishment to the fringes of the Playland floor. Turns out they had stars at every position: Dinah-Mite, Electra Blu, Pussy Velour, and Barbarella were agile, swift jammers. Eight Track and Sedonya Face were a wall of defense at the front of the pack as pivots. Their blockers—Dirty Deeds, Cheap Trixie, and Reyna Terror—were annoyingly good at getting in the way. But even more powerful than their individual skaters was how they'd learned to work together.

The underdogs had been sneaking off to a rink in Bastrop, a quaint town about forty minutes from Austin. The extra practices, the hankering to prove they'd been worth the wait, and their innate athleticism all came together during their first season, and it left the rest of us in the dust. Each month, they handily defeated the opposing teams.

It was hard to begrudge them their victories after a year of their being treated like steerage passengers on the *Titanic.* But that didn't stop the Hotrod Honeys from plotting and planning how we were going to beat them in the championship game. The Hustlers had been undefeated all season, and after losing to them twice, we wanted to capture that season title and the honor of being the Texas Rollergirls' first champs.

The Hustlers and Honky Tonk Heartbreakers line up for a Jam at Playland

Michael R. Osborne

Thanks to Dinah-Mite and the Hustlers, we were all pushed to get better at our game. All of us were realizing there was more strategy and finesse involved in each of the positions than we'd first realized. It took me about six months of practice and play before I could watch skaters in action and really see what was happening. Roller Derby moves dazzlingly fast—like hockey, without the puck to lead your eye—and it's hard not to be overwhelmed by the sensory input. As we all settled into the sport, we started to specialize our roles in the game and the action on the track got a lot more interesting.

As we evolved as players, we stopped thinking of blocking as the "easy position" and recognized that blockers are the heart and soul of the pack. A combination of brawn and brains (and beauty), blockers have to think both offensively (to help the jammer) and defensively (to stop the opposing jammer). We form walls with our bodies or gang up to box in the opposing jammer to trap her midpack. When we're at our best, we keep the pack tight, making it more difficult for the opposing jammer to slice through. Or we split up, one of us hugging the inside line and the other patrolling the outside perimeter, looking for the opportunity to body-check the other jammer into the crowd. (The Hell Marys' jammers are required to take an oath: "I will not attempt to skate around the outside of Eight Track.")

Now we practice two types of blocking: the booty block and the body check. In a booty block, we lower our center of gravity by skating in a squat and position ourselves directly in front of the approaching jammer, anticipating her moves and shutting her down. A solid booty block is the bane of most jammers: what's a girl to do when she's trapped behind a steamroller who's determined to keep her from passing? The body check is the crowd-pleaser—and my favorite, too. It's a full-body battering ram that sends jammers, blockers, and pivots alike through the air, into the audience, and onto the acrylic. There's really nothing more satisfying than plowing my archnemesis into the beer-wielding fans in the front row.

The rules forbid us to push or grab the girls on the other team, but getting physical with our own teammates is one of the best ways to get a jammer through the pack. We Hotrod Honeys snag, pull, push, and crash into each other with hilarious regularity—but a well-timed, controlled push from one of us can give our jammer the extra oomph she needs to break past an enemy booty block.

The best way to rile up the crowd *and* help out a jammer is with a whip. That's when a blocker or pivot reaches back for her jammer, grasps the jammer's hand (or forearm or skirt—whatever she can get a grip on), and swings the jammer forward, transferring momentum to help her blast past the rest of the pack like a slingshot.

As a skater's blocker skills evolve, she can be "promoted" to pivot, which is really just a blocker who has special responsibilities at the front of the pack. A skilled pivot speeds up the pack as the jammers approach, and then slows the pack as the jammers lap their way around the track. Pivots often double-team with their front blockers, forming a wall to prevent the other jammer from getting through.

One of the other special duties for the pivot is recognizing the off chance when she becomes the jammer. During the first pass through the pack, a jammer can sometimes get stuck: maybe her blockers are unable to make sufficient holes, or she might have an atrocious fall that takes too much recovery time. Meanwhile, her opponent has taken advantage of the situation and established herself as lead jammer. If the poor beleaguered jammer can get to her own pivot, she can hand off the star from her helmet and her pivot becomes the jammer. Beers are raised in a toast! Announcers go wild! The refs confer! The new jammer-pivot does her damnedest to score some points. It's like a once-in-a-lifetime sighting of an exotic bird—rarely seen but highly valued—and it's a lifeline for a tired jammer.

As I've already admitted, I was overeager to be a jammer in my early derby career. I wanted the razzmatazz of the spotlight, to be a superstar. I've since realized it's a whole lot of responsibility to be the girl who's got to score, and a good jammer has got to be thinking while she's sprinting. A key piece of strategy for the lead jammer is determining when to call off the jam—which means knowing how many points she's scored and where the opposing jammer is in relation to her. The lead jammer calls off the jam by placing both of her hands on her hips to signal to the ref. Ideally, she calls it off after she's scored at least one more point than her opponent, or when she's trapped—by a blocker or a fall—and needs to stop the other jammer from racking up points.

As our game matured to be more athletic—and Dinah-Mite's reputation for being a Roller Derby superstar grew—the media took notice. Our local all-news station named Dinah-Mite the Athlete of the Week in July 2003 (in Austin, a town that can claim cyclist Lance Armstrong and football star Vince Young as local heroes). The headline on the story: "Roller Derby Athlete May Be Super Hero."

Then I got a phone call that was unexpected and ridiculously exciting. A reporter for CBS had caught wind of what we were up to, and she was coming from New York in October to interview Reyna Terror with her daughter Spawn of Terror, and to tape our championship for a feature segment on *The Early Show.* The news crew would follow Reyna Terror from her volunteer duties at a running race in the morning to our championship bout that night, and capture everything in between. We were going to be on national TV as the Texas Rollergirls. Praise the Lord and pass the bearing grease!

Less high-profile but infinitely more Rollergirl-esque, we were also going to be featured on *Free Beer,* a local television show. We decided we'd make male derby fans everywhere weep with joy with an all-girl fantasy: a faux slumber party for the cameras, complete with pedicures, silly hairdos, pillow fights, whispered confessions, and gossip.

The conceit was that the slumber party was held the night

before the championship game. In reality, we all got together for the taping a few weeks before the big game.

We planned the party for my house, in my studio. Our home is a two-parter: a main house with all the rooms you'd expect, and a second two-room building in the backyard. It's our music-writing-programming studio and playhouse, and we pimped it out with a metallic gold ceiling, a red velvet divan, leopard-print rug, gold throw pillows, and gold lamé drapes. We even spray-painted a bust of Beethoven gold and perched him on top of the piano.

It really took on the feel of a clubhouse when a dozen or so Rollergirls arrived toting props, snacks, skate gear, and twelve-packs of beer. Oh, man! The outfits. I wore vintage black knee-length bloomers covered in rows of lace ruffles, a Texas Rollergirls T-shirt, black Converse sneakers, and showgirl makeup. The other girls wore silk pajamas, baby dolls, feather mules, fuzzy bunny slippers, chenille robes, supersize T-shirts (and little else), lacy lingerie, and *Flashdance*-inspired one-shoulder sweatshirts and leggings. We all assembled in the studio, crashing on the couch or on the floor with sleeping bags. Electra Blu, Ultra Violent, Cheap Trixie, Eight Track and Cassette, her six-year-old daughter, Dirty Deeds, Sparkle Plenty, Derringer, Loose Tooth Lulu, Hot Wheels, Kitty Kitty Bang Bang, Vendetta Von Dutch . . . it was a full house of rivals and pals from three of our teams.

The fourth team, the Hell Marys, had a meeting scheduled that night, so their only member at the party was Mean Streak, winner of the 2003 Best Pivot Award at the Whammies (our annual awards celebration of the best and baddest in the Texas Rollergirls). Off the track, Mean Streak was rarely serious for long. On the track, she was a terror. When I saw her coming at me during a game, I would just kind of batten down the hatches and brace for impact. If she had me in her sights, I knew I was going into the audience.

Since her real approach to getting ready for a bout was low-key, she decided to do her own version of *Whatever Happened to Baby*

Jane? for the pajama party cameras. Her hair was pulled into uneven ponytails that sprang from her head in violent spikes, and her face was powdered white. Dressed in a beige sixties-style peignoir, she flicked a switchblade open and closed, while murmuring in a singsong voice. Then she smeared red lipstick around her mouth, over and over and over. I think the cameraman was truly terrified.

The rest of us indulged in stereotypical, thanks-for-setting-us-back-thirty-years girliness. Electra Blu and I lay on our sleeping bags and munched Doritos, then we painted the interviewer's fingernails bright red, all the better to complement the motor oil facial he'd received from Vendetta Von Dutch earlier that evening. Derringer had brought a shotgun (unloaded), and she sat in the center of the couch, a menacing expression on her face, methodically polishing the barrel.

Across the room, Dirty Deeds, one of my favorite partners-in-crime, finally gave in to the interviewer's request that she hit him, and she nailed him with a pity punch. She's a glamazon: six feet tall, blond, muscular, and always in high heels. She doesn't walk; she strides. Decked out for her interview in a purple, lace-trimmed bustier, zebra-print micro-miniskirt, purple fishnets, and knee-high metallic silver platform boots, she didn't look like a girl who spends her days working for nonprofits as a volunteer coordinator.

At the time, my hair was Billy Idol blond and short. Derringer had put her weapon aside for a while, and was covering my head with rows of itty-bitty ponytails when we heard a knock at the studio door.

Without waiting for an invitation, a buffed-out dude in mechanic's coveralls, tinted aviator shades, and an expertly slicked-back D.A. hairdo clomped into the room.

"Did somebody call a mobile mechanic?" he asked, then hit the play button on his boom box.

What followed was an erotic, smoking-hot, gyrating, undulating strip tease. He peeled off his coveralls to reveal a wife beater and black boxer briefs—with delivery of an impressive package. He made the rounds of the room, thrusting and wiggling and flirting with each girl in succession. Cassette's eyes were the size of Frisbees and her cheeks burned bright pink. The rest of us were in various states of hormone-drunk and hysterics. As the music climaxed, he wrapped his arms and legs around the pole that supports the studio ceiling, and rode that thing like a bucking bronco. When the music ended, he circled the room again, kissing a cheek here, nuzzling a neck there. Then he zipped up his jumpsuit, pulled his sunglasses down his nose to give us a sly wink, grabbed the boom box, and disappeared into the night.

"Holy shit! Was that, like, one of y'all's boyfriends or husbands or something?" the cameraman asked, wiping sweat from his brow.

"Oh, no!" Dirty Deeds said, laughing, "That was White Lightnin'. She's a Hotrod Honey."

★◻★

Michael R. Osborne

𝔇irtp 𝔇eeds #22
HUSTLERS/TEXAS ROLLERGIRLS
POSITIONS: *Blocker, Glamazon*
HEIGHT: *6' something*
DISLIKES: *taxes; math; sorority girls; Bush and his Republican cronies*
THEME SONG: *AC/DC "Dirty Deeds" and ODB "Hey, Dirty!"*
FAVORITE QUOTE: *"Between two evils, I always pick the one I never tried before."—Mae West*
DIRTY DEEDS FACTOID: *Yes, those are her real legs.*

Ms. Deeds was raised in the sultry, seductive clime of Miami, amid pastel palaces and muscle-bound masculine eye candy. Though Latin rhythms and Cuban food soothe her soul, AC/DC calls out to her dark side. When her (dirty) deeds necessitated a getaway, she shimmied west to Austin, in search of soul sisters who could match her crime for crime. The Hustlers are the perfect cover for the long, lean, killin' machine. If you got a lady and you want her gone, Dirty Deeds can help you out—and it's dirt cheap.

AWARDS: *2004 Texas Rollergirls Sweatiest Rollergirl ("I was nominated for Hustler Blocker of the Year in 2005, but Sedonya Face beat me. That bitch!")*
RIVALS: *Sparkle Plenty, Honky Tonk Heartbreakers/Texas Rollergirls*

◻★

Suddenly the door burst open again and an army of maniacs stormed into the room. Wearing Mexican wrestling masks and pantyhose over their faces, they attacked with loaded cans of silly string—covering the ceiling, sleeping bags, couch, walls, beer cans, stripper pole, and us with tacky, multicolored twine, while screeching like howler monkeys. Then they sprinted out the door, but not before we'd all seen a flash of red plaid.

The cameraman followed the trail of masked marauders, and we followed him. A collection of Hell Marys—The Wrench, Muffin Tumble, Devil Grrl, Bloody Mary, Misty Meaner, Deadly Cyn, and Anna Mosity—stood in the driveway, smoking cigarettes and smirking, discarded wrestling masks at their feet.

What can I tell you about Anna Mosity? She's the kind of girl you want to bite when you see her—like, you just know that her shoulder would taste like the first strawberry in June or a cinnamon bun. She's what a fourteen-year-old boy thinks about when he thinks "pretty girl"—the real-life version of Kelly LeBrock in *Weird Science.* Of course, Kelly LeBrock never beat up bikers at the ROT Rally, which I saw Anna Mosity do in the audience of the Jerry Lee Lewis show, with my own two eyes. She was celebrated as much for the panties she wore under her uniform skirt—"Nuns Suck" printed across the butt— as for her aggressive blocking and jamming.

The interviewer took one look into her doe eyes and made a fatal error in judgment.

"Hey, Anna Mosity . . . wanna beat me up for the camera?"

That's like saying, "Hey, cobra snake, just give me a little nip." or "Yo, homie. Bet you can't peg me with that nine-mil."

While the cameras rolled, Anna Mosity dove at the interviewer with her derby-honed flying tackle. In the footage that aired on TV, it looked like a genuine knockdown, drag-out. The two of them tumbled, rolling in the gravel, with Anna Mosity definitely in the power position.

She pummeled him with both fists until he cried uncle. (I think he really was crying.) Then she got up, flipped her hair, smoothed her skirt, and turned a dazzling smile to the camera. The lens followed her as she sashayed down the street, then the camera pivoted back to the interviewer for his show-closing remarks.

"Well, there you have it. I survived. We spent a sexy night with the Texas Rollergirls as they get ready to . . ." His voice trailed off as fear clouded his face. Then he shouted, "No!" as he brought his arms up in a defensive motion around his head. An airborne blur of red plaid and auburn hair knocked him to the ground again. The last shot before the scene went black was Anna Mosity pounding on him like nobody's business.

And that's exactly what it's like the night before every championship game.

☠ ♥ ☠

While the Hustlers and Hotrod Honeys spent the *real* championship eve eating healthy food, drinking water, and getting to bed early, the Hell Marys and the Honky Tonk Heartbreakers—set to play for third and fourth place—were fucking with each other in a way that only the partners in a true love-hate relationship can.

No one will confess to being the brains (or lack thereof) behind the idea, but at some point, the Heartbreakers—who hadn't won a game all season—decided to make their own offtrack amusement by toilet papering the Hell Marys' houses and yards. At casa de Wrench, a top-of-the-line security system—her dog, Ruly—alerted her to the intruders just as they were about to start soaping the windows of the classic muscle car she loves almost as much as her dog. The Wrench bolted from bed as her puppy went nuts barking, waking the neighbors on The Wrench's quiet residential street. She chased the Heartbreakers down her driveway, almost catching them before they escaped in Sparkle Plenty's truck. It's a good goddamn thing she didn't catch them. At Strawberry's house—on the east side—she turned her dogs loose on their gingham-clad butts, and they almost got their keisters blown off by her husband's shotgun—and Amen almost called the cops after the ruckus woke her sleeping daughter.

Phones rang all over town as the Hell Marys communication network ramped up. Revenge was in order, and why wait until it was a cold dish? Anna Mosity and Mean Streak launched retaliatory strikes.

By game time the next day, the mock anger had turned to real, hard, chilly determination to make the other team pay. The Hell Marys were genuinely pissed about being disrespected and having their sleep disrupted. The Honky Tonk Heartbreakers were mad right back at what they saw as the Hell Marys' lack of a funny bone. The game was on.

09

We Are the Champions

To me, our 2003 championship was a celebration. The worry of our first game was long gone. We had CBS cameras in the house, taping for *The Early Show.* A crew was on hand to film the whole shebang for a DVD. Riff Scandell had landed the "It" band of the summer for our halftime show; fresh from an instrument-smashing appearance on *Late Night with Conan O'Brien,* we had . . . And You Will Know Us by the Trail of Dead.

Going into the championship, the standings looked like this:

> *Hustlers 4–0*
> *Hell Marys 2–2*
> *Hotrod Honeys 2–2*
> *Honky Tonk Heartbreakers 0–4*

The Honky Tonk Heartbreakers were announced to rousing applause, and then the Hell Marys took the track. In a show of unity, they skated en masse, rather than reveling in the spotlight with individual introductions. Their usual pranks—flashing ruffled butts, frolicking with demonettes and wheeled priests—were replaced with resolute expressions.

★🔲

(back): Smaximaz #1134, The Crusher #3, Apocalippz #86, Misty Meaner #5, Bea Attitude #40 oz., Bloody Mary #4 (captain). (front): Hissy Fit #54, Muffin Tumble #28, Nasty Habit #68, Disharmony #17, Bunny Rabid #99 (co-captain), Amen #55, The Blade #6", Satina (mascot; with pom-poms). Missing from photo: Deadly Cyn #7.

Rebecca Davis/rebeccadavisphotography.com

Hell Marys 2006

THEIR HYPE: The Hell Marys are canonized by their fans who worship at the altar of the red-and-black plaid. The moral straightjacket of parochial school has only made them more brazen; their attitude problems are out of control. Clutch your rosary and grab some holy water! When these reform-school girls roll onto the track, only divine intervention can save your soul.

THEIR REP: The Hell Marys are known for hitting hard—and often—from the first whistle. The blockers and pivots specialize in repetitive, powerful lateral hits that knock opposing blockers out of the lane, clearing a path for the Hell Marys jammer. The team's jammers are compact and fleet-footed; they excel at watching for the holes opened up by their blockers and play the game at their speed, on their terms.

🔲★

The opening bout of the night was for third place, the Hell Marys versus the Honky Tonk Heartbreakers. First at the jammer line was Buckshot Betsy for the Honky Tonk Heartbreakers and Strawberry for the Hell Marys. The two had a long-standing rivalry. Designated hotties for their teams, they were both petite, fiery-tempered, and evenly matched for speed and skill. But the playfulness that was usually on display between them was gone, replaced with an implacable, closed expression from Strawberry as the announcers recounted the TP incident for the audience. As the crowd booed and aahhed in sympathy with the Hell Marys, the whistle blew, and Strawberry took off like a shot, Buckshot Betsy drafting at her heels.

Buckshot, thanks to a whip from Jen Entonic, was named lead jammer. As the pack hit the second corner, Mean Streak pounded Honky Tonk Heartbreakers like a wrecking ball, but Buckshot continued to rack up points while Strawberry was stuck midpack. Finally, just before the two-minute buzzer ended the first jam of the night, Bloody Mary nailed Buckshot Betsy with a solid hit and sent her into the audience; Buckshot called off the jam. Our color commentator Julio E. Glasses told the screaming audience, "The Honky Tonk Heartbreakers are playing like they haven't before this entire season. They are out for a win tonight."

★✰★

(back): Bettie Rage #12, Derringer #.44, Devil Grrl #666, Moonshine #XXX; (middle) Belle Starr #1889, Loose Tooth Lulu #4X4 (co-captain), Trouble #10 (captain), Sparkle Plenty #00, Dagger Deb #13; (front): Buckshot Betsy #21, Crazy Duke #02, Sic Shooter #06, Jen Entonic #03

Michael Harmon

Honky Tonk Heartbreakers 2006

TEXAS ROLLERGIRLS CHAMPIONS 2004, 2005, 2006

THEIR HYPE: Sweethearts of the midnight rodeo, the Honky Tonk Heartbreakers sure know their way around the ranch. They can rope a Brahman, bust a bronco, take a tumble in the hay, and lasso the heart of an elusive cowboy, all while wearing the shortest denim this side o' the Pecos. Circle the wagons! It's a showdown at the T.X. Corral when these wild Western women have you in their crosshairs.

THEIR REP: The Honky Tonk Heartbreakers are known for fast packs and their excellent lateral maneuverability. The blockers and pivots specialize in the "swoop," an unexpected, full-body block from the outside that uses speed and the element of surprise to take out opposing blockers. The team's jammers are among the fastest in the league; they excel at assessing the pack and adjusting their speed and direction in response.

✰★

Next on the line were Misty Meaner for the Hell Marys and Loose Tooth Lulu, a rookie Honky Tonk Heartbreaker, making her debut as a jammer. Misty Meaner was trapped in the pack by Sparkle Plenty; Loose Tooth Lulu was named lead jammer, but she called off the jam when the mischievous Muffin Tumble landed a solid block and sent her out of bounds.

For the remainder of the half, the teams continued to trade the lead jammer title and the score stayed within a two- to three-point lead, in the Heartbreakers' favor. With only about four minutes left in the half, Barbie Crash hurled her waif-model body at Anna Mosity, concerned more with exacting revenge for the previous night's shenanigans than with the scoreboard. When the refs had untangled limbs and separated the two, they were both sent to Hot Wheels, the Penalty Princess, for punishment. Panting and sweaty, their faces flush with anger and exertion, the girls were sentenced to a one-lap skate duel, with the winner taking home bragging rights and an extra point for her team. Anna Mosity took an early lead and easily won the extra point, while the announcer whooped, "A Rollergirls' fight is like licking a flaming popsicle stick. It hurts like hell, but it sure is sweet."

Back on the track, the skaters seemed more interested in venting their fury than ensuring a win. Bloody Mary—usually coolheaded, calculating, and deadly efficient in the jammer slot—grew frustrated behind Sparkle Plenty's effective blocking. What's a pissed-off Rollergirl to do? Bloody Mary hooked both hands in Sparkle Plenty's studded belt and gave it a yank, sending both of them sliding across the track and into the front row of the audience. Good for morale, but not for the score. The Heartbreakers led by two points with only two minutes remaining in the first half.

The remaining jams in the half were a mess of scuffles, whistles, illegal takeouts, and hard, legal hits that did little to affect the score. In a derbyrific pile-up, Trouble took a whip from Derringer and then The Wrench flattened both of them; all three then crashed into the infield among the skaters waiting on the benches. The last jam—with only fifteen seconds on the clock—was a formality. Strawberry and Sparkle Plenty stood at the line, waiting for the whistle, pointedly not looking at each other.

As the crowd counted down 5 . . . 4 . . . 3 . . . 2 . . . 1 . . . to the buzzer, the scoreboard showed the Hell Marys with 25 to the Honky Tonk Heartbreakers' 27.

At the back of the rink, in a dark corner, I stood in a circle with the rest of my team. It was almost our turn to skate. The last time we'd faced the Hustlers, we'd lost 67 to 51. We were our own worst enemies, and we knew it. A collection of hotheads and powerful skaters, we hadn't yet really gelled as a team.

But I knew that if we could pull together, we could break up the Hustlers' coordinated blocking and put the brakes on the Dinah-Mite scoring machine. Hell, I'd taken Dinah-Mite's ass out in the July bout. Coming down a straightaway, I nailed her with my right shoulder and hip, knocking her to the floor, just out of bounds. Of course, she'd bounced right back up without missing a beat, and it hadn't changed the score, but just knowing I'd gotten her once was a confidence-booster. Sadly, that was also the game in which I'd let Eight Track get to me, which earned me a roll on the floor with her and a trip to the penalty box.

The number one priority for our team was to stay calm and focused. We needed to keep our emotions in check and play a surgical game: stop Dinah-Mite, work together against the Hustlers' defense, and call off the jam when we earned enough points.

But from the first whistle, we were distracted by our own tension, herky-jerky and reactive. During the first-jam jitters, the Hustlers' Electra Blu was named lead jammer against our own Lucille Brawl, but they both scored point-for-point until Electra Blu was taken out by Cat Tastrophe and called off the jam.

★✚✚

(back) Tomcat #5, Riff Scandell #00, Voodoo Doll #29 (co-captain), Speedy Marie #47, Rice Rocket #3e8, Hydra #8, Melicious #11, Eight Track #8, Kitty Kitty Bang Bang #10, Vendetta Von Dutch #13; (middle) Lucky Strike #7, Dottie Karate #57, Lucille Brawl #56, Tinkerhell #23, Pinky #442; (front, kneeling) Pixie #i, Cat Tastrophe #XX (captain), Rebellika #19.

Hotrod Honeys 2006

THEIR HYPE: Don't be fooled by the pink! The Hotrod Honeys make Russ Meyer's babes look like ladies-who-lunch. In their handbags: switchblades and lipstick. In their hearts: fury as black as motor oil. Change your points and top your tank with gas, 'cause when this girl gang revs their engines, they drive like lightnin' and crash like thunder.

THEIR REP: The Hotrod Honeys are known for tight packs, blocking walls, ferociously hard hits, and resilient jammers. The blockers and pivots are adept at working together, combining booty blocks and takeouts to tire their opposition and shut down opposing jammers. The Hotrods' jammers skate low and stay on their feet; they excel at maneuvering through holes and strategically calling off the jam.

✚★

Second at the line were passionate adversaries Cat Tastrophe and Dinah-Mite. Longtime friends from pre-derby days, their rivalry was the spark that impelled each of them to train harder and brag bigger. Just as Dinah-Mite was named lead jammer, Riff Scandell called on the "Stop Dinah-Mite Strategy: Plan B"—if you can't take her out legally, start a fight with someone else and get the freakin' jam called off by the refs. As Riff and Cheap Trixie brawled into the front row of the audience, whistles blew and the crowd began to lose its collective head.

The captains called the same lineup to the track. Cat Tastrophe and Dinah-Mite lined up to jam, and I took my position as blocker three

★🔲

(back) Pussy Velour #74, Reyna Terror #99 (co-captain); (middle): Barbarella #66, Electra Blu #23, Smash Hit #45, Miso Fresh #21, Dinah-Mite #00, Dirty Deeds #22 (captain), Curvette #'76, Cheap Trixie #13, Rollin' Sweet #512; (front, seated): Ellis Dee #12, Sedonya Face #420, Slim Kickins #11. Missing from photo: Lady Stardust #51

Felicia Graham

𝔥𝔲𝔰𝔱𝔩𝔢𝔯𝔰 2006

TEXAS ROLLERGIRLS CHAMPIONS 2003

THEIR HYPE: Bedecked in purple and silver, the Hustlers have mastered the fine art of the grift. No foolin', brotha; they'll swindle you out of your heart and your wallet with a slick-as-satin seduction. You can't outshoot them at pool or outthrow them at dice, and when these divas start their derby dance, they'll roll right on over you.

THEIR REP: The Hustlers are known for coordinated blocking, surgical pivots, and very fast jammers. The blockers get low and pair up, working the zones to shut down the opposing offense. At the pivot, the Hustlers are masters of controlling the pack speed and regularly take out the opposition's jammer. The Hustlers' jammers use textbook-pretty speed-skating form to capture lead jammer status and power through the pack.

🔲★

at the back of the pack. It was my job to stop Dinah-Mite before she could enter the pack and then to assist Cat Tastrophe. The jam started, and I blew it. Before I'd even realized it had happened, Dinah-Mite had passed all of us and was declared lead jammer. She'd cut a clean line on the inside perimeter of the track right past me and in just five seconds, had taken control of the play. But Cat Tastrophe was close on her tail, drafting off her speed, and conserving energy for the fight through the pack on the next lap. The rest of us bobbed and weaved and bounced off each other, trying to stay on our feet while we looked back over our shoulders for the jammers.

The Hotrod Honeys and Hustlers demonstrate the anatomy of a pileup

Michael R. Osborne

> "I asked my boyfriend why he comes to my bouts, and he said, 'Sometimes I just like watching you knock people over.'"
>
> —DAHMERNATRIX, HOBOTS/DUKE CITY DERBY

I saw Dinah-Mite rushing toward me around the curve. I had a clear sight line on her and none of her blockers were anywhere near me. I cut to the right to position myself directly in her path, exhaling as I braced for her to hit me full-throttle. She passed her teammates Dirty

Deeds and Cheap Trixie on the inside, then BLAM! got up close and personal with my backside. The impact knocked my feet out from under me, and I accelerated to the floor, hitting ass-first, then shoulder, my helmet ricocheting against the acrylic. As I rolled sideways, I tripped my own teammate Speedy Marie, and the rest of the pack—Dirty Deeds, Cheap Trixie, Riff Scandell, and Sedonya Face—stumbled and fell around us, driving knees and elbows into soft body parts. In a flash, we were all up and back in the game as Dinah-Mite slid by unscathed and continued to add points to her tally.

I had one jam to rest until it was my turn to take my place at the jammer line. On the benches in the center of the track, my teammates and I alternately hollered at the refs, screamed at our players on the floor, and sulked. Less than six minutes into the game, we were already pouting and had already earned an eardrum-busting lecture from The Boss, our head ref, about how he wasn't going to tolerate dirty play. From the center, we watched Pinky struggle into lead jammer position, and White Lightnin' repeatedly drill the Hustler jammer Pussy Velour with hard hits. Incensed, Pussy Velour turned on the nearest Hotrod Honey she could reach, and she tumbled to the floor with our own Vendetta Von Dutch, both girls scraping, bashing, and kicking at each other as they struggled to get the upper hand before the refs could break it up.

I straightened my skate laces, drank water, and tried to control my breathing. I was going up against Lady Stardust in the next jam, and I was determined to get lead jammer. Evenly matched in speed, she and I couldn't be more different in physique. Stardust is long, thin, wiry—like a whippet—and I'm a bulldog: short, squat, using more power than finesse to get through the pack. We always have a good time jamming together because even though we're both competitive, our mood—even in the games—is usually light. It's like we have an unspoken agreement to take the game, but not ourselves, too seriously. I've sent her out of bounds and into the fans many times—and tackled her like a football player when the spirit moved me—but we always share a wink at the line and a hug before heading home after a game. Her day job is a pet-sitting business; how could I not adore a girl who both loves animals and dresses like Ziggy Stardust?

As I skated to the line, pulling the star helmet cover onto my head, I wondered again why I campaigned to be a jammer. It's so stressful, carrying that burden of trying to score, especially in the championship game. I love to be the center of attention, no doubt about it, but with that "look at me" attitude comes the fear of humiliation. What if I get stuck in the pack? What if I can't catch up to the pack? There's a comfortable, almost-anonymity in blocking. As blockers, we're in the pack, a thicket of arms and legs and wheels and helmets. The beer guzzlers in the audience can barely discern what we're doing out there. But the jammers—they're literally in the spotlight and once they've broken free of the pack, they're like a showgirl performing a solo dance, crossing on the curves and sprinting toward the rest of the chorus girls.

Rolling up to the line is a bad time to have a crisis of faith. I took a deep breath, got into position on my toe stops, and cleared my mind of everything except the word "Go!" as I waited for the whistle.

Lady Stardust and I were side-by-side going into the pack. I tried to take the inside, but got hung up behind Dinah-Mite and Cheap Trixie. I cut toward the outside as we approached the corner and, somehow, Lady Stardust, my teammate Pixie Tourette, and I all smashed into the front row. We leapt back on our wheels. Lady Stardust was slightly ahead of me, but Pixie was on her, nudging her with annoying jab-like body blocks. I sneaked around the inside past Lady Stardust as my teammate Hydra swooped in and knocked Stardust into the crowd again.

My path to the front was cleared by Hotrod Honeys' booties, and I broke free of the pack. I heard over the P.A., "Melicious is our lead jammer!" as Lady Stardust was knocked to the floor again by Lucille Brawl.

I caught the pack, earning points as I passed the Hustlers, and when I got knocked out of bounds on the straightaway, I called off the jam, hoping I'd scored at least one more point than Lady Stardust. The scoreboard announced the good news: we were within one point of the Hustlers with 4:25 to go in the half.

I thanked my blockers for helping me get through the pack and grabbed some water, getting ready for my next turn at blocking. As White Lightnin'—dictionary definition of badass—had taught me: when a jam is over, forget about it. Don't celebrate the things you did well; don't dwell on the things you did wrong. Get ready for the next jam and save the triumph and tears for the afterparty.

The next two jams followed a pattern: the lead jammer was established, Rollergirls were body-checked into the audience, squabbles turned into fights. The Hustlers were ahead, and we were running out of time. With only fifty-three seconds remaining in the half, White Lightnin' lined up against Barracuda—day job: professional badass; hobby: weight lifting.

White Lightnin' was lead jammer and had just made her second lap through the pack, scoring as she passed one, two, three Hustlers. But as she came around the curve to pass Dinah-Mite at pivot and earn that fourth point, Dinah-Mite hunkered down and drove her entire body into White Lightnin'. Our jammer was catapulted into the audience like a cartoon villain rebounding off a punch from Catwoman, her body splayed out horizontally, parallel to the floor. The crowd erupted with cheers and the clock ran down.

The score: Hustlers 31, Hotrod Honeys 27.

☠ ♥ ☠

The wait from the end of the first period, through the halftime entertainment, and then the other teams' second period can be excruciating. Adrenaline and attitude are cranked to maximum overdrive and then . . . it's time to be gracious with fans or family, posing for photos and making small talk. During halftime, I often find myself waiting in a painfully long bathroom line. Playland doesn't have locker rooms—in their defense, how could the owners ever have predicted they'd need changing rooms for sixty glamour-girl athletes?—so we Rollergirls wait like the civilians for a turn in the ladies' room. It can be awkward. There are certainly sexier places to sign autographs and pose for photos than within earshot of a flushing toilet. "Wait, move to your left a little, then we can hide the 'Employees must wash their hands before returning to work' sign with your head."

At our halftime meeting to regroup for the second half, the Hotrod Honeys all agreed that we were mostly doing what we needed to—working together on blocks and assisting our jammer. But the Hustlers were making lead jammer too often for our comfort zone, and we had to do a better job of stalling Dinah-Mite. We were only down by four points. If we could cool it with the fights—are you listening, hotheads?—and shut down their scoring advantage, we could steal the championship right out from under them.

I often have to chew on the inside of my lip to keep from laughing when we talk about strategy. I know the purpose of the meeting is to get us pumped up and focused, but the actual statements can be a little inane. It reminds me of the commentators during a big football bowl game. The head sportscaster repeats ad nauseum, "This game is gonna be all about the special teams, Howard," and his cohost replies—every time—"Yes, and this football team is really going to need to move that ball down the field."

My pal Bloody Mary and I amuse ourselves in our pregame carpool by mocking the sportscasters' platitudes with our own derby version:

"What the girls are really going to have to do today, Bloody Mary, is skate really fast and put some points on the board. Cat Tastrophe is going to have to use all nine of her lives!"

"You're right, Melicious, but I think it's also really going to be about the blockers . . . can Vendetta Von Dutch knock Barbarella into outer space?"

In a circle with our heads together, my teammates and I crossed hands in the center and chanted, "Faster, faster! Kill! Kill! Kill! . . . Faster, faster! Kill! Kill! Kill!" We were definitely going to have to get some points on the board and do some blocking. But first, we had to watch the fourteen-minute infinity of the Honky Tonk Heart-breakers–versus–Hell Marys second half.

"The rivalries forged in the first period come home to roost in the second, ladies and gentlemen," Julio E. Glasses said, just before the buzzer.

He was right. The first jam was aggressive and violent, with just a touch of crowd-pleasing shtick. It was an ideal example of how each of us takes the game really seriously, but can't resist the urge to showboat.

In a repeat of the last jam in the first half, Strawberry and Sparkle Plenty were on the jammer line and both teams had their biggest, hardiest blockers in the lineup. From the first whistle, the pack was a mosh pit, blockers bouncing off each other and the floor while fighting to keep the jammers trapped. Strawberry muscled her way through to become lead jammer and put four points on the board. Just as she called off the jam, Sparkle Plenty lunged at Anna Mosity on the opposite side of the track, and before the refs could get her under control, she'd torn Anna Mosity's "Nuns Suck" panties right off her perky butt.

"Let's all say a prayer, everybody!" said play-by-play announcer Whiskey L'Amour. "Bow your heads."

Unfortunately for the Hell Marys, that was their last moment of levity for the rest of the game. With each jam, the Heartbreakers' advantage grew. Over the course of eleven jams, the Heartbreakers won lead jammer only three times, but their defense kept the Hell

Marys from racking up points. With five minutes left in the half, the Hell Marys were down by 10, and their usual tactics weren't working. The Heartbreakers refused to engage in fights—the rodeo sweethearts gutted up every insult and illegal takedown, keeping their minds in the game and their eyes on the scoreboard.

When the final whistle blew, the Honky Tonk Heartbreakers had won their first game of the season. Final score: Honky Tonk Heartbreakers 54, Hell Marys 20. More than the win, they'd given us all a sneak preview of what we could expect during the Texas Rollergirls second season. New jammers like Trouble and Loose Tooth Lulu looked like they'd been drinking rocket fuel. In a strategic move for which none of us was prepared, the Heartbreakers had shifted the focus from the back of the pack to the front. All of us had traditionally relied on blocker three to stop the opposing jammer before she could get too far, but the Heartbreakers had put their fastest blockers at pivot and blocker one. They consistently trapped the opposing jammer in the pack, allowing their jammer—even though she wasn't in the lead position—to dominate and score, while the lead jammer languished, stuck behind the Heartbreaker pivot.

Watching their game that night, I felt excited and nervous. I was seeing strategy in action and *athletes* skating around that track. Our silly little game was becoming a sport.

In a pregame interview, Hustler captain Electra Blu said without hesitation, "We intend to maintain our undefeated status."

My teammate Vendetta Von Dutch warned, "We're going to completely fucking destroy the Hustlers. They don't even see it coming."

The Hotrod Honeys had only fourteen minutes to prove which of them was right.

The air hummed as Cat Tastrophe and Electra Blu waited at the jammer line. The crowd was roaring, but I felt like I was hearing them from far away. I was pivoting against six-foot/two-hundred-pound Eight Track, with our own clobberer Tomcat, sneaky Lucille Brawl, and quick Speedy Marie in the pack behind me. It was a money lineup. A perfect opportunity to tie up the score on the first jam, then start building a lead.

As the pack rolled into the second curve, Lucille Brawl held Electra Blu in a textbook-pretty booty block, and I whipped Cat Tastrophe around the outside, then laid a shoulder-hit on Dinah-Mite just for grins. The only thing between Cat Tastrophe and lead jammer was Eight Track, and the two were racing well ahead of the pack. From my perspective, it was time for the refs to call the twenty-feet rule that meant Eight Track would have to step aside to let Cat Tastrophe pass.

★▣

Celesta Danger/celestadanger.com

𝕰𝖑𝖊𝖈𝖙𝖗𝖆 𝕭𝖑𝖚 #23
HUSTLERS/TEXAS ROLLERGIRLS
POSITIONS: *Jammer, Pivot, Blocker, Blue Streak*
LIKES: *cute boys with good manners; international intrigue; first-class airline tickets to exotic locales; dancing on the bar; Afros and cornrows*
DISLIKES: *stingy tippers; line dancing; matte eye shadow; the smell of clove cigarettes and patchouli; cheap vodka*
ELECTRA BLU FACTOID: *She has a signature cocktail named after her on Red River: Monopolowa vodka, club soda, cranberry juice, two slices of lime, served in a chilled pint glass.*

A bronco-bustin' cowboy lassoed Electra Blu's heart. But after a long ride to Texas and a whole lotta bull, she two-stepped away from him and swaggered into a downtown nightclub. To her surprise, a girl on roller skates handed her a piña colada. Confused, but thirsty, Electra downed the cocktail and was soon mesmerized by the lights on the dance floor. By midnight, she knew her future was hustling, not rustling, and the Hustlers were born. Known for her trademark blue lightning bolts, she's electric on the track.
RIVALS: *Lucille Brawl, Hotrod Honeys/Texas Rollergirls; Muffin Tumble, Hell Marys/Texas Rollergirls; All of the Honky Tonk Heartbreakers*

▣★

The refs finally finally finally made the call, and Cat was established as lead jammer, with Electra Blu close on her heels. They both sprinted around the track toward the pack to begin scoring points. Cat snuck past Dinah-Mite, took a helpful push from Speedy Marie, and . . . *crash!* Dinah-Mite took Cat out with a clean hit. Cat called off the jam from her position on the floor.

We hadn't closed the four-point gap.

I sat out the next jam and watched Pinky stretching and rolling her shoulders as she took position with Pussy Velour on the jammer line. Pinky was in good hands with another killer lineup: Tomcat, Vendetta Von Dutch, and Pixie as her blockers, with White Lightnin' at the pivot. But as the jammers moved through the pack, it was Pussy Velour who passed the pivots first to become lead jammer. As the pack sped around the curve, Pinky was knocked down by Barbarella. Pinky popped up, headed for the straightaway, only to fall again, this time with Sedonya Face and Rosie Cheeks. Again, she leapt to her feet and sprinted toward the pack, but Rosie Cheeks leveled another shot that sent them both crashing in front of the fans. Rosie disentangled herself from Pinky and skated away. Pinky stayed on the floor.

As the action moved quickly around the track, it took the refs a few endless seconds to realize that Pinky was clutching her shoulder, knees hugged into her chest like a pill bug hiding from a bird. The EMTs rushed to the track and the rest of us waited. It's always horrible when there's an injury because it's not like it is on TV. When a pro athlete is injured on television, the medical staff hits the field immediately and the commentators give the viewing audience a blow-by-blow in soothing, hushed tones. For us, in the middle of the track—amid the shouting fans, yelling refs, pounding music, and thirty Rollergirls simultaneously saying, "What's happening? Is she OK? What's wrong with her?"—there was nothing to do but wait.

"I've just gotten word from Tomcat," Julio E. Glasses said over the P.A., "Pinky has dislocated her left shoulder."

The EMTs attempted to pop Pinky's shoulder back into place while she lay on the Playland floor, but had no luck. They helped her to her feet, and as she slowly left the track, we could see through her skin that her arm bone was separated from the shoulder joint. It was really gross. The crowd halfheartedly cheered her return to vertical, but the prevailing mood was somber. Except for Pinky; *she* looked pissed. She didn't cry or wince, but seemed to be barking at the EMTs while she gestured with her right hand at her left shoulder. If she could have popped her shoulder back in herself and continued to skate, I think she would have done it.

The refs regrouped. The announcers cracked a few jokes to restore the happy fun vibe, and we got ready for the next jam.

As the crowd chanted "Faster, faster! Kill! Kill! Kill! . . . Faster, faster! Kill! Kill! Kill!" I looked at the scoreboard. We had eleven minutes left and the score was 34 to 27. Plenty of time to make up seven points, but we couldn't mess around.

For the next three jams, it was derby business as usual. The Hotrod Honeys' jammers got lead two of the three, but we just couldn't close the gap in the score. With about seven minutes left in the game, Lady Stardust and Speedy Marie were at the jammer line. They'd just taken off when Sedonya Face landed a hard hit on Speedy Marie that pushed her into the crowd on the corner. Just when it looked like Lady Stardust would pass the pivots to be named lead jammer, Tomcat was clobbered by Rosie Cheeks. Rosie's a little thing, but, as our announcers are forever reminding us, "Roller Derby is a game of angles." Tomcat's got about five inches of height and fifty pounds of muscle on Rosie, but when the tattooed wonder hit her, Tomcat crumbled like two-day-old coffee cake. She went down on her tailbone, bouncing hard on the landing. Unfortunately, she didn't get up.

It was disconcerting to sit in the middle and watch the usually amiable Tomcat lying on her side—wiggling and writhing in obvious discomfort—with a grimace stretched across her face. The clock was stopped, and again, the EMTs ran onto the track to tend to one of my teammates. Vendetta had reached her limit. She grabbed the microphone from Julio E. Glasses and said, "You know, I can't help but notice, these hookers right here in purple wanna keep saying that the Hotrods fight dirty, but you notice how many of our players are gonna have to go to the ER tonight 'cause the Hustlers don't know how to play right!"

The crowd booed and oohed in protest and agreement. As Vendetta skated away looking pleased with herself, she almost collided with Sedonya Face, on *her* way to grab the mic.

"Sedonya Face, how do you respond to that?" Julio asked.

"Girl, we practice twice a week," Sedonya said to Vendetta's retreating back, practically snapping her fingers in front of her face with a satisfied "mmm-hmmm." "You should know how to fall so you don't get hurt."

Meanwhile, Tomcat had recovered from having the wind knocked out of her and was back on the bench. There were just under seven minutes left on the clock. We still had a chance. On the next jam, Cat Tastrophe at the pivot laid into Pussy Velour, sending her into an appreciative fan's lap and clearing the way for Lucille Brawl to take lead jammer. As Lucille came past me, about to start scoring points, I gave her a whip that sent her around two sets of blockers, but when she hit the straightaway, Barbarella shoved her with both hands into the crowd. The refs banished Barbarella to the penalty box as Julio, so excited he could barely get the words out, crowed, "That was just a free-for-all on skates."

With just five minutes left, the Hotrod Honeys had a power play while the Hustlers' Barbarella chilled out in the box for one minute. This was our chance to turn the tide. But when Cat Tastrophe and Dinah-Mite met to run out their rivalry again, the Hustlers defense held Cat Tastrophe within the pack, allowing Dinah-Mite again to be named lead jammer. By now, my team was tiring, and the emotional upheavals of the injuries, the fights, and the trash talk were beginning to wear us down. Our play was getting desperate. The pack was strung out, making it easy for Dinah-Mite to glide through untouched. In a heroic effort, White Lightnin' set up to lay a huge hit on Dinah-Mite, cutting from the far outside toward Dinah-Mite on the inside boundary. White Lightnin' did a 180 pirouette, intending to hit Dinah-Mite from the front, but Dinah-Mite was too slippery and glided right past White Lightnin', whose momentum threw her into the infield where she rolled and crashed into one of the refs.

With three minutes left in the half, in the championship, in the season, the score was Hustlers 53, Hotrod Honeys 37. The only way we were going to close a sixteen-point gap was if we broke all of the Hustlers' legs in the next jam. But my team never gives up. Call it blind faith or folly, but we play every jam like it's for all the marbles. And I've got to say, my Hotrod sisters know how to have a good time. The last four jams were filled with wipeouts and takeouts and takedowns that had the fans on their feet. Tomcat tackled Dinah-Mite, and the two tussled on the floor like kids wrestling in the basement rec room. Lucille Brawl waved and blew kisses to the crowd during her jam. Vendetta Von Dutch was banished to the penalty box. Eight Track introduced White Lightnin' to the fans sitting along the left straightaway with a huge shoulder check. Beers flew out of raised hands, and White Lightnin' hit one dude with so much force, his shoe popped off his foot and landed in the middle of the track.

When Barracuda and Cat Tastrophe took the jammer line, our fans shouted, "Faster, faster! Kill! Kill! Kill!" Just before the whistle blew for the last time on our inaugural season, the two jammers gave each other a high five, and then sprinted around the track as the clock ran down and the crowd counted "Five . . . four . . . three . . . two . . . one!"

Final score: Hustlers 63, Hotrod Honeys 46.

Electra Blu's bravado paid off. Dinah-Mite's jamming delivered. The Hustlers were the first Texas Rollergirls Champions with an undefeated season.

★◻

Michael R. Osborne

Dinah-Mite #8

HUSTLERS/TEXAS ROLLERGIRLS

POSITIONS: *Jammer, Blocker, Pivot, Superhero*

This roller dame arose from the glitter of the early days of disco balls. The magic began one night when her parents' starstruck eyes met across the dance floor; Trixie Stardust and Sly the DJ Funkmaster came together in a hustle that made sparks fly. Their passion for groovy tunes and sex-a-licious dancing united, and in a flash, Dinah-Mite was created. Hangin' with the hippest cats and coolest of cool dames, she soon learned that she was a *good* dancer, but a *great* skater. To everyone's dee-lite, she shimmied into the Hustlers lineup to own her birthright as an electric-slidin', funky-jivin', roller-skatin' Hustler in motion.

AWARDS: *2005 Statistician's Award for Best Jammer, 2005 Hustlers MVP, 2005 Hustlers Best Jammer, 2004 Hustlers MVP, 2004 Hustlers Best Jammer, 2003 Texas Rollergirls MVP, 2003 Texas Rollergirls Best Takeout, 2003 Texas Rollergirls Best Jammer, 2003 Hustlers Best Jammer*

◻★

Do You Know Who I F***ing Am?

People wonder why we Rollergirls make up personas. I wonder why more people don't.

Our personas aren't just the uniforms and makeup and silly antics. Our alter egos give us free rein to become the babe of our dreams— a schoolyard bully, a lascivious glamour girl, a fast-as-lightning athlete. A persona can also deliver up an easy scapegoat for bad behavior: "It wasn't me that illegally elbowed Bloody Mary in the third jam, it was Melicious."

Becoming Melicious

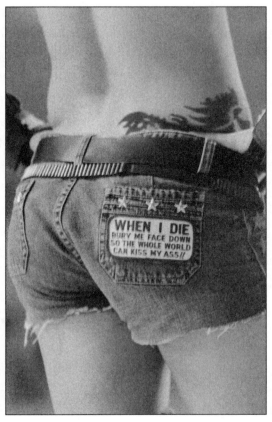

WHEN I DIE
BURY ME FACE DOWN
SO THE WHOLE WORLD
CAN KISS MY ASS!!

Michael R. Osborne

helps me deal with fear and doubt; it's a lot easier to keep anxiety at bay if I remember that the blocker gunning for me is really after Melicious, and Melicious can take it. She's tough.

Someone like Eight Track might not need a persona to make her braver; she was voted Most Feared by our league in 2005. She's a big powerhouse and deflects other blockers like Wonder Woman's magic bracelets. A tap of her hip sends mere mortal Rollergirls crashing into the audience. Of course she doesn't need a persona to manage her fear, but she's one of the reasons the rest of us do.

Developing a Rollergirl persona can go deeper than smoke-and-mirrors entertainment. We Rollergirls have found that our on-track personas can help us in our real lives, too. Even if you're not ready to lace up skates of your own, you might be able to learn something about yourself and better ways to deal with life if you give yourself a Rollergirl name and try on a new persona to see how it fits.

We all use shortcuts to manage the crap that happens every day. Your knee-jerk reaction to something annoying—like your co-worker stealing your yogurt from the fridge . . . again—is a conditioned response. The ability to change your automatic comeback to events and people might seem impossible, especially if you're dealing with something stressful, like a romantic entanglement or a lame-ass boss. But with imagination and patience, you can apply lessons learned by pretending to be someone else and make them part of the real you. By imagining what your Rollergirl persona might do in a particular situation, then acting like her, you could change your ingrained reaction. How cool is that?

"I am now a schizo with two names and one thigh bigger than the other. Roller Derby has taught me how to book a show, skate backward, get money from anyone in the name of a cause, take out a girl who's twice my size, start and avoid a bar fight, stage a debate, hold a mediation, throw an awards ceremony, talk someone out of quitting, talk someone into helping, befriend someone I have nothing in common with, sew a helmet cover, and even, sometimes, keep my big mouth shut."

—CRACKERJACK, RESERVOIR DOLLS/MAD ROLLIN' DOLLS

For centuries, storytellers have used archetypes to make their point. After stringent scientific research—OK, it was actually a few years of talking to Rollergirls about their alter egos—I've identified the idealized varieties of Rollergirl personas that can help you skate through life with fewer bumps in the road. As you develop your Rollergirl persona, ask yourself: What kind of player do I want to be? What kind of person can I become? For your on-track persona, you might pick just one archetype to help shape your new, larger-than-life personality. Off the track, all of the archetypes come in handy once in a while—and all of us have elements of each persona hiding inside of us. We just need to draw them out.

THE SUPERHEROINE

VARIATIONS: Amazon Warrior, Super Spy, Martial Arts Expert

Faster than a juicy rumor. More powerful than a double-espresso. Able to leap male egos in a single bound. It's the Superheroine! Like Uma

Thurman's character in *Kill Bill* or *Tomb Raider*'s Lara Croft, she's a daredevil, a dynamo—with a nimble mind that's as powerful as her punch. She knows that evil exists, but she refuses to give in to it or to her own dark side. Doubt and fear are her archnemeses, but she never backs down from a challenge.

On the Track

In a uniform designed to showcase both her athletic build and allow for maximum movement, the Superheroine is a leader on the track with a laser-beam focus on winning. She doesn't cheat or fight, but skates with heart, skill, and speed. *Mostly* a team player, she'll showboat if the moment is right. The Superheroine is idolized by her fans, but they can also find her a bit intimidating; a good Superheroine will seek them out to make a friendly, inspiring connection.

Off the Track

In "real life," the Superheroine lives with integrity, balancing her physical talents with mental gifts. She recognizes that not every fight requires her fists; that sometimes an honest conversation, perhaps some self-sacrifice, and a touch of finesse go a long way to helping her reach her goals. The Superheroine possesses deep wells of strength that give her the confidence to approach negotiations and demanding tasks—whether at work or at home—with quiet authority.

THE BOMBSHELL

VARIATIONS: Femme Fatale, Pinup Girl, Seductress

"Dangerous Curves Ahead" should precede her wherever she goes. A smooth operator who usually follows her heart, she bewitches men and women with her lethal good looks and understated smarts. Like Marilyn Monroe and Madonna in her Boy Toy phase, the Bombshell is definitely one to stop and smell the roses (and entwine them in her hair while she's at it). She's not afraid of a long-shot proposition because she knows she can talk her way out of anything. Note: This alter ego also has a dark side: the femme fatale who uses her wiles to manipulate the world according to her whims.

On the Track

In a stylish, sexy uniform that showcases her, um . . . assets, the Bombshell is wily and playful on the track. Of course she wants to win, but only if that means her team played well together and with a little flash. She tries her best not to cheat, but sometimes she just can't help herself; accidents happen. Affectionate with her own team—and known for her lighthearted approach to competition by her rivals—the Bombshell is also a fan favorite: warm, flirtatious, and always ready for a photo op or autograph.

Off the Track

Outgoing and charming in "real life," the Bombshell makes her successes look easy. But don't be fooled; the reality is that the Bombshell gets her way by making it easy for her adversaries to say yes. She arms them with the information they need, and knows when to cajole—and when to push—to reach her goals. There's steel beneath her smile, but when things go right, no one but her needs to know that.

THE SEXY LIBRARIAN
VARIATIONS: Teacher/Professor, Scientist

The Librarian is proof that the sexiest part of a woman is her brain. Think Famke Janssen as Jean Grey in the *X-Men* movies or Lisa on *The Simpsons,* and don't be fooled by the logical, matter-of-fact exterior. Beneath her aloof facade burns a passion for life that's rivaled only by her quest for knowledge. She's read about a lot of things, and she's ready to experience them firsthand. She uses her intellect as both a shield and a weapon. Her foible? She can be impatient with those poor souls who are ignorant, either by choice or circumstance, and she can be frustratingly stubborn when faced with opposition.

On the Track

The thinking woman's Rollergirl, no detail of the Sexy Librarian's uniform is left to chance, and she helps her team win with her mastery of strategy. She's got the other players' numbers—stats, foibles, secret weapons—and she'll only cheat when she's calculated the pros and cons of a trip to the penalty box. Never daunted by new challenges, her approach to changes in competitors, venues, and rules is "We can figure this out." The Sexy Librarian makes fans feel comfortable with small talk on just about any subject, and she's a natural at promoting her league.

Off the Track

In "real life," the Sexy Librarian thinks before she acts; she does her research so she's rarely suprised, and can present a calm, assured face to everyone around her. But that doesn't mean she always *feels* calm. At work and at home, her passion for what she's doing runs deep, and she needs to work on containing her frustration so she doesn't bury an irritating co-worker—or frustrating soul mate—in a barrage of indisputable facts that demonstrate her mastery of details and logic.

THE HOTTIE HOMEMAKER

VARIATIONS: Wiseass Waitress, Frisky Flight Attendant, Naughty Nurse

A nurturer to the nth degree, the Homemaker fights for the underdog and provides TLC when the world is too cold and cruel, like Martha Stewart magically mixed up with Samantha from *Bewitched*. Her soothing demeanor disguises a heart that beats with the power of a mama bear defending her cubs. She gets a lot from listening to others and offering sage advice, but the recipients of her kindness best not cross her or disobey her wishes: "If Mama ain't happy, ain't nobody happy."

On the Track

In her uniform with just-so, handmade touches, the Hottie Homemaker nudges and nurtures her team to victory in the game. She's an expert at doing her job, while also making sure that everyone else is doing what they're supposed to, shouting directions in the pack and pushing her blockers into position. Though cheating isn't her preferred method, she'll do what needs to be done to get points on the board. Her philosophy? "If you take my advice, we'll all be fine." Her teammates find her alternately bossy and caring, but fans are unanimous: her willingness to chat and friendly demeanor make her a favorite.

Off the Track

The real world Hottie Homemaker is the first to come to the rescue in times of crisis or to offer sensible advice—even when her friend would prefer she *didn't*. But her intentions are always pure: she wants to make sure that co-workers, teammates, family, and friends succeed at their hearts' desires. All the better if they take advantage of her experience and guidance.

THE WISECRACKIN' DAME
VARIATIONS: Gangster Moll, Intrepid Reporter/Photographer, Detective's Sidekick

In the old days, she was the girl with spunk and moxie; now, she's the one most likely to grab a beer with the guys, but look all-woman while she's doing it. Like Frenchy in *Grease* and *Superman*'s Lois Lane, she's the sidekick that keeps her best friend out of trouble. Supportive and reliable, the Wisecrackin' Dame always has a smart-ass comment at the ready, but her feelings run deep. She's true to her dear ones to the end, defending them with words and (when necessary) an occasional fist to the jaw or kick to the shin.

On the Track
The Wisecrackin' Dame looks great in her uniform, but she's not overly concerned with external appearances—she knows it's the skill and drive *inside* the uniform that really counts. She's the queen of smack talk in the pack, and she's got the goods to back up the big promises her mouth makes. She may talk dirty, but she plays clean, and her intense team loyalty smoothes ruffled feathers when she criticizes as often as she compliments. For her, the game of Roller Derby is one big lark, and her fans laugh and cheer right along with her.

Off the Track
An idea-generating machine, the Wisecrackin' Dame can make convincing arguments on both sides of an issue, which makes her an asset to her league and her "real life" co-workers. This girl loves a challenge and can sweet-talk, harangue, or joke the people around her into a can-do attitude that gets the job done. She's also got a kind word and "We'll get 'em next time" when plans go awry.

THE GANG LEADER
VARIATIONS: Outlaw Cowgirl, Sophisticated Socialite

Like Lori Petty in *Tank Girl* and real-life whistle-blower Erin Brockovich, the Gang Leader is all-woman on the outside, but is a bruised, idealistic child on the inside. Cynical, charming, and charismatic, she knows what makes people tick and can see through their attempts to deceive. Though she's adept at rallying followers to a cause, her survival instincts create a gulf between her and the ones who love her. Others' kindness occasionally pierces her armor, but she retreats quickly, embarrassed to have lost her wits in a fog of emotion. The members of this rabble-rouser's posse are fiercely loyal and would follow her anywhere.

On the Track
She looks tough and intimidating in her uniform, and it's no act. She's a force on the track: formidable and all about the game . . . *winning the game.* She wants clean victories and has no patience for skaters who cheat. She rallies her team with no-nonsense pep talks, and the Gang Leader's interactions with her fans is minimal. She's not a Rollergirl to make friends; she's got a job to do.

Off the Track
The Gang Leader knows how to get shit done. Though she may sometimes seem brusque, she also inspires action. Friends and co-workers are impelled to act by the example she sets and by her belief in what she's doing, whether it's saving a historic landmark, planning an important work-related seminar, or rallying the troops for just one more stop on a bar-hopping expedition. The Gang Leader is driven, and her gang's actions help her deliver on her zeal.

THE DOMINATRIX
VARIATION: High-powered Executive, Military Officer, Prison Guard

This lady is a master manipulator who demands respect, and she doesn't give a damn if she makes waves along the way. Think bad mamma jamma Pam Grier as Foxy Brown or Julie Newmar's Catwoman. Decisive, opinionated, goal-oriented, and not open to negotiation, she ensures that everyone around her bends to her will (and she knows they secretly love it). Although she can be a tough number, everything works out perfectly when she's in charge.

On the Track
While her uniform may be so sultry it borders on impractical, the Dominatrix is very focused on winning—exposed body parts be damned. Physically dominant, psychologically tricky, she cheats if she wants to and, from time to time, compels her teammates to do the same. She's not really a joiner, but has a knack for knowing when to support her team and when to challenge them, and her tough-love approach endears her to them. She exudes a beguiling, dangerous vibe that attracts fans; intimidated by her, they enjoy every second of the fear.

Off the Track
With a solid understanding of the ins and outs of humans' wacky behavior, the Dominatrix intuitively knows how to give people what they want, even when they don't consciously know themselves. At work, she assigns her employees to projects at which they'll excel, and among her friends, she's a trusted ally for honest advice that may be hard to hear, but is right on the money. The Dominatrix embraces her power and, most of the time, uses it for the good of those around her.

THE GIRL NEXT DOOR
VARIATIONS: Tomboy, Catholic School Girl

A real salt-of-the-earth kind of gal, the Girl Next Door is pretty, decent, responsible, and resourceful. Like Rachel on *Friends* and Dorothy in *The Wizard of Oz,* she's not a fan of confrontation, but she'll do what has to be done. Only a fool would mistake her kindness for weakness; she won't strike first, but she has tremendous strength of will. She *wants* to see the world as a basically good place, so she can sometimes be too trusting, but don't underestimate her. She can take care of herself.

On the Track

In a cute uniform that's attractive, comfortable, and game-ready (the scorekeepers can easily read her name and number), the Girl Next Door is a consistent player who gives her all. While she might not be the star of the team, she's never going to cheat, either. She joined Roller Derby to make friends and have fun; winning might be the icing, but she really loves the cake. She's approachable and inclusive with her fans, always ready to make them feel like part of the Roller Derby family.

Off the Track

In her "real life," the Girl Next Door is an ideal team member: hard-working, genial, the kind of girl managers and co-workers are pleased to have on their projects because she gets the job done with a smile and minimal fuss. Among her friends, she's prized for her easygoing nature and thoughtfulness. She's not a pushover, but believes that life is better when everyone gets along. She can turn on the fireworks when appropriately inspired—but it's a relief for her to return to an even keel.

☠ ♥ ☠

In most cases, each of the Rollergirl personas will give you a completely different set of reactions to a given situation: the Bombshell's response to an illegal push from behind is radically different than what the Dominatrix and her teammates might do in retaliation. Remember: by adopting a Rollergirl persona, you can change whatever your *natural* reaction might be. Take me as an example. Off the track, if I'm not bothered too much by a lame move by someone else, I might shrug it off. But my reaction to an illegal derby move when I'm Melicious is to deliver the hardest body block I can muster next time around the track.

Some situations give you the chance to try on multiple Rollergirl personas. Like . . . your league has invited a rival team from another state to your home turf for a grudge match, and you've been named the interleague ambassador. In the weeks leading up to the big night, you might be the Sexy Librarian, learning as much as you can about the other team—their lineup, their signature plays, their weakness for whiskey—to help your home team in their pregame preparations. Then, thinking like the Hottie Homemaker, you might make gift baskets for the visiting team to ensure they feel welcome before the on-track battering begins. When bout day arrives, your Wisecrackin' Dame might surface to make sure that the rival team knows the game is on. (When the last whistle blows and everyone heads to the local watering hole, the Bombshell might help you "make friends" at the afterparty, but that's another story. . . .)

WHAT'S YOUR ROLLERGIRL NAME?

Rollergirls are (in)famous for their punny names, equal parts hubris and humor. The questions below can help you come up with a Rollergirl name of your own. Of course, you could always rely on the porn-star name formula (name of your first pet plus the name of the street on which you grew up), but then you could end up calling yourself Fluffy Maple. And that just won't do.

Here are some examples to get you started on the name game:

Does your real name lend itself to something naughty?

Melissa/Melanie, aka Melificent, Mel Feasance, Mel A. Noma (and, of
course, Melicious)
Annie, aka Annie Social, Annie Hero
Dee, aka Dee Generate, Dee Stroyer, Dee V. Ant
Meredith/Mary, aka Merry Death, Merry Go Round
Anita, aka Anita Drink, Anita Mann
Marsha, aka Marsha Law
Or simply, Randy (or go Porn Star: Randie with a smiley face over the *i*)

What's better than a little sex and violence?

Melicious = malicious + delicious
Dee Fightful = delightful + fight
The Knock-out
Kitty Kitty Bang Bang

Do you have a personal attribute you can exploit? hair color? ethnicity?

Blond Bomber
Rice Rocket
Ragin' Cajun

Concerned with formal social salutations?

Miss Fit

Miss Creant
Ms. Behavin'
Madame X-rated

Can you twist a celebrity's name?

Payne Mansfield
Raquel Welcher
Bettie Rage
Pattie Hurts
Bratty Duke
Mia Hammer

Or pair up with a pal?

Rolletta Lynn & Patsy Crime
Spank Sinatra, Dean Smartin', Slammy Davis Jr.
Moonshine & Jen Entonic

How 'bout a fictional character?

Boobarella
Skaterella
Cruella de Kill
Hotlips Hooligan
Nancy Drewblood
Jane Ire
Lady McDeath

Or a writer?

Judy Boom
Agony Christie
E.M. Forcer
Rudyard Cripling
Bomb Clancy (She's a Clear and Present Danger.)

Or your favorite cocktail?

Jen Fizz
White Lightnin'
Bloody Mary

Can you adapt the name of a band?

Freakwood Smack
Rebellika
Uzi Quatro
Kid Vicious

Or use alliteration or rhyming?

Blitzkrieg Betty
Julie Jawbreaker
Dottie Karate

Can you find something you like in the dictionary?

animosity, becomes Anna Mosity
degenerate, becomes Dee Generate
anti-establishment, becomes Annie Establishment

Can you corrupt a cliché?

Robbing the cradle, aka Robin d'Cradle
Eve of destruction, aka Eva Destruction
Alive and kicking, aka Olive N. Kickin'

Is gambling the answer?

Asa Spades
High Roller
Crushin' Roulette

Maybe you identify more with an object?

The Wrench
The Crusher
The Vise
The Blade

Or a profession?

Hydra (hydrologist by day, skater by night)
The Professor
The Assassin
The Enforcer

Or can you appropriate a film title?

Kitty Kitty Bang Bang
Debbie D. Dallas
Robin D'Hood

Maybe a porn star name isn't so bad?

Trixie
Pixie
Bambi
Brandy
Candy
Boom-Boom
Cha-Cha
Sin-D

Wanna be threatening?

Celia Fate
Faye Tality
Juana Rumble

Or maybe inflict a little pain?

Billie Club
Dagger Deb
Bella Donna

Bonus points: Can you combine more than one category?

Miss + stripper name + dictionary = Misty Meaner
personal attribute (red hair) + celebrity name + violence = Lucille
    Brawl
real name + booze = Jen Entonic
booze + celebrity name = Whiskey L'Amour

I've got to level with you. I may introduce myself as Melicious and tell everyone that my Melicious persona is bleeding over into my real life, but I don't always wake up feeling Melicious-y.

The real me, at least as I see me, is pretty square. Definitely the kind of girl you could bring home to Mama. I didn't have a teenage rebellion until my mid-thirties, and when I did, I used my corporate salary to buy myself tattoos. I don't drink often, and I don't smoke. I've never tried any recreational drugs, because the buzz I catch from caffeine packs enough of a wallop. I never had a promiscuous or experimental sexual phase in college. So all those stories that begin, "You know we've all tried it once . . ." Um, no. No, I haven't.

I like to watch *Jeopardy!* on TV and shout the answers at Alex Trebek (while flipping him off). Left to my own devices, I fall asleep at 10:00 p.m. and wake up, alert and ready to bound out of bed, at 5:45 a.m. I say "fuck" a lot, but I don't like dirty jokes. *Jane Eyre* is my favorite book. I think men should act like men, women should behave like ladies, and the world would be better if we all remembered to use impeccable manners.

I believe that cleavage and bare midriffs don't have a place in the light of day, unless the displayer of said body parts is a) on the beach, or b) on her way to the Kit Kat Klub ('cause then she's got a professional obligation). One does not upstage the bride when attending a wedding, nor wear crimson lipstick to a job interview. Don't accept the invitation to the party if you don't intend to go, and do not, under any circumstances, go to dinner at a friend's house without bringing something for the hostess, no matter how many times she insists you should come empty-handed.

Yeah, I like rules. I hold myself to a high standard of exemplary, good-girl behavior. Yes, it can be a drag. But it's also the only way I know to get things done right in real life.

On the track, it's a whole other story.

I know only two people who would want to see the straightlaced, teetotaler, bookworm, classically trained pianist version of me on skates. Their names are Mom and Dad.

Before I joined Roller Derby, the words "sexy" and "hot" were not the ones I heard used to describe me. Organized. Smart. Reliable. Those were my stock-in-trade. But oh! How I longed to be like a reckless, hotheaded femme fatale on the cover of a pulp novel. Dangerous. Mysterious. Desirable. Hell on wheels in a black dress.

The first step in my transformation was a search for the perfect Rollergirl name. If it had somehow been my choice, I wouldn't have picked Melissa Kathryn Joulwan from the baby name book on May 1, 1968. (But it is better than the name I missed by a hairbreadth: Thomasina. I guess my dad wanted a boy.) I might have chosen Claire or Samantha or Natasha. A name that hinted at international spy or rock star. But our names are like the safety dress we all have in the back of the closet: comfortable, familiar, the reliable choice when everything else is going to hell in a handbag. You might get a new last name when you get hitched, but your first name is who you are.

Until you become a Rollergirl. Then you get to choose. What fun! What freedom! What pressure.

> "I chose the skate name Devil Dog because I'm a former marine, and that was the nickname for marines in World War II. Our enemies came up over a hill, saw the look in our marines' eyes, and screamed that we were hounds from hell."
>
> —DEVIL DOG, GARDA BELTS/MINNESOTA ROLLERGIRLS

I had a few criteria for my new name. It had to fit into our team theme, hinting at characteristics of a fifties girl gang filtered through eighties punk rock—like the chicks in a Russ Meyer film. And it couldn't be too punny. I wanted something clever and playful, but not silly, and definitely not raunchy. (I'll never forget how scandalized I was by the name "Connie Lingus" at my first bout.)

Like my tattoos, I wanted the name I chose to have personal significance. Names based on characters and celebrities are clever, but I wanted a name just for me. If possible, it would be something short and snappy that would look great on the back of a shirt, and dance off the announcer's tongue—like Madonna and Fantasia.

In the same way that a girl named Lolita is required to be an ingénue and anyone named Ethel—poor girl!—sounds like she wears orthopedic socks, I wanted a name that would be an extension of my uniform and my behavior, something so evocative, it suggested the personality of the skater behind the moniker.

For days I flipped through the thesaurus and magazines. I did brainstorming maps fueled by online searches. I muttered possibilities to myself under my breath, and shouted them randomly at Dave to gauge his reaction.

I considered Glamour Puss, for its Bond-esque appeal, but rejected it for its close proximity to the not-so-nice slang for a part of my anatomy I hold dear. Other girls aren't so shy; Pussy Velour, I salute you.

My next choice was Kitty Kitty Bang Bang. It didn't fit the short-and-snappy criteria, but I thought it was funny and cute. Plus, I love the movie *Chitty Chitty Bang Bang,* and there's a group called Shitty Shitty Band Band, and . . . well, I thought it was hilarious.

Dave gave it a thumbs-down: "It's a cute name, but I don't think it suits you." (A prescient decision, because later, it became the name of one of my best derby friends. Cheers to you, Ms. Bang!)

The name Melicious came to me from an unlikely source: a casual comment at the bottom of an e-mail from an acquaintance years ago. In all honesty, I think the guy had a crush on me, and he'd creatively mangled my name in an ill-advised attempt to win my heart.

FAVORITE NAMES

If you could name yourself whatever your heart desires, would you choose Jack Assley, as one of our short-timer rookies did? Nope, me neither. But here are some of my favorites from around the country.

18-Hour Broad, Sake Tuyas/Atlanta Rollergirls
Audrey Rugburn, Shotgun Betties/Denver Roller Dolls
Babe Ruthless, Bad News Beaters/Arizona Roller Derby
Bea Attitude, Hell Marys/Texas Rollergirls
Bitch Cassidy, Saddletramps/Tucson Roller Derby
Black Sabbatha, Highrollers/Rose City Rollers
Bolshe Vixen, Iron Curtain/Tucson Roller Derby
Bonnie Rotten, Atomic Bombshells/Minnesota Rollergirls
Buster Cheatin', Referee, Detroit Derby Girls
Carmen Geddit, Psych Ward Sirens/Houston Roller Derby
Celia Fate, Debutante Brawlers/Carolina Rollergirls
Charla Malm, Debutante Brawlers/Carolina Rollergirls
Cleo Splatra, Atomic Bombshells/Minnesota Rollergirls
Crash N. Burnadette, Prim Reapers/Alamo City Rollergirls
Crazy Duke, Honky Tonk Heartbreakers/Texas Rollergirls
Crescent Wench, Big Easy Rollergirls
Cruel Ella, Rockits/Minnesota Rollergirls
Curvette, Hustlers/Texas Rollergirls
Darth Hater, Hostile City Honeys/Philly Roller Girls
Deadly Cyn, Hell Marys/Texas Rollergirls
Debbie Taunt, Dixie Derby Girls
Elle McFearsom, Detroit Pistoffs/Detroit Derby Girls
Erin Blockabitch, Kansas City Roller Warriors
Goldie BloXX, Burlesque Brawlers/Houston Roller Derby
Jayne Manslaughter, Sugar Kill Gang/Rocky Mountain Rollergirls

Joan of Anarchy, Quad Squad/Mad Rollin' Dolls
Jodie Faster, Wicked Pissahs/Boston Derby Dames
June Carter Crash, Suicide Shifters/Dallas Derby Devils
Kim Reaper, Derby Liberation Front/Rat City Rollergirls
Leggs Luthor, Brooklyn Bombshells/Gotham Girls Roller Derby
Malicyn Wonderland, Slaughterers/Dallas Derby Devils
Margaret Thrasher, Announcer, Gotham Girls Roller Derby
Mr. Wonder Foul, Referee, Tampa Bay Derby Darlins
Pam Demonium, Reservoir Dolls/Mad Rollin' Dolls
Pound Cake, Unholy Rollers/Mad Rollin' Dolls
Punk Tart, Dixie Derby Girls
Queen of Hurts, Referee, Boston Derby Dames
Rita Hateworth, Atlanta Rollergirls
Roxanne Rolls, Dagger Dolls/Minnesota Rollergirls
Ruby Bruiseday, ShEvil Dead/B.ay A.rea D.erby Girls
Rumbelina, Toxic Shocks/Atlanta Rollergirls
Sadie Masochist, Manic Attackers/Windy City Rollers
Sandra Day O'Clobber, Broad Street Butchers/Philly Rollergirls
Sid Vixxen, Band of Brawlers/Ohio Rollergirls
Slammela Anderson, Boston Derby Dames
Tawdry Hepburn, Burlesque Brawlers/Houston Roller Derby
The Notorious R.I.P./Biggie Mauls, Sake Tuyas/Atlanta Rollergirls
Tootsie Roll, Atomic Bombshells/Minnesota Rollergirls
Track Daddy, Referee, Tucson Roller Derby
Tura Skatana, Devil's Night Dames/Detroit Derby Girls
Val Capone, Manic Attackers/Windy City Rollers
Vanna Whitetrash, Quad Squad/Mad Rollin' Dolls
Winona Fighter, Red Ridin' Hoods/Rocky Mountain Rollergirls

I'd long ago ditched the dude, but during my brainstorming phase, I remembered the name. I knew I really liked it because I didn't tell anyone right away.

Melicious.

I kept coming back to it, like the clearance rack at a Hot Topic store. Was it a treasure overlooked by everyone else, or was it just junk?

I imagined a lovelorn fan whispering it in awe as he watched me skate around the track. I heard feet stomping and saw fists pumping in the air, as the crowd chanted, "Mel-i-cious! Mel-i-cious!"

Like delicious and Melissa in a mash-up. Both better for having been merged. Vicious. Ambitious. Capricious. Superstitious.

Melicious.

> "Tinkerhell embodies all that Peter Pan's Tinkerbell did—bitchy, jealous, mischievous, dainty, prissy, and sometimes, just plain mean. But I'm just a little more evil than that! . . . I'm taking my uniform to an even darker place: tougher, more dangerous. I've been training hard, and I want the outside to reflect my new attitude on the inside."
>
> —TINKERHELL, HOTROD HONEYS/TEXAS ROLLERGIRLS

My name was ready to be silk-screened onto the back of my uniform shirt. All that remained was to develop my persona, the substance behind the style.

I wanted to be Mean and Intimidating—like The Wrench. She's retired now, but when she was skating, she was something to see. Friendly and approachable off the track, The Wrench played with an intensity that was as daunting as her height and strength. She was adored by her fans for her brusqueness and had a no-talking rule when she was in character. In lieu of words, she'd grunt at fans, grabbing them in a headlock, then shaking them like a puppy with a rag doll. The abuse sent her fans into paroxysms of glee.

"Wreeeeeeeench," they'd crow, "I loooooooove you, Wreeeeeeeeench!" But I knew I couldn't pull off a persona like that. I can't convincingly sing the nasty Danzig song "Mother," and even in the most dire circumstances or drunk off my ass, I speak in full sentences.

I was also intrigued by the idea of being a Sexpot. When I first joined the league, I don't think there was anyone hotter than Strawberry and Holli Graffic. In their blue plaid miniskirts, open-to-there white blouses, and ponytails, they were a rolling anime fantasy. Strawberry was sassy and street; Holli Graffic was like a postmodern gun moll. Their skating style was quick, cagey, determined, and flirty. The words, "Ladies and gentleman, Strawberry is our lead jammer," were Strawberry's cue to wave to her adoring fans, blow them a kiss, flip her skirt, shimmy her shoulders . . . something to show them that she knew they thought she was fabulous. I saw her cheer so hard for herself once, she lost her balance and crashed to the floor. The crowd only screamed louder. Strawberry and Holli Graffic had a lock on the vixen angle.

> "My skate name is Barbarella, and I wear purple and silver spandex . . . it looks great on the track. To get into character, I just make sure my breasts look good."
>
> —BARBARELLA, HUSTLERS/TEXAS ROLLERGIRLS

I turned to the real me for ideas about my persona. All that self-examination was unsettling, like looking in the mirror in direct sunlight, all the fine lines, flaws, and bumps highlighted. But it was for a good cause. Nothing to do but gut it up.

Here are some of the things I noticed that I'm willing to share:

Melicious Characteristic #1: Bratty

I hate being the butt of jokes, but oh! Is there anything more delish than mocking others (with love, of course)? Ted Casablanca on E! The Egotastic.com blogger. GoFug Yourself. These are my peeps. I heard someone say once, "If you don't have anything nice to say, come sit by me," so I grabbed a seat and stole their line as my own.

Melicious Characteristic #2: Glamorous

My fashion ideal is old-school Hollywood style—liquid eyeliner, lush lips, smooth hair, a come-hither glance, a few diamonds. Like Marilyn Monroe in *Gentlemen Prefer Blondes;* Bettie Page in her leopard-print bathing suit; Rita Hayworth in *Gilda.*

Melicious Characteristic #3: Lighthearted

Doesn't matter how much I wish I was dark, moody, and mysterious; I have a sunny outlook, and I like to laugh. I'm naturally cheerful. I want to brood, but I can't help but smile.

Melicious Characteristic #4: Social Distortion's Number One Fan

I love the music of Mike Ness and Social Distortion so much, I can barely talk about it. The shift from competent, educated woman to duct-tape-and-wire-cutters-wielding fanatic is instantaneous from the first strum of a Social D song. My earnestness about and glorification of Mr. Ness's gravel voice and heartfelt lyrics is embarrassing.

Melicious Characteristic #5: Honest

I can't bring myself to lie, cheat, or steal, even when it really would work in my favor.

★◻★

Rebecca Davis/rebeccadavisphotography.com

Melicious #11

HOTROD HONEYS/TEXAS ROLLERGIRLS

POSITIONS: BLOCKER, PIVOT, JAMMER, DICE THROWER

LIKES: *things that sparkle; fishnet stockings and big black boots; Social Distortion and the wisdom of Mike Ness; Sun Sessions Elvis and Boy Toy Madonna*

DISLIKES: *bad tattoos; pointy-toed shoes; nude hose; mullets and bad dye jobs; Jumpsuit Elvis and Kabbalah Madonna; liars; think-straight sinners*

LUCKY NUMBER: *Yo-leven*

FAVORITE VICES: *shooting craps; Jim Beam straight outta the bottle; 5:00 a.m. pepperoni pizza; makin' out in the backseat*

FAVORITE SONGS: *Social Distortion, "When She Begins"; Elvis, "Hard-headed Woman"; Stray Cats, "Fishnet Stockings"*

FAVORITE QUOTE: *"I sold my soul to the devil, and then I stole it back."—Mike Ness*

HEIGHT: *5' 4" of fury*

Melicious was conceived in the rumble seat of her daddy's hotrod in the backwoods of Pennsylvania. With the ragtop dropped back and the stars twinkling like rhinestones in the night sky, her mama thought that the parking lot of the Willow Lake Skating Rink had never seemed so romantic. And there were two things her mama could never resist: the perfect little black dress and a good-lookin' boy with a guitar in one hand and a cold beer in the other.

Melicious shared her mama's passion for fashion and yen for men, and she knew early on that she was meant for more than the flannel shirts, Aqua Net, and dime-store fragrances of rural PA. As her mama told Melicious, "There ain't a man in this town worth putting on makeup for, baby."

Melicious wept at the thought of leaving her mama and the roller skating rink, but when the small-town blues just hit too hard, she packed up her feathers and safety pins and lipsticks and leather to find a place with flattering light and a man with an appreciation for an angel in combat boots.

At first, the bright lights of Hollywood beckoned, then the sparkle and sin of Las Vegas proved tempting, but eventually grew dim. It was in Austin at Lovejoy's Tap Room that Melicious finally found her destiny.

Looking for a safety pin to solve a fashion emergency, she was distracted by a gang of girls lookin' like punk-rock royalty in pink and black. Soon they were powdering their noses, lining their eyes with kohl, and debating the merit of wooden versus acrylic floors for skating speed and traction. Her words of wisdom for her new friends? "There's never a bad time to be glamorous . . . especially when you're kicking someone's ass."

AWARDS: *2005 Crowd Favorite, 2003 Best Rack, 2003 Miss Texas Rollergirl*

RIVALS: *Hissy Fit & The Wrench, Hell Marys/Texas Rollergirls; Belle Star & Devil Grrl, Honky Tonk Heartbreakers/Texas Rollergirls; Dirty Deeds & Sedonya Face, Hustlers/Texas Rollergirls; Ivanna S. Pankin, Neander Dolls/Sin City Rollergirls*

◻★

Melicious Characteristic #6: Tougher than you think

A corollary to all of the above: I think a lot of people—including myself—mistake my innate kindness and good intentions for weakness. Sure, I'm rarely the first aggressor, but if you push me, I'll push back. I'll smile and apologize while I'm doing it—and maybe feel a tiny bit bad about it later—but I'll definitely shove back.

So I sat down with my list of traits, summoned the spirit of Damon Runyon, and pretended I was an *Us Weekly* reporter, writing a profile of an up-and-coming A-lister. The result is my Texas Rollergirls bio—my marching orders every time I hit the track.

I feel most like Melicious when I walk into Playland before the bout. The kids from the afternoon birthday parties have cleared out of the rink, and the Texas Rollergirls crew hasn't yet set up our track and stage. It's just an enormous, dark, cool blank canvas—and it feels like the space is waiting for us to fill it up with our energy and noise. It's familiar and magical at the same time. Before the bout starts—before the fans filter in and beer is spilled on the floor and girls have had fights or moments of glory—it's all possibility.

"Roller Derby made me face my fear of being in the spotlight, or being the center of attention. I had no problem with big groups under somewhat formal circumstances, like public speaking. But I had never been comfortable doing anything showy in front of people—and certainly nothing silly in front of 1,100 spectators! My parents are pretty low-key, conservative Christians. The part of derby that shocks (and tickles) them the most has been seeing their somewhat introverted, brains-over-brawn oldest daughter become a performer."

—BLOODY MARY, HELL MARYS/TEXAS ROLLERGIRLS

To get to that feeling takes hours. I spend most of game day sloughing off Melissa Joulwan—the girl who worries about paying the bills on time, who monitors the nutritional value of every morsel of food she eats, who had her heart broken by the boyfriend who declared Chopin boring and asked, "Why can't you play some Billy Joel?"

On game day, from the moment I wake up, open my eyes, and stretch, to the moment I line up in my first jam of the bout, everything I do is a step toward becoming Melicious.

> "Roller Derby challenges my ideas about myself. The 'You Suck' voice that says, 'You're not athletic. You have no business doing this. You're too old/slow/fat/thin ... whatever.' I love derby so much, and I have such respect, admiration, and affection for other skaters, that I constantly face down my fears. Instead of hiding from myself, derby gives me reasons to stand and deliver."
>
> —HELL'S KITTEN, HIGH SEAS HOTTIES/DALLAS DERBY DEVILS

I know a group of girls in our league with a standing date to eat brunch together on game day. I envy them their mimosas and margaritas, sipped on a porch somewhere in the sun. Their cheese omelets and hash browns or blueberry pancakes. I've got nutrition rules that really shouldn't be broken, so my breakfast on game day is carefully calculated to make sure I have enough energy to last through the whole bout. Eggs (or, more specifically, one whole egg and two egg whites) scrambled with low-fat ham and two-percent cheese, a whole-grain English muffin, heart-healthy margarine, one cup of coffee with Splenda (no sugar!) and sugar-free vanilla-flavored creamer, and an orange. Plus, at least two glasses of water and my horse pills: Vitamin C and a multivitamin. Breakfast of wannabe champions.

Some other Rollergirls go to work before coming to the bout; I don't even get dressed on game day. I shuffle around the house in my leopard-print pajamas and black fuzzy slippers until it's time to get dolled up. I drop the thermostat to 68, set the AC fan on high, and mute the volume on the phone. I don't do a lot of talking on bout day—usually just a quick "Be careful!" call from my mom and that's it.

I read through our team lineup, the carefully concocted, overly scrutinized schedule that lists which team member will play each position and when. Putting the lineup together is a political nightmare for the captains and co-captains. Our "by the skaters, for the skaters" philosophy trickles down to our teams, too, which means everyone believes they have a right to voice their opinion on the lineup. For a bunch of hard-asses, we're a sensitive lot. The number of times a player's name appears in the bout lineup can be perceived as an unspoken assessment of their value to the team.

"Being a captain has made me a stronger leader. I tell people on job interviews, 'If I can manage sixteen of the most strong-willed, independent Roller Derby bitches you've ever met, I can supervise your secretary.'"

—DIRTY DEEDS, HUSTLERS/TEXAS ROLLERGIRLS

Around 2:00 p.m., I start seriously reviewing our game strategy. I crank up my iPod with my Melicious playlist—I like my music angry or happy and not much in between—then I sit on the floor and clean my skate wheels with a pink towel. I have a hard time tossing out old pairs of sneakers because I get sentimental about the miles they walked, the steps they climbed, the ropes they jumped. I feel the same way about my skates. They're trashed. The toes are torn and scuffed, the tongue on the right is barely still connected to the boot, the insoles need replacing. Again. But I'm attached to them like the teddy bear my dad gave me on my first Christmas. Those skates and I have been through a lot together. We've stared down threatening blockers, recovered from nasty falls, slid into the audience, zigzagged through cones, and leapt over fallen comrades. There's a reason so many Rollergirls bind their skates with duct tape, and it only marginally has to do with finances. Who dumps an old friend just 'cause they're rough around the edges?

DERBY PLAYLIST

This is the playlist I use to get ready for a bout. It's a mix of songs that I associate with being powerful, aggressive, and sexy—the emotions I try to channel when I hit the track. I set my iPod on shuffle and visualize myself taking out the other team's jammer over and over while the crowd cheers.

The Bloody Tears, "I Wanna Testify"

Bullets and Octane, "Caving In"

Charlie Sexton, "Beat's So Lonely"

Christina Aguilera, "Fighter"

The Clash, "Brand New Cadillac"

Elvis Costello, "Mystery Dance"

The Explosion, "Here I Am"

Grandmaster Flash, "The Message"

Green Day, "She's a Rebel"

Jesse Dayton, "Arkansas Chrome"

Joan Jett, "Bad Reputation"

Kid Rock, "Cocky"

Mike Ness, "I'm in Love with My Car"

The Misfits, "Where Eagles Dare"

Peter Elliott & the Sellouts, "Suzette"

Pink, "Trouble"

Rockland Eagles, "Wanna Take a Ride"

Road Kings, "Harder Than Your Heart"

Social Distortion, "Cold Feelings"

Social Distortion, "She's a Knockout"

Stray Cats, "Fishnet Stockings"

Tsar, "Band-Girls-Money"

ZZ Top, "I'm Bad, I'm Nationwide"

I check for frayed laces, make sure my bearings don't need grease, tighten the stoppers so they don't fall off midgame, and tie fresh pink ribbons into the first two eyelets of my skates. While my hands strip the fuzz, dirt, cigarette ash, hair, and other unidentifiable and disgusting substances from my wheels, my brain walks through the game. Whatever lame objections I might have had to the lineup are gone, and I embrace it as gospel, thinking through my goals for each jam.

Packing my gear is part of the ritual, too. My skate case was a gift from my mom long before I moved to Austin. It's shaped like an old-fashioned suitcase, glossy black patent leather on one side, fuzzy leopard print on the other. I carted it from one residence to another—from the houseboat in Sausalito, to the apartment in San Francisco, to the duplex in Austin, to my permanent home—and it never had a designated purpose. I couldn't part with it, but there was no way to use it. Until Roller Derby. Now it's decorated with stickers: a cheesecake shot of two shirtless actors from *Saved by the Bell.* A dancing tooth that says, "I was brave." A red-white-and-blue #1 inscribed with "Girls Rule." A photo sticker of Devil Grrl looking impish. If I put my skates in the box just so, then add my wrist guards on the sides, elbow pads crosswise, and knee pads on top, everything fits. I shake my mouthguard case to make sure my favorite piece of safety gear is where it should be, and my equipment is locked and loaded.

Now is probably a good time to come clean with some ugly truths about pretty Rollergirls. We wear stinky pads and if our feet were literary characters, they'd be Quasimodo.

Don't believe me? Here's a typical scene from Roller Derby practice. Over time, each of our four teams has marked its territory in the lobby of Playland. Now and then, someone will cross over into the Hustlers area for a quick conversation, or slide down to the end of the bench to the Honky Tonk Heartbreakers corner. But we're all stubbornly set in our ways, and have staked our claims to our "spot."

So there we are, sixty or so Rollergirls, pulling pads and skates and socks out of our skate cases while we gossip and yell insults at each other across the room. And then . . .

<sniff> <sniff>

"Do you smell that?"

<sniff> <sniff>

"Who *is* that?"

Around the room, Rollergirls gamely shove their noses into their own pads—and the pads of their neighbors—to identify the offender.

It's a singular stench, this malodor of seasoned and aged Roller Derby pads. In case you've never had the distinct pleasure of experiencing it for yourself, imagine the aroma of the inside of a milk carton left in the trunk of a car during August in west Texas, then rubbed down with a salami sandwich, and smeared with Vick's VapoRub.

It's worse than that.

Once it gets into your pads—and up your nose—it's almost impossible to eradicate. I've washed my pads with extra-strength detergent and doubled the recommended amount of Wildflower-Fresh fabric softener. I've tucked Summer Rain dryer sheets inside and around them for days at a time. I've run them through the dishwasher. Sprayed them with Febreze. Doused them with Nature's Miracle ("the number-one-selling pet accident stain and odor remover"). And, combining an old trick for removing spaghetti sauce stains from Tupperware with Arm & Hammer knowledge, I've coated them with a thick dusting of baking powder and let them roast in the sun.

At some point, we all have to accept there's a time for home remedies, and there's a time to buy new pads.

But it's not always the pads—sometimes it's the girl. There I was, in the middle of the track, lined up with my leaguemates for five-line bouting. (That's a scrimmage in which the pack consists of ten random Rollergirls, rather than five players from each team. It's a great way to learn how to play with anyone and to make sure team barriers never become insurmountable.)

We're lined up, waiting for our turn to jam, when . . .

<sniff> <sniff>

"Oh, man! I *really* stink," one of the girls said, her voice thick with repulsion, as she sniffed her own armpit.

Simultaneously, a dozen other girls threw an arm overhead, tucked their own snouts into their underarms, and inhaled.

Let me tell you about my feet.

They're big. And wide. I'm only five feet four and most girls my size wear adorable doll shoes in size six or seven. I wear size nine-and-a-half. Boats.

A few years ago, I got them tattooed. The tops of both of them, from ankle to piggies, are decorated with traditional tattoo elements—dice, roses, a sparrow and red heart, dots and stars, a horseshoe, and cherries—with the sage advice "Don't gamble" (on the right) "with love" (on the left).

When I told my mom, she said, "But you hate your feet."

Exactly.

After three hours of abuse from the tattoo gun, my feet puffed up to twice their original size. I shuffled around in slippers for weeks until they healed, then I hit the boutiques and bought a wardrobe of sexy shoes to show them off. Mary Janes. Clear acrylic sandals. Strappy platforms. I was a shoe glutton, snatching up any pair that would display my art. I developed a crush on my feet and gazed at them lovingly at every opportunity.

Then I became a Rollergirl.

I spend roughly eight to ten hours a week with my dogs wrapped in duct tape and two pairs of socks, then strapped into leather skate boots—not a friendly environment if you want twinkle toes. Bumps, calluses, blisters, blisters on top of calluses, odd dark spots, shiny patches, black toenails, lost toenails, corns, bunions—my feet are a gnarled mess. We've all got a "no sloughing" rule with the pedicurist, and vacations are a mixed blessing. Too much time spent in the pool or on the beach means tender, baby-soft tootsies—and weeks of torturous derby practice to rebuild the lizard-like protective coating. Strappy sandals? Not a chance.

☠ ♥ ☠

I'm very superstitious. To other people it might just look a lot like T.G.I. Friday's flair. But to me, all the crap on my uniform—and the associated assembly ritual—is essential to my Melicious mojo. I like to keep my lucky charms and tchotchkes nearby. I never owned an iron before I joined Roller Derby; now I use the damn thing regularly to keep my uniform spiffy.

Just after the coup, during the crappy, confusing time when we weren't sure if we even owned our Rollergirl names, my team decided to take a punk-rock approach and use safety pins to attach our names and numbers to our backs, rather than silk-screening them. In defiance, I cut a scrap from an old Hellcats shirt to use as a back patch. Then I made an iron-on from my inkjet printer and ironed it onto the scrap. I've worn a DIY back patch ever since.

The first step in the uniform rite is pinning my name on the back of my shirt. Then I attach a skull-and-crossbones pin I found in an alley to the pink bow on front. After winning the Best Rack award at our Whammy Awards ceremony a few years ago, I decided to put a big bow on my boobies, like they're a present I give to our fans every month. I like the contradiction of the dangerous accessories and the girly bows: "I'm cute and pink and cuddly . . . I might kill you."

> "I'm a huge fan of the Sex Pistols. I'm also big into dressing up and theatrical makeup. My helmet has a Union Jack on the side; my uniform is covered in punk-rock patches. My favorite is a caricature of Jerry Lewis's face that says 'I'm skating for Jerry's Kids.' I always pose with my two-finger salute (the UK equivalent of the middle finger). I love putting on my uniform and becoming a sneering, trashy punk."
>
> —BONNIE ROTTEN, ATOMIC BOMBSHELLS/MINNESOTA ROLLERGIRLS

On my right sleeve, I wear a black patch printed with a pink kitten; it says, "Pretty Messed Up." On the left, a collection of buttons: Cat Tastrophe's lovely face to remind me to "Hit, or be hit." A skull-and-crossbones from the band Teenage Harlots. Pink and silver zebra stripes printed with WILD! that was given to me by my number one fan, Charlotte. I HEART TXRG. A pink cartoon kitty.

Around my neck, I wrap a pink vinyl studded choker that Dave gave me, and on my right wrist, a pink leopard cuff. I have to remove it when it's time for wristguards, but there are always photo ops before then. On my left wrist are the bracelets I never take off—the silly rubber bracelets Cyndi Lauper and Bananarama had crawling up their arms in the eighties. No, I haven't been wearing them since then, but I've worn an odd number on my left wrist for years. They don't commemorate anything in particular, but I'm too superstitious to remove them.

The only thing better than a supportive friend is a supportive bra, and the importance of the right bra for Roller Derby can't be overstated. I know some guys think loose-and-free is a turn-on, but they're wrong. It's one of the truths of the universe—blame physics—that when we skate forward, our breasts want to dance side to side. Pretty boobies are supported. Perky. Strapped in for safety, but not squished.

Which is why jog bras don't really work. The tickets have got to be front and center for the jam. I've found my foolproof derby bra, and if it's ever discontinued, I think I'll be even more upset than I would be if my hair stylist moved.

The bottom half of the undergarments is crucial, too. A little flash of somethin'-somethin' under a short skirt is cute. Flirty. Provocative. A full-frontal *Basic Instinct* is a definite no-no. We've had some wardrobe malfunctions on our track throughout the years. Like the newbie who forgot to wear panties under her nude-colored support hose and flashed her entire business when an opponent used the uniform as leverage for a whip. Or the veteran who forgot she was only wearing a thong. One fall was all it took for 1,100 people to know her really, really well. For every member of the crowd who loves the peep show, there are a handful of Rollergirls laughing with malicious glee at their roller sister's misfortune. After I've pulled my fishnets on (always black, always with seams), I top them with black satin tap pants with tiny pink bows at the hem, or pink briefs covered in rows of ruffles.

In November 2003, Rolletta Lynn—one of our Honky Tonk Heartbreakers—was selected to participate in the reality show *Switched!* The program recruited two folks with opposite lifestyles and dropped them into each other's lives; *Freaky Friday* for the new millennium. Rolletta Lynn had no idea where she was going or what she'd be doing; the producers refused to divulge even the weather forecast for her destination. That meant her switchee had no idea that she was about to be made an honorary Rollergirl, complete with a new persona, practice requirements, and a special bout in front of a live audience and TV cameras.

I was among the Rollergirls on the airport welcoming committee. We waited with balloons at the bottom of the escalator, scrutinizing the crowd for our new rookie. We expected the producers to pull a fast one and argued over whether we should be looking for an ultra-conservative, right-wing, young Republican type, or a bouncy-haired, bubble-headed sorority sister.

"I used to be a shy, nerdy, tomboy, music geek, who hid behind my shaggy hair and glasses. Joining Roller Derby actually brought out the woman in me. I'm physically and mentally stronger and tougher than I ever imagined I'd be. I also have a new wardrobe full of fish-nets and miniskirts and a phonebook full of cool chicks' names like Patsy Crime and Donna Matrix."

—ROLLETTA LYNN, QUEENS OF PAIN/GOTHAM GIRLS ROLLER DERBY

Our rookie spotted us first, because it never occurred to us to look for a young African-American male. His name was Eric, and he was from Grambling, Louisiana. While he underwent Rollergirl training, Rolletta was taking his place as drum major in the "finest band in the land," Grambling State University's Tiger Marching Band.

We'd been sworn to secrecy by the producers, so we couldn't tell Eric anything about what was in store for him. After peppering him with questions about his life back home, Sparkle Plenty challenged him to guess our identities.

"What do you think we do?" she asked as we drove into town.

"Um . . ." Eric said, hesitating. "Are you dancers?"

Sparkle Plenty almost ran us into a ditch as she shrieked, "Strippers! He thinks we're strippers!"

Later that night, the Honky Tonk Heartbreakers gave Eric gifts to hint at his new role: makeup, a push-up bra (from me), Ibuprofen, and Band-Aids. A text message from Rolletta delivered the news that he had just three days to learn the ropes before being thrown into a jam. Eric was on his way to becoming Psilent Predator.

A good Southern boy, Eric was painfully polite, a trait I found endearing. At skating practice, he was very serious and focused, his face splitting into a heart-melting smile when he conquered the crossover. In conversation, he was quiet and deliberate. Imagine what he must have thought in those first few hours, surrounded by Rollergirls in all our cussing, hyperactive, bawdy, unrestrained glory.

Eric might have been overwhelmed by us, but *Psilent Predator* held his own. After a weekend of skating drills, he was ready for the Sunday morning invitational bout. We'd recruited a few hundred friends, family, and fans to join us for the taping of the Honky Tonk Heartbreakers—with special guest Psilent Predator—against the Hell Marys.

People milled about with cups of coffee and breakfast tacos, instead of beer and nachos, waiting to see the first-ever male Texas Rollergirl. Psilent Predator rolled onto the track in jeans and a blue Western shirt with a snappy red bandanna. He wore a gigantic Afro wig topped by a glittery cowboy hat. The retiring young man was gone, replaced by a bobbing, shimmying madman. He lapped the track like a pro, and the crowd went wild. Later in the game, when he nailed Strawberry into the audience with a clean block, he was named lead jammer in his very first Flat Track bout. Behold the power of a Rollergirl persona.

CHAPTER
CHAPTER

11

Welcome to Playland

The Texas Rollergirls still hold bouts at Playland Skate Center, but our games are dramatically different than the first time I walked onto that lavender floor. We've got a full-blown production that takes our audience—and us—to a fantasyland where glamazons do battle on eight wheels.

Our audience is as much a part of the show as the performers, and it's filled with contradictions. Five-year-olds who want to run and play mix with jaded preteens who think everything is a bore. Tattooed boys drink beer with men who usually wear neckties to work. Manicured women trade tips in the ladies' room with chicks who know their way around Manic Panic hair color. Old-school derby fans cheer alongside lifelong football fanatics.

When the game starts, the audience is unified, because our sport is based on a simple, but irresistible, formula:

Pretty Girls + COMPETITION + LIVE MUSIC + *COLD BEER*

It's the A-list of life's all-American pleasures. If they're not careful, fans can go home with a broken nose and a broken heart. They line up hours before the bout to ensure a floor seat within a few feet of the track's edge, called the Blue Line. Later, they brag about the bruises they got when a Rollergirl landed in their laps. (Worn by a skater or a fan, a bruise is a badge of honor.)

"Between the bands, the beer, and the strong women on wheels, it feels like you've fallen into that scene in *Pinocchio* where the boys start turning into donkeys because they're having too much fun."

—D THE B, DERBY WIDOWER/TEXAS ROLLERGIRLS

The show really starts in the Playland parking lot. In thigh-high silver boots and black teetering stilettos, pointy-toed cowboy boots and chunky Doc Martens, customized Converse and prim saddle shoes, the Rollergirls strut and stomp across the lot, unfairly judged by the sun, like Vegas neon at noon. Individually, we can look out of place or over-done in the suburban daylight, but standing together, we make sense. That's what our fans see when they pull their hotrods and minivans into the parking lot—an assembled roller army, ready for flirtation and combat.

We're all in persona as we walk past the early fans lined up along the outside of the building. (Buckshot Betsy has been known to feed the prebout line of fans with homemade fried chicken.) But once we're inside, we again become regular girls for a short while: every-one's got a job to do before the bout. The transformation of the rink from children's birthday party venue to derby arena is like one of those old-timey, sped-up, time-lapsed films of a crew putting up a circus tent.

Our Production Manager jogs from one end of the rink to the other, solving last-minute crises, both big ("The lightbulb in the scoreboard projector is burned out, and we don't have a backup!") and small ("Where's the duct tape?"). A crew labels the chairs in the VIP section. Another group hangs sponsor banners on the walls around the rink. In the back corner, our dressing room is assembled from PVC tubing and curtains, while team captains track down their skaters—"Has anyone seen Sedonya Face?" "Where's Hissy Fit?"—and give copies of their lineups to the scorekeepers.

Meanwhile, the Beerland staff wheels tall stacks of beer cases into the snack bar, burying the cans in car-trunk-sized metal tubs of ice. Members of the opening band load in, sneaking glances at the cleavage and fishnets bopping around them. Watching their reactions to the Rollergirls is amusing. They're either completely bedazzled by us—tripping over cables and tongue-tied—or totally unfazed, like they've seen it all before and we should just get over ourselves. I enjoy both responses.

Just inside Playland's front doors, the merch booth starts to take shape as volunteers hang T-shirts and display posters, and get caught up on the gossip since the last bout. Across the lobby, the spotlight charity for the night—Bikers Against Child Abuse, or Texas Hearing and Service Dogs, or Keep Austin Beautiful, or Whole Women's Health—displays its promotional materials.

In the center of the rink, a team of cute boys and martial-arts experts from Lonestar Jiu Jitsu ("Here to protect YOU from the Rollergirls") wear red T-shirts with SECURITY printed across their backs. They lay the track and mark off the "flying skater zone" with blue tape, establishing the Blue Line that separates the boundary of the track from the audience. Our playing area is an 88-by-53-foot oval outlined by red, white, and blue rope lights. Devised by our own Electra Blu, the track layout was adopted by WFTDA as the standard. It was designed to accommodate how a skater at high speeds naturally moves within the track, and its dimensions were calculated to ensure that it was no easy task for a jammer to make it through the pack to score (see page 10 for a neat illustration). Thanks to the "Look ma, no railings!" setup, the only thing between the edge of the track and our fans is luck.

In the middle of the oval, light towers go up, casting a warm yellow glow on our track, and adjacent to it, the scorekeepers climb the eight-foot ladder into their crow's nest to record our stats. By 6:00 p.m., when most of the setup is complete, the EMTs from the Motorcycle Special Events Team take their position next to the track, the DJ cranks the volume on "Sex on Wheelz" by the Thrill Kill Kult, and the announcers start the countdown to doors.

When our fans walk into Playland, they're usually greeted by a handful of Rollergirls distributing programs and talking shit about the game. The opening band plays on the stage just inside the door, and on the track, Rollergirls from all four teams skate warm-up laps.

That's when the fun starts for me. Until then, I'm antsy and cross, obsessively reading and rereading our lineup, applying and reapplying lipstick, trying to redirect my nervous jitters into aggressive energy.

When I hear "Five minutes till doors," and the band starts their set, the Rock 'n' Rollerderby has begun. The first fans in the doors park their asses in the prime spots along the Blue Line. Veterans know that if they sit on the straightaways, they'll have an unobstructed view of the action—but if they nab a seat on the outside of either curve, they're likely to get a lapful of Rollergirl.

I love that time, the feeling of being part of a big show. It's exhilarating to skate to live music—there's a different energy and edge. Even though I'm part of it now, when I see my friends from all of the teams, skating on the track together, I'm starstruck all over again. Everyone looks fit and focused, unyielding. The colors of their uniforms—pink and black and red and blue and purple—are like confetti as they zoom around the track.

★🔲

Ziv Kruger

𝔅𝔲𝔠𝔨𝔰𝔥𝔬𝔱 𝔅𝔢𝔱𝔰𝔶 #21

HONKY TONK HEARTBREAKERS/TEXAS ROLLERGIRLS
AUSTIN TEXECUTIONERS, 2006 DUST DEVIL NATIONAL FLAT
TRACK CHAMPIONS

POSITIONS: *Jammer, Blocker, Pivot, All-around Badass*
FAVORITE QUOTE: *"The best revenge is pissing on someone's toothbrush."*
BUCKSHOT BETSY SPEAKS: *"When I retire, I'm gonna take up boxing. I hope to kick Tonya Harding's ass one day."*
Buckshot Betsy got her name from her mama because her favorite toy as an infant was her daddy's double-barreled shot-gun. She's been known to shoot one of her five brothers in the ass at least once a year and has developed quite the reputation as a rootin', tootin' cowgirl. Born and raised in Floresville, TX, her accomplishments include Miss Flores-ville 1994, Hog Tying Champion 1996, and still having all of her own teeth.

AWARDS: *2005 Honky Tonk Heartbreakers MVP, 2005 Texas Rollergirls Most Fashionable, 2004 Texas Rollergirls MVP, 2004 Honky Tonk Heartbreakers MVP*

RIVALS: *Babe Ruthless, Tent City Terrors/Arizona Roller Derby; Doe Holiday, Saddletramps/Tucson Roller Derby; Roxy Rocket, Trauma Queens/Carolina Rollergirls; "At home, I like to take it out on Eight Track."*

🔲★

During the warm-up, Sparkle Plenty and Buckshot Betsy—both members of the Honky Tonk Heartbreakers—like to bash into each other full-force. Buckshot says she'd rather have the first hit of the night come from her friend than from an opponent. I like to practice hugging the inside line. Or I tease the blockers on the opposing team by skating next to them, as closely as possible, without touching, or pacing just in front of them, keeping them trapped behind me. If they move left, I do, too. I try to imagine what an annoying little sister might do, and do those things—with the most intense Melicious scowl I can muster (the mouthguard helps a lot).

At 7:00, the opening band plays their final number and the announcers—like carnival barkers—start to spin a tale for the audience, drawing them into our derby drama. On a small stage next to the rink, Whiskey L'Amour (play-by-play), Jim "Kool-Aid" Jones, and Julio E. Glasses (color commentary) sit at a table behind a bank of microphones, like a press conference. Chip Queso, crowd wrangler and cheerleader, leaps, bounds, dances, marches, runs, and skips around the perimeter of the track, riling up the audience, waving his hat in the air, and sassing the other announcers like a one-man Greek chorus.

(back) Whiskey L'Amour, Hot Wheels, Jim "Kool-Aid" Jones; (front) Julio E. Glasses, Chip Queso

In his trademark yellow Western shirts—customized with patches, skulls, and appropriately cheesy photo buttons of long-lost eighties bands—Chip is a gen-u-ine cowpunk. He's been skateboarding so long, no one can remember a time when he wasn't dropping into a bowl, and he tells any Rollergirl who'll listen, "Our four wheels came from your eight wheels." His name is a Tex-Mex-icanization of his old college nickname: Fondue. Like the chips-and-dip that inspired his persona, he's gooey and irresistible.

The Iron Announcer, our color commentator, was formerly known as Julio E. Glasses. But a derby-fueled caper forced him to change his identity. His previous persona was inspired by his fiancée's adoration of Enrique Iglesias. Why did he choose to emulate Iglesias the elder? "I'm old-school that way," he says with a shrug.

As any fashionista will tell you, the key to defining a personal style is identifying that one special accessory—and for Julio, it was his multicolored serape. But in a tragic kidnapping and Jägermeister debacle during the Dust Devil tournament in February 2006, Julio's serape was snatched. Photos of the serape in compromising positions surfaced online; a return was negotiated.

While the serape was MIA, Julio was reborn as the Iron Announcer. In a pristine white counter coat, black pants, shirt and tie, and chef's toque, he's the master of color commentary—his words, the garnish on the play-by-play served up by Whiskey L'Amour.

A spiral fracture brought Whiskey's skating career to an end, but it couldn't stop her flip sense of humor and cockeyed point of view. When she mixes her wiseass hanky-panky with her knowledge of the game, we've got the perfect guide to navigate our fans through the ins and outs of our sport. Whiskey takes the notion of a persona to its extreme; she wears a different costume for each and every bout. In getups ranging from Winnie the Pooh to Red Sonja—and so many male fantasies and therapy sessions in between—the real Whiskey L'Amour remains an elusive and enthralling mystery.

If Chip Queso is the playful younger brother of the announcer family, his troublemaking older sibling is Jim "Kool-Aid" Jones. Kool-Aid's real-life story is so preposterous, he didn't need to create a fictional bio to go along with his alter ego. Born in Greece to hippy-love-cult parents, he had no choice but to preach the gospel of Flat Track Derby. In 2006, he unveiled his new vestments: a suit—with matching Bible cover—made entirely of red Cherry Kool-Aid packets. Stitched by hand from hundreds of packets, it shimmers in the Playland lights and crinkles with Kool-Aid's every move.

Hot Wheels started her career as a skater, but found her true calling as the Penalty Princess. Isn't it better to dole out punishment to skaters than to take it yourself? Like a psychotic Julie Andrews, Hot Wheels lists among her favorite things the crack of the whip, spankings, leather and vinyl apparel, and loud rock 'n' roll music like Adam Ant's "Beat My Guest."

Whiskey and the Iron Announcer explain the rules to the audience before the game, but it's never clear whether anyone is listening. Then Kool-Aid provides vital beer-drinking instructions. Spilled beer on the floor of the kitchen is annoying; a few drops of beer on the track mean a dangerously out-of-control wipeout for Rollergirls. So Kool-Aid has developed a brief training program for the fans who sit at the Blue Line. With the exaggerated, self-conscious patience of an elementary school teacher, he explains that when a Rollergirl flies out of bounds, it's the responsibility of each and every audience member to lift their beers above their heads, "Because if you spill your beer, and the Rollergirl falls, she'll kick your ass . . . but *not* in the way you would like." The whole rink practices together: "You grab your beer and you . . . LIFT! LIFT!"

Then it's the moment we Rollergirls have been anticipating since we arrived two hours before: introductions and the starting whistle.

As our game has evolved to be more competitive, much of the silliness within the jams has been lost—no one wants to blow a game by pulling some loony stunt. But before things got so serious, crazy shit used to happen. A masked player would skate out onto the track in the middle of the jam and tackle another skater. Or a one-on-one fight over nothing would explode into a bench-clearing brawl that sent the referees into a whistle-blowing frenzy. Now, most of the goofy stunts and melodrama are planned for the team introductions.

The Hustlers have established themselves as the dancing queens, getting down with their bad selves to seventies songs ranging from rock to disco to funk. Over the past few years, the Hell Marys have been escorted onto the track by a band of bagpipers, a twelve-foot nun on stilts, and a roller-skating cleric named Jason Priestly who led the audience in the team's chant-along, "Hell Marys! Hell, yeah!"

The Honky Tonk Heartbreakers are known as much for their zany intros as they are for their two-year undefeated streak. When they took on a team from Seattle's Rat City Rollergirls, they dressed as pest exterminators in biohazard jumpsuits and gas masks. Another time, they reenacted the opening of the game show *The Price Is Right,* running onto the track to the strains of the show's theme song, while waving their arms overhead like a first-time-in-California homemaker who finds the rapture in Broyhill dining room sets. And once, they sang that old favorite from childhood—"Little Bunny Foo Foo"—while a six-foot-two man frolicked around the track in a fuzzy pink bunny suit.

My team usually glides onto the track between two black-and-white-checkered flags waved by our pit crew, adorable girl greasers decked out in mechanics' jumpsuits and Hotrod Honeys flair. Sure, we might mock Bunny Rabid with a carrot on a stick when she lines up to jam, or steal a microphone from the announcers to add our own commentary to the game when our opponents have stretched the bounds of our patience, but in general, we don't go for cutesy crap. By the time we're skating out for our intro, we're in rumble mode, shouting "Faster, faster! Kill! Kill! Kill!" with the folks sitting on the pink and black cushions in our fan section.

But at the 2005 season opener, after finishing the previous year with only one win and seven consecutive losses, we knew we needed to exorcise our demons, so we put on a passion play to get back our mojo.

Our leading lady that night was Voodoo Doll. Six feet tall, with a body like a centerfold and long auburn hair, Voodoo is everything and nothing you'd expect. Men are transformed into drooling idiots by her physical assets, oblivious to the icepick-sharp brain tucked inside her lovely head. She seems amused by their flattery, simultaneously humoring and mocking them by posing for obligatory cheesecake photos with them. No dummy, she knows when to bring out the brain—like when she turned Andy Warhol's iconic Campbell's soup can into a can of Smackdown Soup for a Texas Rollergirl's flyer—and when to bring on the bod—like when she agreed to be the star of our bad juju exorcism.

Michael R. Osborne

Hotrod Honey Voodoo Doll uses an elbow to put the brakes on the Hustlers' Jammer, Electra Blu

Voodoo Doll was crammed inside a full-size black wooden coffin; our pit crew served as pallbearers. The rest of us draped eerie, sheer black veils over our helmets and slowly rolled onto the track in a somber processional. A mournful dirge played over the P.A. while we held miniature black crepe parasols over our heads and clutched black silk roses. One by one, we circled the coffin, dropping our roses to bid a final farewell to our losing season.

As the last blossom fell, the music changed to a jubilant New Orleans march, and the coffin lid slowly slid back to reveal one long, lean, fishnetted leg, extending up and up and up toward the ceiling. A second leg appeared and the rest of Voodoo Doll followed. Gyrating and undulating like a high priestess, she pointed her skull rattle to each corner of the rink, summoning our rookie teammates—the fresh hope for a new season—and the rest of us tore off our veils, gathered the roses, and tossed them to our fans. The ritual was a success. We put a gris-gris on the Hell Marys and won the game, 54–24.

☠ ♥ ☠

When every skater has been introduced and had her moment in the spotlight, Kool-Aid moves on to the next step in the derby tradition: the national anthem. He does his shtick, which is rewarded with a huge laugh from the audience: "Ladies and gentlemen, would you please rise and join us now in the singing of the national anthem . . . Gentlemen, please remove your hats . . . Foreigners, please play along."

The audience stands, and our entire league rolls on to the track. In unison, all of us turn toward the rear wall. Dead center is the most pandering video I've ever seen of a glorious flag, rippling in a pixel-induced breeze. We hold our helmets over our hearts and for once, the Rollergirl chatter is silent as the anthem begins. Although I wouldn't describe myself as patriotic, I admit to getting a lump in my throat during the singing of "The Star-Spangled Banner."

We vary the performers each month, and we've had some real clinkers over the years. Like the Canadian dude who, after fumbling the lyrics—even though he read them from a crumpled computer printout—stopped midsong to blurt, "What do you expect? I'm Canadian!" Or the bombshell wannabe who tried to imitate Marilyn Monroe's "Happy Birthday" flirtation with JFK with a breathy, "Oh, say can you see . . ."

Some renditions have been stirring. Blues Traveler's John Popper surprised us at a bout once and played a jazzy, improvised rendition on his harmonica. Another time, a nineteen-year-old guitar whiz named Curtiss did his own blistering take on Jimi Hendrix. Whiskey L'Amour played a solo version on her piccolo! And to celebrate our 2006 championship, local favorite Peter Elliott sang all four stanzas—bet you didn't know there were four!—at double-speed with just the right mix of reverence and attitude.

As soon as the last notes of the anthem die away, the pivot and jammer for each team wrestle their helmet covers into position on their heads—a star for the jammer and a stripe for the pivot—and the ten girls slated to play in the first jam line up on the track. The DJ's music pounds—Sex Pistols or Motorhead—and people in the audience cheer so loudly the cords in their necks throb. Kool-Aid leads us in a countdown to the starting whistle:

"Five . . . four . . . three . . . two . . . one . . ."

The ref blows the whistle, launching the pack on their first lap around the track, and the jam clock starts counting down from two minutes. When the pack has made a quarter-lap, the ref gives two sharp whistle blasts, and the jam is on.

While the first five members of our team are skating, the rest of us huddle on the benches in the center of the track. We drink water. We anxiously fire questions at our manager: "When am I in?" "Who's my blocker one?" "Where's the freakin' pivot helmet cover?" And always, we're yelling, because it's almost impossible to hear each other over the cacophony of the music, the fans, the grunts of the skaters in the jam, and the refs' whistles. In between the jams, we have only twenty seconds to assemble our lineup on the track, or we skate short. It sucks to have only two blockers versus the other team's three—or worse, no jammer—because we couldn't get our shit together to get to the line on time.

When it's my turn to hit the track, I like to find someone in the audience—a friendly face in a Hotrod Honeys shirt or, even more amusing, a fan of the other team—and wink or blow 'em a kiss. Then when the whistle blows, all thoughts of the people in the audience evaporate as I try to do my job: clobber the other team's jammer, keep the blockers off my jammer, and help get my jammer through the cluster of limbs and wheels around us.

The first big hit of the game is startling. One second, I'm looking for the jammer over my left shoulder and the next—WHAM! It's the sound of my knee pads and wrist guards clattering on the floor that makes me realize I've been nailed. We have tricks that are meant to keep us from falling down and being blindsided, but it still happens. (We wouldn't have an audience if it didn't!) I'm stable when I skate in a squat position, with my feet wide and elbows out, like a radar antenna scanning for the enemy. But sometimes, if the other blocker gets me just right, maybe with a hip check, or sneaks in around my elbow, down I go.

"When I took my first really huge hit, I was mad about it for weeks. How come I didn't see her coming? How did she manage to send me flying? When is my bruise gonna heal? And then I realized that it was okay because I stopped being afraid of getting hit. I share that with the new girls: 'There is this moment when you stop worrying about falling down.' When I see them learn the lesson, it brings me to tears because I know they are strong, but more importantly, *they* know it."

—JERSEY RUNAWAY, SUICIDE SHIFTERS/DALLAS DERBY DEVILS

So far, I've been able to say "Falling doesn't hurt," and mean it. The worst I've endured is countless black-and-blue marks on every part of my body, a crick in my neck, and a recurring twinge in my right shoulder. And the fishnet burn. I have fishnet burn scars on the backs of both thighs—my trophy for repeatedly skidding my skin across the acrylic floor in fishnets. A good fishnet burn is both fascinating ("Wow! It looks like you sat on a waffle iron") and a total gross-out ("Eeeeu! Each of those little squares is oozing," and later, "Dude! You have, like, forty square miniscabs").

With games once a month, the previous bout's fishnet wounds have just about healed when I hit the deck to refresh the burns. I hear the sickening, unmistakable sound of sweaty skin meeting acrylic, then feel the familiar sting. I go to sleep most postbout nights with a healthy slathering of Neosporin and a bag of frozen peas applied to my butt. I could stop wearing fishnets—or stop falling—but where's the fun in that?

I've been quite lucky. I've yet to visit the EMTs or the emergency room. Some Rollergirls argue that it's not a question of *if,* but *when,* we'll all get our turn in the MRI machine. Looking at the list of derby medical emergencies we've had in our league alone, I hope they're not right: torn ACL, LCL, MCL, and PCL; meniscal tears; broken noses and wrists; snapped tailbone; cracked ribs; concussions; sprained and broken fingers; black eyes; lacerated chins; fractured elbows and collarbones; chipped and knocked-out teeth; dislocated shoulders; detached retinas; and bruises, contusions, hematomas, and abrasions raging from pinprick to dinner-plate-sized. Not to mention pregnancy.

CHAPTER

12

Breakin' the Rules

The Hotrod Honeys finished the 2004 season with a 1–7 record. Our fans liked to say we "never gave up" and "played with a lot of heart." The truth is that we were frustrated, and in every game, we fought—ourselves and the other team—to the last bitter buzzer.

We played the Honky Tonk Heartbreakers at the March bout. In direct contrast to us, they were enjoying an undefeated season. During a jam in the second half of the game, Vendetta Von Dutch and Derringer lined up together. Derringer is a six-foot-tall blocker who usually plays at the back of the pack. Her height and large frame had always been a challenge for us, but that season she'd become fast and agile, too. She seemed to be everywhere at once, knocking down blocker three, then racing along the inside line to block the jammer at the front of the pack. She'd become very effective, and it was annoying as hell.

Vendetta Von Dutch is an elementary school librarian—soft-spoken, loving, and adored by her students and their parents. But on the track, she lives up to her name. She has a memory like a Mafia don and the threat of violence is only partially a put-on. She can't abide a half-assed commitment from herself, and she certainly won't tolerate it in others. Winning isn't *a* thing, it's the *only* thing.

In the mess of elbows and skate wheels that was the pack, Derringer propelled Buckshot Betsy with a push into the lead jammer position, then laid into Vendetta with a body block. Like a game of telephone with hits instead of secrets, Vendetta set her sights on Barbie Crash, another Heartbreaker blocker, and took *her* out with a legal hit.

FIGHT! FIGHT! FIGHT!

"I'll fight anyone, anywhere. I'll fight you on your mama's bed. I've even been known to fight a fan or two or three. . . . If I can, I'll take out five or so fans with my enemies' sprawled bodies, and I'll clean up the beer with my opponent's uniform."

—EIGHT TRACK, HOTROD HONEYS/TEXAS ROLLERGIRLS

Even with eyes closed, there's no mistaking when a fight breaks out on the track. The roar of the crowd increases exponentially and the air crackles with energy. The announcers provide play-by-play of every moment of the tussle, while the refs do their best to separate the offenders as other skaters jump onto the pile to join the mêlée.

Whether it's two Rollergirls trying to settle some personal score, or a bench-clearing brawl, fights are definitely the chocolate sprinkles on top of an already decadent sundae. Did the scuffle start with a legal hit? Or was it the result of an illegal but effective tackle? Is there blood? Did the refs call off the jam, or is the rest of the pack still skating—and scoring? Observant fans will quickly see that while the personas may be fictional, the fights are real.

In the next jam, Sparkle Plenty plowed into Vendetta, ratcheting up Vendetta's ire. When Trouble came around the curve as lead jammer, Vendetta forgot the rulebook and took Trouble to the floor with fists flying. By the time the refs pulled them apart, Vendetta had a split eyebrow and blood rolled down her face, into her eye. She laughed coldly at our captain's admonitions to see the EMTs, gritted her teeth, and, with chin lifted, stubbornly lined up for the next jam. Just before the whistle blew, someone painted a target on Loose Tooth Lulu with six final words to Vendetta: "Don't you let that jammer go!"

WHEN WE'RE GOOD, WE'RE REALLY, REALLY BAD

The list of forbidden moves grows as Rollergirls devise new ways to wreak havoc on each other. The current list of no-no's looks a little something like this:

- No use of any part of the arm below the elbow.
- No tripping.
- No hitting from the rear.
- No grabbing, holding, or pulling an opposing player (or her uniform).
- No throwing elbows.
- No falling in front of an opponent and/or blocking from the floor.
- No head butting.
- No punches to the face.
- No spitting on the track.
- No cutting the track.

And as D the B always says, "If you brag, don't cheat. And if you cheat, don't brag."

As the pack rolled around the track, fighting for position, Vendetta tackled Lulu, kicking off another brawl. Our ref The Boss had enough, and as he pulled the two apart, he ordered Vendetta off the track. "You're out!" he yelled, pointing toward the exit doors. Without saying a word, Vendetta stood and hurled her helmet. "I felt crazed," she says, "like I could have chewed someone's face off." Her helmet skittered across the floor and came to a stop when it hit the fans sitting on the Blue Line. For the second time that night, she was ejected from the game, by our other ref Quicksilver.

A few months later, Vendetta's black eye was healed and the drama had been mostly forgiven, if not forgotten. It was the last practice before our rematch with the Heartbreakers, and we were having a go-for-broke scrimmage with the Hustlers.

Vendetta was blocker three, looking over her right shoulder for the jammer. Most of her weight was on her right foot as she rolled into the curve. Suddenly—BLAM!—a solid hit on her left side. She did a complete 180 spin and landed—hard—on the floor with her left shoulder. She says now that she heard a pop and tried not to puke when she felt her collarbone snap.

At the bout a few days later, she was still angry—at the skating gods, at her collarbone, at the doctor for putting her out of commission for three months—and she got her revenge with a megaphone. The anti-cheerleader, Vendetta spent the entire bout striding angrily around the track, hurling insults and barbs, put-downs and wisecracks at the Honky Tonk Heartbreakers, the refs, and unsuspecting audience members.

To Sparkle Plenty, as she waited at the line to jam: "Hey, Sparkle! Are you what my skeleton looks like under all my meat?"

To the Heartbreakers, as they huddled for a pep talk: "Damn! There's a lotta gingham over there. Are you 'hookers' planning a picnic? I'll bring the fried chicken; who's bringing the potato salad?"

But mostly she just bitched about the reffing and the scoring.

Until she crossed the line and dared to step onto the track in her shoes. The normally placid, kitten-loving, self-possessed Quicksilver sped to Vendetta and, nose-to-nose, demanded, "GET THE FUCK OFF MY TRACK!"

The ranting through the megaphone continued, from a referee-approved distance behind the Blue Line.

That year at our Whammy Awards ceremony, Vendetta was voted Crowd Favorite by our fans and honored with the Best Injury Award from the league.

☠ ♥ ☠

I have to admit that my favorite Roller Derby play blatantly breaks the rules. Known indelicately as the ClusterFuck, the play was invented by the devious minds of my beloved Hotrod Honeys. Whether we're up by a wide margin, or doomed to lose, our captain calls this dastardly play whenever the mood strikes, much to the delight of the audience and my team.

When the whistle blows to start the jam, we take off, as usual . . . but on the second whistle that signals the jammers to sprint toward the pack, every member of the Hotrod Honeys—including the jammer—tackles her counterpart on the opposing team and introduces her to the floor. It's wildly satisfying to see the astonishment on the face of my nemesis-of-the-moment. Sure, the payback can be a bitch—and the refs turn red with anger, pointing vehemently toward the penalty box—but working on my Ann Calvello attitude makes it all worth it.

Now that I've glorified the misdeeds that garnered awards and infamy for some of our skaters, it seems like a fitting time to talk about the folks who try to keep it all under control: the scorekeepers and the referees.

I honestly don't know why our refs and coaches put up with us.

During a game, they banish us to the penalty box, and we refuse to go. At practice, they give us instructions for a drill, and we grumble under our breath. They tell us to shut up and skate, we talk louder. We generally behave like teenagers who scream, "I hate you!" at their parents before running to their rooms and slamming the door. We cuss them, ignore them, argue with them, and question them at every turn.

And we adore them.

Our ref crew is a family affair. The Boss is our speed coach at practice and the disciplinarian on the track during a game. His real-life daughters—affectionately known as the Twin Towers—along with Quicksilver do their best to keep us in line. They identify the lead jammer, call penalties, blow the whistles that begin and end the jams, break up fights, and confer with the scorekeepers on the number of points earned in each jam.

That's their official capacity. But it's only a small part of the story. The Boss and Quicksilver are two of the important people who help us in our crusade to be the best skaters we can be. They're our constant companions at practice, forcing—and encouraging—us to repeat drills over and over to improve our skating form, increase our speed, build our endurance, and hone our strategy. They're both accomplished speed skaters, and from the get-go, they always treated us as athletes.

The Boss isn't loose with the compliments—he's kind, but not a pushover, and he doesn't toss off praise lightly. One of my best derby moments was at a practice during our off-season. I'd been working hard off the track: lifting weights, doing kickboxing to improve my reflexes and balance. I fervently hoped someone would notice the leaner, meaner, faster me.

The Boss challenged us to see how many laps we could skate in five minutes. I put my head down and tried to not think about the flames that seemed to engulf my lungs. During the last two minutes, while I was huffing like a freakin' freight train, I heard The Boss shout,

"Look at Mel! Y'all better catch her!" That's when I realized I was keeping pace with—and about to pass—some of the jammers. Later, The Boss pulled me aside and said that I was doing "real good . . . like a bat outta hell."

Quicksilver is the kind of no-nonsense gal I envy. Her philosophy is brilliantly straightforward: If you want to feel good, you eat healthy. If you want to skate faster, you train. There's no drama involved. No big secrets, or heart-to-heart conversations. Zip your lip and get out there and do whatever it is you're going to do. We dubbed her Quicksilver because, like mercury, she's smooth and fast and elegant and seemingly indestructible when she skates. I've seen her fall only twice in almost five years, and both times were because some dingbat Rollergirl tripped her. We all *think* we're badasses; she *is* a badass.

We're fortunate that both The Boss and Quicksilver were able to look beyond our juvenile behavior and slutty practice clothes to see the athletes we could be. When they believed in us, it helped the rest of us have faith, too. Sure, we grumble during the squat-sprint drills—and I doubt that a roomful of Rollergirls will ever listen more than they talk—but we'd be lost without our coaches, and every one of us knows it.

The refs' partners in law and order are the scorekeepers. They sit in a perch, eight feet above the track, and count the points earned by the jammers as they pass their opponents. When the refs and scorekeepers are in agreement about the results of the jam, they pass the info along to the scoreboard operator, who updates the computer-generated scoreboard we project on the wall.

Sometimes a Rollergirl misbehaves so badly, perpetrates a deed so heinous, she incites the wrath of the refs and the Rollergirls. Unfortunately for Bettie Rage of the Honky Tonk Heartbreakers, April 24, 2005 was her night. Her team, the 2004 Champions, had been undefeated for nine consecutive games, and they showed no signs of letting up on the competition.

★◻

Sonny "The Boss" Felter & Debra "Quicksilver" Smotrilla

Larry Stern

The Boss

LIKES: the squat-sprint drill; clean bearings; quad skates; amateur sports and playing with heart; tight skating floors; being the man with the whistle

DISLIKES: boys who are mean to his Rollergirls; illegal take-outs; bald skate wheels; slippery rinks; busted knees

FAVORITE QUOTE: "Pain! We love pain!"

BEST DERBY MOMENT: When the Texecutioners brought the Dust Devil National title home to Austin. ("I never had so much fun in my life. I was on cloud nine.")

WHY THE BOSS IS A HERO: He started competitive quad skating in 1954. In 1971, he was a member of the senior four-man relay team that won the Nationals and set a new national record. In 2000, he competed in a veterans division and took third place.

THE BOSS FACTOID: His daughters, aka the Twin Towers, are speed skaters and are part of the Texas Rollergirls referee team.

Larry Stern

Quicksilver

LIKES: shiny wooden floors; training "slow and low" to skate fast; peanut butter; mercury thermometers; black-and-white stripes; the Veloway

DISLIKES: handsy players; falling; digital thermometers; moving tables and chairs; arguments about the score

FAVORITE QUOTE: "Ladies . . . listen!"

WHY QUICKSILVER IS A HERO: She's a member of the Texas Speed Team and races on both inline and quads. At the 2004 Texas Road Rash Inline Marathon, she took third place in her division with a time of 1:48:38 and an average speed of 14.2 mph. In 2005, she cleaned up in her division at the National Indoor Speed Skating Championships in Pensacola, Florida:

Inline: 1st place (time 38.435)—300 Meters, 1st place (time 1:04.639)—500 Meters, 1st place (time 1:33.450)—700 Meters, 2nd place—2000 Meters Relay (with Donna Shelton)

Quad: 1st place—Ladies 2000 Meters Relay (with Kasey Felter, one of the Twin Towers), 3rd place—Mixed 2000 Meters Relay (with Tom Atkins)

◻★

In the first game of that night—between the Hustlers and Hotrod Honeys—my teammate Eight Track had wrapped Dinah-Mite in a headlock and dragged her to the ground. Eight Track earned a minute in the penalty box—but she also enjoyed whooping cheers from the crowd and our team bench.

That image was still fresh in Bettie Rage's mind as she hit the track for a jam against the Hell Marys. The Heartbreakers' jammer had been sent to the penalty box for some now-forgotten indiscretion, so the Heartbreakers would begin the play without a jammer. If the Hell Marys jammer Misty Meaner could get through the pack, she could score unmatched points for a full minute, until the Heartbreakers jammer returned to play. The Heartbreakers were ahead, but Rollergirls never take a lead for granted.

When Misty Meaner rolled around the curve, she came up on Bettie Rage in the blocker three position. Bettie Rage prepared to nail her, but Misty Meaner slowed down. The hit was too early; Bettie Rage was going to miss her. Instead of chasing Misty Meaner for another attempt at a legal hit, Bettie Rage threw herself to the floor. She landed in front of Misty Meaner and with a "whatever it takes" attitude, kicked out her foot to clip Misty Meaner directly in the skates. Bettie Rage said later that her only thought was that she had to take Misty Meaner out—that "sometimes taking the foul is better than losing the point."

That statement could cause a raging debate among Rollergirls until well past last call. But Bettie Rage *did* suffer the consequences of her actions.

She'd tripped Misty Meaner directly in front of the Hell Marys bench. Although Misty Meaner was unscathed—she flew through the air like Supergirl and landed in a half-skid that had her back on her feet in a flash—the Hell Marys were vexed.

From the audience, I watched a furious, swarming mass of red plaid pile onto the track. The Wrench dove on top of Bettie Rage, using her body as a shield to protect Bettie from the now rabid Hell Marys.

"I was like, 'Oh, shit!' The benches cleared and they were all coming out, I thought, to kill me," Bettie Rage says. "I remember Anna Mosity hit me before I became engulfed. When the refs pulled the girls off me, the first thing I saw was Anna Mosity sitting next to me, so I bopped her square on top of the helmet: BOP!"

It's the number one rule of playing dirty tricks in Roller Derby: the player who *reacts* is the player who gets caught. Anna Mosity may (or may not) have hit Bettie Rage first, but the refs certainly saw Bettie Rage hit Anna Mosity. And that was it. Bettie Rage's game was over— she was ejected.

The refs are in charge; they are the one true law. Doesn't matter who actually did what to whom and when. The refs' version is all that matters.

So what really happened in the Bettie Rage vs. Hell Marys skirmish? Bop or hit? Aggressor or reactor? Worth the penalty or bad decision? Bettie Rage, Anna Mosity, and the Hell Marys won Best Fight at that year's Whammy Awards.

All I can say is Roller Derby. . . . Fuck, yeah.

(ROLLER)GIRLS JUST WANT TO HAVE FUN

CHAPTER

13

Rollin' into Times Square

At 5:00 p.m. on Tuesday, August 3, 2004, I was on a plane to New York with Misty Meaner, Electra Blu, Buckshot Betsy, and Whiskey L'Amour. ABC's Diane Sawyer and the rest of the *Good Morning America* cast needed a Roller Derby tutorial.

Much as I hate flying, I was happy to finally have my ass in the United Airlines seat. The whirlwind had started with a phone call the previous day from a *GMA* intern. Her producer had seen an article about us in *The New York Times* and maybe wanted us to come to New York for a live broadcast. She was just giving us a heads-up, nothing was definite. Talk to you soon. Love you, mean it.

The rest of Monday was filled with frantic e-mails and cell phone messages that traveled from me to Whiskey to Buckshot Betsy to Electra Blu to Misty Meaner and back again. We were in a tizzy. Hesitant to get too excited, in case the invitation to be on live national freakin' television should evaporate—but too keyed-up to think about anything else. We went to bed Monday night believing it was a long shot and that since we hadn't heard anything definite, we probably weren't going.

On Tuesday at 11:17 a.m., out of the blue, we got our flight information. It wasn't until I was tucked into my seat, purse stowed securely beneath the seat in front of me, that it hit home: we were appearing live on *Good Morning America* in less than twenty-four hours.

I have bad flying karma. I get to my destination eventually, but I seem to spend a disproportionate amount of time stalled on the tarmac for mysterious reasons or waiting in the terminal for mechanicals to be fixed. I shared my curse with my traveling companions. Our flight was scheduled to depart at 5:21, but we didn't take off until around 7:00. For almost two hours, we sat on the runway. No explanation. No drinks. No foil packets of peanuts. Five amped-up Rollergirls with nowhere to go.

So I fretted.

Am I gonna look fat on TV? How many people watch *Good Morning America*? What if I say something stupid? What are they going to make us do? Is Diane Sawyer really going to wear roller skates? I wonder if any celebrities are going to be on the show?

Meanwhile, in Pennsylvania, my parents were scrambling, too, hand-lettering signs and packing suitcases so they could be in the Times Square studio audience for our appearance.

We were met at Newark airport around 1:00 a.m. by the intern (cheerful), a van (standard), and a driver (sullen). I'd like to say we were whisked away to the Millennium Broadway Hotel in a music video montage of neon lights and skyscrapers and stretch limos. In reality, the ride felt never-ending. Our happy anticipation had disintegrated into weary, bedraggled, overwrought, and dehydrated.

In the van, the intern read from her bulging Daytimer.

"Five a.m. rehearsal with Diane. To answer your question, Melicious, you're all responsible for your own makeup. Our makeup artists have a packed schedule tomorrow."

She looked up from her notes with a broad grin, "But I'm sure you guys will look great! You're pros. You brought your uniforms, right? And the extra skates for Diane?"

☠ ♥ ☠

The *Good Morning America* studio has several sets. Upstairs, it's homey, with terra-cotta brick walls lined with bookshelves. Flower arrangements and throw pillows are strategically placed around the room. A U-shaped brown leather couch dominates the middle of the setting, backed by a bank of windows that face Times Square. In another conversation nook, armchairs are parked on top of an Oriental rug. Downstairs is the fishbowl studio that looks out on the foot traffic of Times Square. Outside its windows, *GMA* fans press their noses to the glass or look up, slack-jawed, at the enormous video screen and LED scroll that displays the scene home viewers watch on their TV screens.

The intern took us into the fishbowl and explained that we'd be skating there, with a live audience standing around the perimeter of the makeshift rink. The room was about a quarter the size of Playland when it was empty. We watched as equipment was slowly loaded in and positioned around the room: multiple cameras the size of Volkswagens. A miniature stage set with armchairs for Diane and her interview subject of the day. Wall-sized sheets of corrugated tin. Brass poles with a velvet rope to keep the audience safe from our skating mischief. Soon, we were left with a minirink—maybe twenty feet across, barely enough room to take two strides—in which we would somehow convey to America the wonder and thrill of Roller Derby.

The intern disappeared and reappeared while we stood in the fishbowl, fully suited-up in skate gear, suitcases at our feet. The seven letters in the word "awkward" only barely hint at my discomfort level. When I'm really nervous, the tip of my nose tingles, and my hands feel like baseball mitts dangling at my sides. I tried to focus on breathing in for four beats and out for eight as the intern explained that the news had taken an unexpected turn. We wouldn't be rehearsing and taping, she said, we'd do our segment live instead.

The sets had warm, filtered lighting, but the passageways

between them were a dark obstacle course of thick cables, mysterious metal boxes, chair legs, and long curtains that pooled on the floor. We picked our way to the greenroom on our toe stops, trying to simultaneously stay out of the way—there were people rushing everywhere— and avoid a humiliating wipeout in the hallway.

The greenroom was both a relief and a disappointment. It was a bland white rectangle dominated by several televisions suspended, hospital style, from the ceiling. A Formica counter with coffee, water, pastries, and fruit ran along the wall under the TVs. A round table sat in the middle of the room, surrounded by molded plastic chairs that looked like they were really hip in the seventies. An assortment of other chairs, obviously pilfered from a variety of offices and thrift stores, were scattered around the room and along the outside wall.

People in headsets and security badges wandered in and out, barking into walkie-talkies. Without exception, the eyes of every person who entered the room—crew, interns, on-air guests, security, admin folks—went immediately to the TV screens and stayed there until they left the room. I watched an intern pour coffee, add sugar, spread cream cheese on a bagel, and peel an orange without looking away from the television.

Our intern materialized with her producer in tow. He talked like an auctioneer, rattling off instructions. We would regroup downstairs in the fishbowl to quickly run through our new assignment. Forget the taped interview and Roller Derby instructions. Instead, we would demonstrate a variety of skating tricks as the lead-in to the weather updates and commercials throughout the last hour of the show.

Downstairs, we practiced our maneuvers. Our first bumper— that's what we showbiz people call them, bumpers—began with us skating in tight circles and ended with a dramatic fall and slide toward the camera. We practiced it over and over again so the cameraman could get the angle just right. In between takes, we ran through the list of moves to make sure we didn't forget anything.

"The first time, we skate, then fall and slide. Then on the next one, we do blocking, right? Then we—"

"Wait! I thought we were doing blocking on the first one, then whips on the second one."

"What? We're doing whips? How are we gonna do a whip in here? There's not enough room—"

"God! Shut up! Listen! I know what he said—"

The fishbowl was now crowded with New York City tourists eager to wave to the folks back home. There was a group of young girls with matchstick arms and braces, holding a sign that said in glitter paint, "Happy 11th Birthday, Bethanie!!!" And a pair of middle-aged men in mint green T-shirts that advertised a candy shop with "Life Is Sweet, Glen Ellyn, Illinois." My roller sisters and I were clearly an affront to their Midwestern values. In photos of us with the audience, everyone else is smiling, but Mr. Life Is Sweet stands with his hands on his hips, peering into the camera with flat eyes.

Across the room, a soft-looking couple in coordinating outfits stood near contestants from the National Miss American Coed Pageant. Miss Connecticut and Miss Washington loved us—even if their mothers didn't. The girls—decked out in white satin sashes, summer skirts, and tiaras—waved us over to pose for a picture.

"You want us to smile, or pretend to beat you up?" Whiskey asked.

"Beat us up!" they said in unison.

Jamie Foxx, there to promote his latest film, had entered the fishbowl, and people were in a dither. He worked the room like a politician, shaking hands, kissing cheeks, mugging for digital cameras. When he got to us, he turned on the magic. He checked us out from head to toe stop with an exaggerated leer, and murmured in his lady-killer voice, "Mmm . . . mmm . . . mmm . . . I do love the Rollergirls."

On the monitor, Diane was wrapping things up on the homey set upstairs, getting ready to join us in the fishbowl. She beamed into the camera. "Remember the Roller Derby? Well, it's back . . . with middle-aged but resuscitated Roller Derby queens!"

Middle-aged?

The cameras were trained on us now. We skated in tight circles, whipping each other and trying not to crash into the camera, the velvet rope, and the movie star. Midlap, I wondered if I was showing too much décolletage for the breakfast set, but the in-studio audience, which included my mom and dad, didn't seem to mind the view. My mom's pink blouse was a beacon in the audience, and Dad held a sign above his head that said, "Melicious is Delicious." Next to him, Jamie Foxx stood with his arms folded, nodding appreciatively.

During the commercials, we got our instructions for the next bumper. We'd skate in the background while Whiskey L'Amour talked about the Texas Rollergirls with the weatherman. Then when he said the magic words, we'd execute our fall-and-slide maneuver toward the camera as the stations flipped from the national broadcast to local weather.

Our first bumper had gone off without a hitch, and we'd won the heart of Jamie Foxx. In spite of Diane calling us middle-aged, we were feeling sassy. A sassy Rollergirl is a dangerous Rollergirl. As we prepped for the next bumper, one of us decided that Buckshot Betsy should body-check my dad during her lap around the minitrack. To the home-viewing audience, it would look like a maniac Rollergirl had tried to flatten an innocent bystander. Television gold!

We got the signal from the producer that they were about to come back from the commercial—our cue to start skating in circles and look like professionals.

Buckshot Betsy ran on her stoppers to pick up momentum, then crossed her feet on the curve to gather speed. As she circled close to the velvet rope, she hurled herself at my dad, scoring a direct hit. My dad—king of the corny joke and hearty laugh—had decided to embellish with a comic touch of his own. But he hadn't shared his plans with anyone else.

When the Buckshot Betsy projectile hit, he wheeled backward, pretending to fall, arms akimbo, panic on his face. It was a pratfall for the ages. But he hadn't counted on being quite so close to my mom. Physics took over: force equals mass times acceleration. Dad hit Mom. Mom wobbled . . . in the fastest slow motion I've ever seen. Her arms helicoptered, and she fell backward, bumping one of the corrugated tin sheets hanging behind her. It clanged on the floor, metallic thunder echoing through the studio. Time stood still and sped up as my mom landed on the klieg light behind her. The crew scurried toward her as the producer said, "And we're back in three . . . two . . . one . . ." Meanwhile, back in the audience, Mom learned one of the lessons of Roller Derby: the fast lane to a man's heart is to take a header at his feet. Jamie Foxx helped her up and asked if she was OK. "Then he gave me a hug and kiss. Twice."

☠ ♥ ☠

I didn't see her enter the fishbowl, but I could tell when Diane Sawyer arrived because the energy in the room shifted. The audience stood up a little taller, stretching to get a peek. The crew went on high alert, and Jamie Foxx arranged his face into a charming-yet-modest expression.

Diane was lovely. She walked with purpose across the set and took her place across from Jamie. They exchanged pleasantries until the camera began to roll, and like someone flipped a switch, Diane's demeanor changed. Her body language and the expression on her face made it seem like Jamie was the only person on the planet and what he was saying was the most fascinating thing she'd ever heard.

When their interview ended, Diane turned her charisma back to the home audience and said, "Up next . . . roller blading!"

Roller blading?

Somewhere in the endless file folders of information she must keep in her noggin, she realized she'd uttered the wrong words.

Her face made the slightest correction, the laser light in her eyes flickered for a millisecond, and she blurted, "Roller Derby! Roller Derby!"

We'd been at the studio for more than four hours. In that time, we'd been on the air for a total of approximately forty seconds. We'd posed for photos. Made multiple trips to the restroom. Almost destroyed the set. Beat up beauty queens. Bummed out Midwesterners.

At no time during the preceding four hours had there been any discussion of speaking on the air.

Until now.

Thirty seconds before we were going live for the final segment of the show, the producer gathered us around him and said, "OK, guys! Ready? Which one of you is doing the talking?"

Blank looks all around. Then four familiar voices said in unison, "Melicious!"

While we'd been flirting with Jamie Foxx, Diane's coanchors had geared up in Texas Rollergirls T-shirts, helmets (with the price tags still attached), pads, and skates. As the producer did the countdown to live, they rolled into the studio, and Diane materialized at my side.

And three . . . two . . . one . . .

"Roller Derby is back, big time," Diane said to her five million viewers. She smiled at me like we were sorority sisters catching up over cocktails. "And you've been doing it your whole life?"

My baseball mitt hands were back, and a puppet master somewhere pulled the string that made my mouth move. I smiled back at Diane and said, "Yes, I've been skating since I was eleven."

For the next two minutes, I explained basic Roller Derby moves while the other Rollergirls demonstrated proper technique so that the coanchors could pretend to misunderstand the instructions. Our honorary Rollergirls shrieked in mock fear as they fell onto their unscuffed knee pads and gamely tried a whip.

I had to laugh. It was too much fun. We really could make anyone a Rollergirl. Even Diane got into the act, trading one of her perfect pumps for my skanky, derby-scarred, beat-up, broken-down skate. Balanced on one foot—four little wheels—she pushed off the floor with her other foot, still in her high heel. As she rolled unsteadily across the floor, ten pairs of hands reflexively reached out to catch her, haunted by visions of the golden girl of *GMA* crashing face-first at their feet.

At 9:00 a.m. sharp, the set lights dimmed, the cameras stopped rolling. "That's it, everybody. Thank you."

Just like that, TV Diane was gone. She graciously signed a few autographs and posed for pictures with audience members, but all of her pizzazz seemed to have been consumed. She was still physically there, but it was like she'd been wrapped in gauze or turned into a character in a pointillist painting. We Rollergirls signed a few autographs, too, thanked the crew, and posed for photographs.

Good Morning America cast with Texas Rollergirls

We all left the studio, *twired*—tired and wired—from our experience. I went with my parents to my dad's favorite New York restaurant, the Carnegie Deli. The rest of the girls went in search of strong Bloody Marys, which they found in a nearby steakhouse. They were immediately recognized by some folks at the bar—because they'd just been on national freaking television.

14

Story of My Life

Anyone who knows me knows my favorite band is Social Distortion, and that its founder, singer-songwriter Mike Ness, is my hero. In case you come from a punk-impaired background, here's a brief 101: Mike formed Social Distortion with some friends in 1979. Growing up in Republican-rich Orange County, California, gave him plenty of things to be angry about, and the band's early music is raw, frenetic, and totally pissed off. In 1982, Social D went on a DIY tour with Youth Brigade that resulted in the documentary *Another State of Mind,* a love letter to the boredom, hedonistic pleasure, and angst of being an outcast on the road. Mike's restlessness and vulnerability in the film were no act—he spent the next few years tangling with drug addiction and the law. But by the late eighties, the boy in the film had grown into a man— accountable to himself for his flaws and able to move beyond his past.

Social Distortion's string of successful albums was the evidence and the result of his redemption. For a lot of people, punk rock is a comic book stereotype—a Sid Vicious sneer, ripped T-shirts, safety pins, and music that isn't very lyrical. But to Mike, it's meant living the way you know is right, without worrying about what your neighbors might think.

That rocks.

The first time I saw Mike Ness perform live was in 1999 at the Seventh Note in San Francisco. For weeks, I'd listened to nothing but his solo CD *Cheating at Solitaire,* and I was beyond excited about the show. When the lights dimmed, the audience stomped their Doc Martens on the floor, and Mike strode onto the stage.

Narrowed eyes. Smirk. Tattoos crawling up his neck and across his knuckles. He wore a black cowboy hat, an embroidered black Western shirt, Dickies, and black workboots. I was nothing but zigzagging molecules, lost in a testosterone cloud. Breathing was an effort, and my mouth was dry. Moving anything—a toe, an eyebrow— felt like an impossibility.

It wasn't his looks that knocked me on my ass. (Although, for the record, yes, he's a good-looking man.) It was coming face-to-face with the living, breathing human who had sung me so many amazing stories of what he'd done, and what I could be if I had the guts to stare down my demons, too.

☠ ♥ ☠

Fast-forward to 2004 and the Texas Rollergirls Semifinals. When I found out that Social D was going to be in Texas the same weekend as our big game, I swallowed the shreds of my pride. It's my dream to have Social Distortion play at halftime during a bout. Not likely. But the next best thing would be to have Ness and company in the audience. I was going to make it happen, or embarrass the hell out of myself trying.

I sent a package to Social D's manager with our championship DVD, stickers, and an invitation to the game. I waited an anxious week, then nervously called to follow up. I got what I'd expected: an extremely polite, but no-way-am-I-putting-you-on-the-phone-with-my-boss handler who said, basically, "Thanks, but no thanks."

Next I wrote e-mails to everyone I knew in Austin who might have the remotest chance of helping me: to Bob, the radio sales dude who gave us a great deal on middle-of-the-night, fifteen-second commercials. To the DJs who'd invited us to their morning shows, then asked if we were all lesbians and if we had pillow fights after the bouts. To Chris Gray, the music writer for the *Austin Chronicle.*

> Hi, Melicious of the Texas Rollergirls here.
> I have a favor to ask... (I know, typical Rollergirl...
> completely self-absorbed until we need help.)
> Saying Social Distortion is my favorite band is, like, the
> understatement of the century. I can't even really talk
> about how much I love that band without turning into a bum-
> bling dork.
> They're going to be in town the weekend of our semifinals. I'm
> trying to figure out a way to invite them as our VIP guests.
> How do you get a hold of rock stars comin' through town?

Radio Sales Bob replied. He couldn't help me get Social D into the Texas Rollergirls audience, but he did put me on the guest list for a special acoustic, in-studio performance by Social D. Score!

I didn't hear anything from Chris Gray until the *Chronicle* was published a week later. At the bottom of his column, was this:

> The Texas Rollergirls would cordially like to offer
> Social Distortion, who plays Stubb's Sept. 27, VIP passes
> for their Sept. 26 semifinal bout. SD reps should con-
> tact melicious@txrollergirls.com.

No matter how many times or how hard I pressed when I clicked "Check Now" in my e-mail, I didn't receive messages from Mr. Mike Ness, or his people, enthusiastically accepting my invitation.

Then, with just four days until the semifinals, I got an e-mail from Chris at the *Chronicle.*

> May have some good news for you vis-à-vis Social D. I interviewed Mike yesterday for my TCB column and he seemed interested. He gave me his tour manager's number. Give Doug a call. Good luck.

I programmed the number he gave me into my cell phone. I copied it into my journal. I typed it into my computer's address book. Then I wrote it on a scrap of paper and stuffed it in my pocket. I picked up the landline and set it down. Then I did it again.

I walked around the kitchen staring at the number pad on the phone. My palms were sweaty; my heart did the rumba.

I dialed 1 and the area code and hung up.

I decided to wait a day. Melissa was not up to making the call. At all. I needed Melicious, and she was nowhere to be found. The phone went back into the cradle. I touched the scrap of paper in my pocket to make sure it was still there.

☠ ♥ ☠

Two days later, Dave and I were on our way to see Social Distortion in San Antonio, about ninety minutes south of Austin. We had plans to meet Doug before the show. I—or, I should say, Melicious—eventually worked up the guts to call. As I dialed, I fervently hoped he wouldn't answer. Then I prayed that he would. Fate stepped in and gave me his voicemail. After a few rounds of phone tag that helped take the edge off dialing, I finally talked to Doug in person. He was enthusiastic and receptive when I invited him, the band, and the crew to the semifinal bout the following night. We were still negotiating whether or not they would actually take me up on the offer.

When we got to the venue in San Antonio, I called Doug from

my spot in the audience: front row, body pressed against the barrier between the bouncers in the stage-front moat and the raging fans all around me. I had a Texas Rollergirls goodie bag ready to hand off to him: a DVD, a pile of T-shirts, a handful of guitar picks, and enough stickers to brand every one of their guitar and amp cases.

I was flustered, and I felt like someone had implanted titanium bars where my collarbones should have been.

"Breathe," Dave said, laughing. "He's just a guy, OK? Breathe. It's gonna be fine."

It was. Doug was noncommittal about the bout, but gracious about the gifts. We talked for a few minutes about Roller Derby and the semifinal; he promised to deliver the merch and that he'd give me a call to let me know if the band would be coming to the bout. "You have my number," he said. "Call me anytime you want to come to a show." Then he shook my hand and went to the backstage holy land.

☠ ♥ ☠

When Mike stalked onto the stage to kick off the show that night, it was just like the first time for me: a total physiological meltdown. I pogo'd. I banged my head. I traded elbows with the kids in the pit around me. We sang and screamed and cursed and thrashed and generally acted like idiots. By the encore, we were sweaty and happily exhausted. But not too spent to cheer and stamp until the band returned to the stage for an encore.

Mike returned to the stage for "Ball and Chain," my favorite Social D song. Though the lyrics outline a hard-scrabble life that's vastly different from mine, I understand the sentiment it expresses—the desire to get out from under the things that keep us down.

In the third verse, Mike usually sings about his local bar and the seedy motel room where he passes the time. He's out of cash, and he's "been drinking since half past noon."

BABY, I'M A STAR

I'm not the only Rollergirl who's had brushes with fame and run-ins with favorite celebs . . .

- When classic rock legends **Cheap Trick** learned about their namesake Rollergirl Cheap Trixie, the band gave her two tickets to their show and a shout-out from the stage.

- Lucky Strike, Nasty Habit, Buckshot Betsy, Voodoo Doll, Misty Meaner, Vendetta Von Dutch, Eight Track, and Punk Rock Phil all appeared in the Frank Miller/Robert Rodriguez film *Sin City.*

- Voodoo Doll was a cannibal chick in Adam Rifkin's caveman comedy *Homo Erectus.* She ran through the forest in a Raquel Welch–style fur bikini and chased the stars of the film with spears. A fur-covered actor was in Voodoo's way, so she decided to hit him with a Roller Derby side block. "He crumpled like a dish rag! But when I looked back over my shoulder, I realized it was a woman. A gorgeous woman: **Ali Larter.** A very gorgeous angry actress in the movie."

- **John Popper** gave Nasty Habit his harmonica when she proved she knew all the words to his song "Hook" by singing it to him at a bout.

- **Dave Grohl** accidentally spit on Apocalippz—from the stage during her favorite song "Monkey Wrench"—at the House of Blues in Las Vegas.

- Rosie Cheeks's date at the 2003 Whammy Awards was **Jason "Wee Man" Acuña** from the MTV show *Jackass.*

- **Avril Lavigne** wore a Windy City Rollergirls T-shirt on stage at a Las Vegas show.

- **Shirley Manson** from Garbage is a Mad Rollin' Dolls fan.

- After Jane **Wiedlin** of the Go-Go's saw the Tucson Roller Derby, she told an interviewer, "I loved it loved it loved it. . . . Tell those Roller Derby girls to come to our show."

That night, in the audience, skinny teenage boys and fresh-faced girls and old-timers like me mouthed the words, beaten up from the moshing and blissed out from the music. In the middle of the third verse, Mike looked my way—looked right at me—and sang: "I've been drinkin' with a Rollergirl all afternoon."

I flipped out in a way I'm not proud of; it was the best show ever.

☠ ♥ ☠

Social Distortion never did make it to the semifinals that weekend, but I don't think that I honestly ever expected them to. It was a fun day-dream. The anticipation—what *might* be—was intoxicating. A few days later, at the radio station show, Mike told me that he and the crew had watched our DVD and that it was "really cool."

CHAPTER

15

Roller-fans Rock

The transformation of an audience member from first-time attendee to Roller Derby fan is endlessly amusing.

There's the initial shock: "Holy shit! They can really skate!"

Then joy.

During a particularly cleavage-fishnets-and-ruffled-panties-infused catfight, a first-timer—sporting a fine pompadour and motorcycle boots—toasted his equally well-coifed buddy with a Lone Star tallboy. Holding the beer aloft, he crowed, "Dude! This is the happiest day of my life."

It's been a strange sensation to realize that I have fans. It was both freakish and flattering the first time someone nervously asked me to pose for a photo with them. I'm sure I blushed and stammered like a ding-dong. But now I've learned to ask the all-important question when posing for the camera: "Nice or mean?" Nine times out of ten, the answer is a jubilant, "Mean!"

Sometimes, bountiful cleavage and short stature collide to produce the Roller Derby novelty photo of a fan's dreams. I haven't yet experienced what we've codified as the "booby hug," but I've seen Voodoo Doll and Apocalippz almost send fans to the EMTs in ecstatic cardiac arrest after giving them one.

A fan—usually a male, but sometimes an enthusiastic woman (straight or otherwise)—cautiously approaches a Rollergirl for a photo op. When they're face-to-face, both realize a happy set of circumstances: the fan may be vertically challenged, but his/her head has a direct sight line to the Rollergirl's "tickets." Much grabbing and mushing of the head into the happy pillows ensues. Photos are snapped. Memories are made.

The first time I signed an autograph, I was unprepared—it looked like my signature on a bank check. The fan seemed happy enough, but I was disappointed. An autograph needs to have flair, personality, sex appeal, a certain je ne sais quoi that I hadn't captured. If a fan was going to hand me a Sharpie and offer up his neck, chest, bicep, or belly button for an autograph, he deserved something more than the ordinary. (Yes, I've signed all of those body parts on different fans. My dad is very proud.)

It's one thing to write my name myself on a fan's body—it's another when a fan emblazons himself with a Rollergirl name as a sign of devotion, like Dinah-Mite's number one fan. For two years, he attended every game . . . shirtless, with DINAH-MITE spelled out in three-inch block letters across his bare chest. He'd sit by the edge of the track, right against the Blue Line, behind a shrine of candles and Lone Star beer cans.

I suppose we should all be delighted that our sport and personas inspire our fans to get wacky. Our audience would definitely be less colorful without Clif, the inaugural winner of our Biggest Fan Award at the 2003 Whammy Awards. He demonstrates his allegiance to his favorite team by wearing his own Hell Marys uniform to our bouts: red plaid miniskirt with leopard print pleats, fishnet stockings, a Hell Marys logo T, and black boots. Hell Marys, hell, yeah!

But sometimes a fan does cross the line from fun to fanatic. Like the dude who offered one of our security guards $40 to steal Bunny Rabid's cotton tail for him. Or the fella who e-mailed Cheap Trixie repeatedly to ask her how many times she'd been spanked in our SWAT team penalty.

The most devoted derby fan in the nation might be Costa from New York City. In the last three years, he's traveled to Florida, Boston, Tucson, and Austin (three times) to attend fourteen Flat Track bouts. He knows all the players and teams throughout the country, along with their stats—and he can be found on derby-related message boards anytime of the day or night.

He's easy to recognize. Just look for the guy with the irrepressible grin and a whiteboard where he displays a running commentary on what he thinks about the game, the refs, and the players. An equal opportunity cheerleader, he claims to love all Rollergirls, but when pressed, he confesses to having a few favorites.

In 2004, Costa was in the audience for the Texas Rollergirls Championship—the Honky Tonk Heartbreakers versus the Hustlers. He'd met Bettie Rage online, and they bonded over their Greek heritage and passion for Roller Derby. At the afterparty, while Bettie Rage celebrated her team's victory at the bout, Costa gave her another gift: he had registered a star in her name with the International Star Registry. Somewhere in the night sky, Bettie Rage winks down on all of us.

☠ ♥ ☠

We've all heard celebrities complain about being tabloid fodder and whine about being chastised for their unbecoming behavior: "I never wanted to be a role model."

Well, I do. I'm proud to say that I have a fan that trumps the shrine guy and the star registry. My favorite fan is a sassy, smart, challenging, inquisitive, precocious eleven-year-old named Charlotte.

Growing up in the age of Britney Spears and Paris Hilton isn't easy. When I met her, Charlotte had yet to go through puberty, but she was already experiencing body-image issues. Her mom worried about the things Charlotte overheard at school—stuff about sex and abuse— that she was too young to understand. We thought that the Rollergirls—opinionated, independent, physically strong—might be a good influence on Charlotte.

So her whole family came to our season opener in 2005. I gave Charlotte a VIP pass and a Hotrod Honeys T-shirt to wear to the game, along with a black-and-white-checkered flag to wave from her front-row seat in our fan section. She was shy at first, hiding behind her mom as she was introduced to me.

But she was curious about me, too, and she peeked around her mom's waist to give me a once-over from head to toe stops and back again. Then the questions started: Why do you wear the bow? Is that girl over there on your team? When is the game going to start? Why is the music so loud? I'd forgotten that kids' unabashed honesty means they don't care if they look a little silly; Charlotte grimaced and plugged her ears with her index fingers until the opening band finished its set. Her complete lack of guile and pretense was endearing. Despite the action swirling around her, she retained a serious expression, her eyes wide—verging on suspicious—behind her glasses. I made it my mission to make her smile.

That was the night the Hotrod Honeys banished our bad mojo with Voodoo Doll's magic spell. When we tossed black roses into the audience at the end of our intro, Charlotte caught one, and I blew her a kiss. In return, I got the beginnings of a smile, just the slightest upturn of the corners of her mouth. No teeth, but it was a start.

At halftime, we posed for a picture together and Charlotte asked me a few questions about the game. I didn't get to see her again that night—they'd had to leave early for bedtime—but I got the full report the following Monday. Charlotte had talked about Roller Derby and me to her friend so much, the other little girl had finally said in exasperation, "OK. You told me about Melicious already. Jeez. I get it."

> "I like the light in little girls' eyes when they muster up the courage to come and ask for an autograph. I *know* that look, and I'm proud to be the source of it ... that mixture of awe and inspiration."
>
> —KIM SIN, FURIOUS TRUCKSTOP WAITRESSES/TUCSON ROLLER DERBY

D the B

Melicious with her number one fan

After that, Charlotte came to every bout—sometimes with her mom, sometimes with her dad, and once in a while, with the friend she'd so frustrated with her Melicious stories. Each time they came, their outfits were more Rollergirl-ish: pink bracelets, pink ribbons in their hair, black-and-white-checkered shoelaces, fake Hotrod Honeys tattoos, broad grins.

At home, Charlotte pilfered a frame from her dad's office and replaced the certificate inside with the photo of the two of us. Then she had her dad hang it in her room, next to her bed, where she draped it with the miniature checkered flag and the black rose. Later that summer, she dyed her hair blue so she would have colored hair like me. It's the sweetest compliment I've ever received.

CHAPTER

CHAPTER

16

We're Bad.
We're Nationwide.

Call it coincidence or great minds thinking alike, but while the Texas Rollergirls were chasing after our first championship, a punk-rock painter in Arizona—who didn't know anything about our start-up league in Austin—was literally dreaming of Roller Derby.

This was before she became Ivanna S. Pankin, founder of the Arizona Roller Derby and later, the Sin City Rollergirls. Before she wore a tiger-print skirt as a member of the Neander Dolls. Before she found her calling as an unofficial Roller Derby Ambassador. When she was an artist living in the San Francisco Bay Area, thinking about female warriors on wheels.

A rink rat in fifth grade, little Ivanna skated whenever she could. She imitated the older kids at the rink and begged the DJ to play "TNT" by AC/DC. She dreamed about being a Roller Derby queen. In 1999, goofing around online, she searched for Roller Derby and found the Bay City Bombers, the famous old-school Roller Derby franchise. Even though the popularity of the banked track sport had faded, there was a loyal, stubborn contingent keeping it alive in the Bay Area. There were no games scheduled, but Ivanna joined their online mailing list anyway; the allure of seeing them play or skating with them someday was irresistible.

A few months later, an invitation to open tryouts arrived in her mailbox. But she'd already reserved a truck and packed her house; she was moving to Arizona. She followed through on her move to Phoenix and tried to forget what she thought was her one shot at playing her dream sport.

A few years later, a friend—who teased her but understood her desire to be a Roller Derby queen—gave her a German poster for the 1972 B-movie *Unholy Rollers. Viva los* exploitation films! *Unholy Rollers* is among the best. Its heroine, Karen, quits her job at the cat food cannery to join the fictional L.A. Avengers. She's no team player, and soon her ambition and rising star cause jealousy among her teammates, leading to big-screen derby drama. The headline on the American version of the poster is "A Locker Room Look at the Toughest Broads in the World."

The poster from Deutschland, the one under which Ivanna lay daydreaming, read *"Samstags wird gerockt—Sonntags wird gerollt."* (Saturdays would rock—Sundays would roll.) She was taking a break from the canvasses she'd been painting; inspiration was in short supply. Crashed out on the couch, half-awake, half-asleep, the woman on the poster—with blond hair streaming out from under her helmet, not unlike Ivanna's—gave her an idea. She'd paint a Roller Derby queen! She rolled off the couch and headed for the studio, mentally drawing Anna Mosity, number 22, the star of her imaginary Roller Derby team.

The idea and paint were flowing, when Ivanna stopped for a smoke break. Without warning, she was suddenly enraged. She felt like her whole life she'd been reading or writing or painting about the things she wanted to do. She lived vicariously through others, recording their adventures in paint.

She ground out her cigarette, stomped to the computer, and posted a message to the azpunk.com message board: "Who wants to join my Roller Derby team?"

By August 2003, her start-up league was skating together at a local rink. Then they learned they weren't alone. Ivanna discovered the Texas Rollergirls online and e-mailed us—and we learned we were no longer alone, too. It was thrilling to know there were other Rollergirls out there, but I don't think any of us realized then how our wheeled freak show was going to galvanize punk-rock, pinup girl, wannabe jocks all over the country.

> "We include all women. Not just the white ones or the rich ones ... we enthusiastically accept professionals, homemakers, punk chicks, every ethnicity, religious or not group.... Vegans play with bacon-lovers. Lesbians bout against housewives. And we don't just play together—we run our businesses, our leagues together, cooperating as this big, amazing group."
>
> —IVANNA S. PANKIN, NEANDER DOLLS/SIN CITY ROLLERGIRLS

Ivanna S. Pankin and the rest of the twenty-member Arizona Roller Derby (AZRD) divvied themselves into two teams—the Bruisers and the Quad Squad—and played their inaugural public bout in November 2003. A line of hundreds of punkers and sports fans wrapped around the parking lot—twice!—as the ticket takers behind one tiny ticket window struggled to keep up with the crush. The nine hundred folks who made it in the door generated a mighty racket as they watched their hometown girls skate for the first time.

Now in their fourth season, AZRD has its own theme song and four home teams:

> Bad News Beaters: *A disorderly baseball team in powder blue and yellow, these girls are a troublemaking grand slam.*
>
> Bruisers: *No Florence Nightingales, these naughty nurses will raise your heart rate. When they break your bones—and your heart—they'll give you a li'l kiss to make it better.*
>
> Surly Gurlies: *The most dreaded sirens on the high seas, these pirate girls in corsets and striped skirts will have you crying, "Aye, whatever you say, my churlish wench!"*
>
> Smash Squad: *Pretty-in-punk cheerleaders, they replace cheer with fear. Yes, yes, yes, they do! They've got spirit, and they'll kill you.*

Arizona's travel team—a group culled from all four home teams to represent the league in interleague competition—is the **Tent City Terrors.** They take their name from a controversial prison program established in Maricopa County, Arizona, by Sheriff Joe Arpaio, the self-proclaimed "toughest sheriff in America." Opened in 1993, Tent City is the country's largest tent prison, and its inmates follow strict rules: no coffee, no cigarettes, no nudie magazines, no TV, except for a nightly bedtime story broadcast by the sheriff himself. The temperatures in the Arizona desert regularly top 100 degrees, and the inmates—male and female—are forced to wear old-fashioned prison stripes and pink underwear.

That's where AZRD's Tent City Terrors found their inspiration— and an opportunity for typically Rollergirl subversive social commentary. Like a pack of scheming prisoners on furlough, the members of the Tent City Terrors dress in black-and-white-striped inmate uniforms—with pink ruffled undies—and are wrangled by a no-nonsense sheriff who keeps them in line: Sheriff Shutyerpaio. (Say it fast, out loud: Shut-yer-pie-o.)

☠ ♥ ☠

Kim Sin, the founder of the Tucson Roller Derby, was one of the cool kids at the skating rink back in the day. Her family moved around a lot, and the first thing she did in a new town was find the rink. Her dad—whom she adored—gave her rides to the rink on his chopper. When she and the rest of the kids streamed out the doors after the skating session, her dad was waiting for her with his friends, Harleys rumbling. She had her first French kiss at a rink near Victorville, California, and she spent holidays at skating lock-ins, eating hot dogs and snack bar junk food and skating all night long.

★□

Liam Frederick

𝕶𝖎𝖒 𝕾𝖎𝖓 #00
FURIOUS TRUCKSTOP WAITRESSES/TUCSON ROLLER DERBY
POSITIONS: *Blocker, Team Founder (retired)*
FAVORITE QUOTE: *"You're dead meat!"*

Conceived during a romp in the backseat of a fifties-era Buick outside Tucson's Rodeo Drive-In, Little Kimmie Sin had a raucous start. Raised by her grandmother on the downside of town, Kim spent her first two years in the Four Star liquor store on South Sixth Avenue. With a pet monkey and three-foot plastic promo bottles of whiskey in her playpen, she was no stranger to the real wheelings and dealings of life. And as a teenager, she never lost a fight, regardless of the odds stacked against her. Her favorite Tucson landmark? The Tucson Truck Terminal (TTT). It's no surprise this freewheelin' rock 'n' roll outlaw started a Roller Derby team that honors America's hard-working Furious Truckstop Waitresses.

AWARDS: *2005 Most Penalties, Tucson Roller Derby Wheelies Awards*
RIVALS: *"Everyone on the track. I don't have a persona. I'm a mean girl at heart, was quite the bully growing up. Never lost a fight to a girl—or a group of girls, for that matter—so it's just me out on the track, with no reason to be polite or nice."*

□★

In 2003, rink rat days long behind her, Kim was on tour with a band traveling through Austin when she ran into girls that looked like her kind of chicks at a Red River bar; they were Rollergirls. The skaters she met had an undeniable energy and enthusiasm for Roller Derby; they seemed unable to talk about anything else. Kim hadn't seen anyone on quad skates since junior high, and she thought about those Rollergirls on the long ride back to Tucson. News travels fast in the underground, and it wasn't long before Kim caught wind of what her old pal Ivanna S. Pankin was up to in Phoenix.

There was no way Kim was going to let Phoenix outshine her hometown of Tucson. At the beginning of December 2003, she hosted her first Roller Derby meeting with thirteen girls who would become the original skaters of Tucson Roller Derby. Initially, TRD was a branch of Ivanna's league in Phoenix, but the girls quickly realized the commute was going to kill them. Kim Sin and her Tucson girls became the Furious Truckstop Waitresses, making the old punker credo FTW (Fuck the World) their own. In April 2004, just five months after their initial meet-and-greet, the TRD skaters played their debut bout against their rivals, the Arizona Roller Derby.

How did that game go?

"They kicked our ass!" Kim says.

Tucson Roller Derby has thrived since their less-than-auspicious beginning. The league now has three home teams:

> Furious Truckstop Waitresses: *Pretty in pink, these soup jockeys are slingin' hash and kickin' ass. You'll eat what they serve you, and you'll like it.*
>
> Das Iron Curtain: *Forged after the disintegration of the USSR, these former KGB agents, cosmonauts, and genetically engineered vixens vow to restore the Union and conquer the world (in skates and red minidresses).*
>
> Vice Squad: *Forget the letter of the law—bring on the police brutality! In cadet blue uniforms, these girls mix a little pleasure with the pain of incarceration.*

Tucson's travel team, the **Saddletramps,** is a posse of brazen Wild West outlaws, rode hard and put up wet. Messing with these girls is like stepping in a nest of ornery rattlesnakes.

☠ ♥ ☠

Soon, the newfound Flat Track community was like that old Herbal Essence commercial from the seventies. "She told two friends, and she told two friends, and so on and so on and so on." Leagues were willed into existence by DIYers in New York (Gotham Girls Roller Derby), Raleigh (Carolina Rollergirls), Seattle (Rat City Rollergirls), and Minneapolis (Minnesota Rollergirls). In Austin, Hydra received e-mails from girls all over the country with questions about how to join a league, how to start a league of their own, how to skate, what kind of skates to buy.

At our monthly Texas Rollergirls league meetings, we debated how much of our "insider" information to share with other leagues. (By "debated," I mean talked for hours and threw hissy fits and cussed and then stomped off to the bar to get another beer because maybe this conversation will finally be over when I get back.) Wisely, a generous spirit eventually prevailed. Plus, we realized if we helped other leagues get up and running, we could kick their asses on the track sooner. Along with reps from the other start-up leagues around the country, the United Leagues Coalition (ULC) was formed.

The group shared training drills and insurance information, commiserated about the challenges of hanging out with so many women, and debated the pros and cons of establishing LLC structures versus nonprofit status. We were all figuring things out as we went along, and it was helpful to find ourselves part of a community that was building a new sport from the wheels up.

The Texas Rollergirls rep to the ULC was Hydra, and there was no one better to take on that job. Hydra is the superhip sister I always wished I had. She's mellow most of the time—I don't think I've ever heard her raise her voice. But just when I think she's made of cotton candy, she reaches some internal patience limit and issues a remark that is biting, dead-on, and calmly delivered.

"I was that girl who wore combat boots and had a wacky haircut. I never used to have girlfriends. But now I've met so many women that I would never have met under other circumstances. I like that our friendship revolves around an athletic activity and doing community events together."

—HYDRA, HOTROD HONEYS/TEXAS ROLLERGIRLS

She's a hydrologist—a water-quality scientist for the United States Geological Survey—so she's got the whole brainiac thing going on. Conversations about environmental challenges and the latest derby gossip are equally engaging. And her record-keeping! Need the scores from a game two years ago? Hydra's got them. Racking your brains try-ing to remember who won that scrimmage back in 2003? She'll remember. She's fierce on the track—she's won the award for Best Hotrod Honeys pivot every year since our inception—but also univer-sally liked because she's a no-drama player. The newbie Rollergirls got the best possible godmother to take them from rookie to high roller.

★□★

Ziv Kruger

Hydra #4
HOTROD HONEYS/TEXAS ROLLERGIRLS
POSITIONS: *Blocker, Pivot, Hydrologist*
FAVORITE QUOTE: *"I hold more grudges than handbags."*

As her name implies, Hydra loves water. It all started when she heard the tales of mermaids of yore, who tempted sailors to their demise by singing a sweet song and luring those swarthy seamen to the deep blue depths. Hydra realized that she, too, could reel in a good catch with her Pacific-blue eyes and hypnotic smile. But fishin' can get boring, so she went looking for thrills and found 'em not at sea, but on wheels. It's been said that oil and water don't mix, but when Hydra met the Hotrod Honeys, it was clear that a little grease from the slickest girl gang in Texas just might benefit from the refreshing H_2O Hydra had to offer.

Whether splashing around or drinkin' it down (with some fine single-malt to rev her engine), Hydra can't get enough H_2O. It's a good thing, too, 'cause all those fluids keep her engines from overheating and help her run all over her opposition, leading them to their demise like sorry sailors of the sea.

AWARDS: *2005 Miss Texas Rollergirl, 2005 Best Hotrod Honeys Pivot, 2004 Best Hotrod Honeys Pivot, 2003 Best Hotrod Honeys Pivot*

RIVALS: *Sparkle Plenty & Loose Tooth Lulu, Honky Tonk Heartbreakers/Texas Rollergirls; Sedonya Face, Electra Blu & Dirty Deeds, Hustlers/Texas Rollergirls; Misty Meaner, The Crusher & Muffin Tumble, Hell Marys/Texas Rollergirls*

IN THE OTHER LEAGUES, MY RIVALS ARE THE WOMEN I LOVE: *Ivanna S. Pankin, Neander Dolls/Sin City Rollergirls; Crackerjack, Reservoir Dolls/Mad Rollin' Dolls; Whiskey Mick, Hard Anya & Barbicide, Saddletramps/Tucson Roller Derby*

□★

During the summer of 2004, it was like someone spiked the cocktails of outsider chicks across the country with a Roller Derby roofie. We learned about new leagues almost every day and for a short while, I think some of us mourned the loss of our "there's no one like us" status. We quickly learned that while we thought we were pretty damn special, we weren't unique. The girls in the photos—from Kansas City, Madison, Denver, Minneapolis, Portland—looked just like us. After the initial sting of realizing I was not a rare and delicate flower, I eagerly began to look for the alterna-Melicious in the other leagues.

One bit of minor drama that I don't think any of us anticipated was the ownership of Rollergirl names. Before the establishment of the ULC (and, eventually, a name registry that, in 2006, listed more than five thousand bona fide Rollergirl names), newbies from other cities often chose names for themselves that were similar, or in some cases, identical, to existing Rollergirls. It was not well-received by most skaters. I posted mildly bitchy e-mails to our Texas Rollergirls message board, telling the whiners to grow up. I just didn't see what the fuss was all about.

Until I learned that another skater—also née Melissa—wanted to rename herself Melicious. You never saw anyone crack open a thesaurus so quickly. I sent her an impassioned plea for the sanctity of my identity, along with a list of what I thought were reasonably attractive alternatives: Mel Adjusted, Melvelous, Melitant (military theme!), Melancholy (gothy fun!), Miss Melo Drama (go diva!), and Mel O.D. (streetwise!). The almost-Melicious, a member of the Carolina Rollergirls' Trauma Queens, chose Militia.

"OK, ladies, which is more annoying? To show up at a cocktail party and find another woman in the same dress, or to arrive at a Roller Derby extravaganza and find another skater with practically the same name? Imagine the tension: The Carolina Rollergirls have a 'Shirley Temper,' while Gotham Girls Roller Derby has its 'Surly Temple.'"

—JACK BROOM, REPORTING FROM THE DUST DEVIL NATIONAL CHAMPIONSHIP
(From "Rollerblog: Rat City Rollergirls on the Road," *The Seattle Times*, February 23, 2006, http://archives.seattletimes.nwsource.com)

It was startling at first to see how Rollergirls really did seem to be the same everywhere. We're women who grew up and found that working forty-plus hours a week—even if you're well-compensated—can be drudgery. That no one worth knowing is going to discriminate against us if we have tattoos or piercings or funny-colored hair. That we can have kids if we want to, but the get-married-have-children rule doesn't necessarily need to apply. After eschewing sports as either a childhood battleground or the domain of overachieving, testosterone-drunk lunkheads, we've learned that building muscle and working up a sweat feels really, really great.

> "I quit sports in high school when it just wasn't fun anymore. I always liked sports—it was just the people who played them that sucked."
>
> —SUZY HOTROD, QUEENS OF PAIN/GOTHAM GIRLS ROLLER DERBY

So without burning our bras or pumping our fists in the air, we simply said, "Why not?" We figured out who we wanted to be and how we wanted to look and who we wanted to spend our time supporting, and we started a Roller Derby revolution.

Hallelujah, and hell, yeah!

Three other outstanding girls who joined in the early Flat Track Roller Derby revolution are the Donnelly sisters. They hail from Minnesota and are half of a six-child family. In 2000, the girl who would become Head Trauma moved to California, where she joined an ice-hockey team to play the sport she'd grown up on. But it didn't quite take; it just wasn't the same as the Land of 10,000 Lakes. She decided she wanted to move. Maybe back to Minneapolis or to Chicago because the Windy City Rollers were about to launch their league—but not to Texas ("too hot!"), despite the fact that an article in *Jane* magazine had her obsessed with the Texas Rollergirls.

ROLLERGIRLS INDEX

70	Years Roller Derby's been in existence
4	Years Flat Track Derby's been in existence
2	Flat Track Derby Leagues in the U.S. in 2003
8	Flat Track Derby Leagues in the U.S. in 2004
34	Flat Track Derby Leagues in the U.S. in 2005
135	Flat Track Derby Leagues in the U.S. in 2006
41,984	Projected number of Flat Track Derby Leagues in U.S. in 2010 (assuming current growth)
5,437	Flat Track Derby skaters in the U.S.
2,487	Flat Track Derby widowers (men and women who've lost their lovers to derby)
1,100	Fans at monthly Texas Rollergirls bouts
100,000	Fans at monthly Flat Track Derby bouts across the U.S.
88	Feet in length of Flat Track
53	Feet in width of Flat Track
5,560	Number of potential Rollergirls born every day in the U.S.
2014	Projected year when every woman in the U.S. will be a Rollergirl (assuming current growth)
11	Melicious's number (also worn by Raquel Welch in *Kansas City Bomber*)
2	Minutes in a Roller Derby jam
45	Gallons of beer consumed at typical Texas Rollergirls bout
12	Dollars to purchase an advance ticket to a Texas Rollergirls bout
12	Average number of days it takes to heal a bruise
90	Dollars to purchase pro-level knee pads
7,000	Dollars to purchase reconstructive knee surgery
125	Dollars to purchase derby-worthy speed skates
2,000	Dollars to purchase gold tooth
3	Dollars to purchase deluxe one-size-fits-all mouthguard
25	Dollars to purchase custom-made mouthguard
40	Dollars to purchase skating helmet
Priceless	Dollars to replace your noggin

She returned to her old stomping grounds and joined a rugby team to find the athletic outlet and social circle she needed. But that disappointed her, too. A grueling work schedule that included flying to L.A. every week meant she couldn't master the ins and outs of rugby. When she realized her team wouldn't let her scrimmage (or, as she says, "didn't have the balls"), she knew she needed to make a change.

Roller Derby skated back into her thoughts because by then, she was reading about leagues in Seattle, Raleigh, and New York. She learned something temptingly wonderful: the girls she read about and met online had started their leagues themselves. She knew if they could do it, she could, too. Especially if she recruited the help of her perennial partners-in-crime: her sisters.

So in 2004, the Donnelly sisters—Head Trauma, Rolls Wilder, and Flogging Molly—jumped in their ride and hit the road to Texas, on a mission to meet Misty Meaner and to see the Texas Rollergirls live and in person. As the Rollergirl community has grown, it's become standard operating procedure to open up our homes—a couch, a futon, a garage apartment—to visiting Rollergirls. The Donnelly sisters were treated to the full Misty Meaner/Hell Marys experience. They even attended the Hell Marys final team meeting before their July bout against the undefeated Honky Tonk Heartbreakers.

The Hell Marys did what they always do before a game; they systematically went through the Heartbreakers roster and talked about each skater. Along with the usual strengths, weaknesses, blocking style, jamming habits, and strategies to use against her, they threw in the occasional smart-ass comment, just to keep it lively. Head Trauma was blown away by the meticulous way they dissected each player.

The next night, she was in the screaming crowd for her first Flat Track bout. It was intimidating and scary and so much fun. The Donnelly sisters were hooked.

They hightailed it back to Minneapolis and threw a recruiting party, where they showed the Texas Rollergirls 2003 Championship

DVD. When the sisters held a follow-up meeting at Head Trauma's house, twenty girls showed up, ready to get down and derby—and in November 2004, they closed recruiting. They had a league.

At the league's coming-out party the following January, they played a minibout on a quarter-sized track and introduced their teams. On the coldest night of the year—remember, this was January in Minnesota—1,500 people waited in line to meet their four hometown Rollergirls teams:

> Atomic Bombshells: *In their radioactive orange dresses, these girls aren't just out to play—they're on a mission to rid the roller world of hazardous waste. Beware their radioactive flammability!*
>
> Dagger Dolls: *The most feared babes in Toyland, you can dress 'em up—in their pink and black baby doll dresses—but you won't take 'em out.*
>
> Garda Belts: *Forget the luck 'o the Irish! These Irish Police lasses ensure state security and public order with force of limb, speed of skate, and the perfect little plaid skirt and green shirt.*
>
> Rockits: *Feared and revered throughout the universe, these cosmonaughty girls—in Mars red flight suits—are outta this world. One hit from a Rockit, and you'll be knocked out of orbit.*

The Minnesota Rollergirls played four bouts of their first season in a traditional skating rink, but when the NHL players went on strike in 2004, the league got the inside track on a new venue: the Roy Wilkins Auditorium, a 4,500-seat sports arena. It took two months of negotiation to ensure the league could preserve some of the quirks that make a Flat Track bout special—like general admission seating and the Blue Line—but the Donnelly sisters stuck to their guns and it's paid off. Happy fans. Happy venue. Happy Rollergirls.

☠ ♥ ☠

I've got another tale of sisters. But this one takes place in two cities: Austin and Madison, Wisconsin.

In Austin, Lucille Brawl. She began her derby career as Honey Hotrod, but when the Texas Rollergirls revolution forced us to choose new team names, she sacrificed her alter ego to our team (Voilà! Hotrod Honeys) and reinvented herself as Lucille Brawl. The name couldn't be more apt. You know how Lucy Ricardo was prone to mishaps and accidents that embroiled her in chaos and mischief? Remove the word "accidents" and you've got our beloved Lucille Brawl. She always has some 'splaining to do. The stereotype of the fiery redhead? She's the proof. All those adjectives applied to wisecracking broads in the forties—moxie, spunk, sass? She's got 'em in spades.

She and I met at a boxing gym and bonded over jumping rope. I should have know she was trouble when she insisted on learning how to crisscross the rope instead of just jumping like a normal person. When I joined Roller Derby, I talked about it so much, I think she finally decided she had no choice but to join me. Good-bye gloves and punching bags; hello wheels and punching girls.

In the other corner, Crackerjack in Madison, Wisconsin. As far as I can tell, Crackerjack is a lot like Lucille Brawl—only more so. Troublemakin' spirit? Check. Sharp sense of humor? Check. Ability to laugh off just about anything? Check. Red hair? Oh, yes.

According to family reports, the two sisters were mostly friends while growing up. Both sisters were good students, both did gymnastics. ("She was always better than me," says Crackerjack.) Lucille had been a Texas Rollergirl for more than a year and her older sister had never seen her play, so when Crackerjack was graduating from college, Lucille gave her sister a trip to Austin to see a bout as a "Hooray! You're a grown-up" gift. What better way to celebrate the shackles of adulthood than a weekend of derby debauchery?

Long before the game was over, Crackerjack had decided that the next step in her personal growth would be starting a Roller Derby league in Madison. She and pal Pam Demonium found twenty-five willing women and just five months after she saw her baby sister killing it as lead jammer, Crackerjack skated in the premiere bout of the Mad Rollin' Dolls. Each month, eight hundred fans show up to cheer for their favorite teams:

> Quad Squad: *Decked out in green and silver, these renegade superheroes fight for truth, justice, and the American way. . . . Aw, who are we kidding? They just fight.*
>
> Reservoir Dolls: *White shirts and black ties on the outside; cold blood on the inside. Murder on the track isn't personal. It's just another day in the roller crime syndicate.*
>
> Unholy Rollers: *Gothic beauties in red and gold, these biker vampires are so seductive, it hurts. Clutch your cross and grab your holy water—their feet are as deadly as their fangs!*
>
> Vaudeville Vixens: *These burlesque broads have a lot of tricks up their sleeves. They'll bedazzle you with their pink and brown corsets, and bamboozle you with their blocks.*

Mad Rollin' Dolls' travel team is the **Dairyland Dolls,** sweet-as-buttermilk farmers' daughters in blue and white maidens' frocks. Corn-fed and seeing red, they're hearty girls from America's heartland.

Still the best of friends, Lucille Brawl and Crackerjack now have a healthy rivalry on the track. "I don't have a lifetime history of taking it easy on her," Crackerjack says in mock sorrow. Then, with a malicious glint, "I do have a lifetime history of kicking her ass. And on the rink, Mama can't save her."

𝕽𝖔𝖑𝖑𝖊𝖗 𝕯𝖊𝖗𝖇𝖞 𝕾𝖎𝖘𝖙𝖊𝖗𝖘 & 𝕽𝖎𝖛𝖆𝖑𝖘

★□

Maraya Chasney/c-hphoto.com

𝕷𝖚𝖈𝖎𝖑𝖑𝖊 𝕭𝖗𝖆𝖜𝖑 #56

HOTROD HONEYS/TEXAS ROLLERGIRLS
AUSTIN TEXECUTIONERS, 2006 DUST DEVIL NATIONAL FLAT TRACK CHAMPIONS

POSITIONS: *Jammer, Blocker, Pivot, Rebellious Redhead*
AWARDS: *2004 Texas Rollergirls Best Ass, 2004 Hotrod Honeys Best Jammer, 2003 Hotrod Honeys Best Jammer*
RIVALS: *Crackerjack*

Timothy Hughes/timothyhughes.com

𝕮𝖗𝖆𝖈𝖐𝖊𝖗𝖏𝖆𝖈𝖐 #100

RESERVOIR DOLLS/MAD ROLLIN' DOLLS

POSITIONS: *Jammer, Blocker, Pivot, Leaning on the Bar*
CRACKERJACK FACTOID: *Crackerjack's fans are known as "Crackerbackers" and one of 'em wears a shirt made entirely of Crackerjack boxes.*
AWARDS: *2005 Season MVP, 2005 Fastest Doll*
RIVALRIES: *Sheriff Shutyerpaio/Helen Wheels and the entire Arizona Roller Derby Tent City Terrors team; every member of the Gotham Girls Roller Derby; Lucille Brawl*

□★

The Internet has been instrumental in bringing together misfit girls to fuel Roller Derby mania. The Texas Rollergirls coup was plotted on a Yahoo! group. Ivanna S. Pankin began her Roller Derby odyssey with an online search. The United Leagues Coalition message board was a virtual headquarters for leagues across the country. And who knows how many Rollergirls were inspired by the photos on our Texas Rollergirls website?

That's how Dirty Britches and Princess Anna Conda, the founders of the Kansas City Roller Warriors, felt themselves drawn into the Roller Derby vortex. Killing time online at the library, they discovered the Texas Rollergirls website and were hooked. At first, they didn't realize the game had rules—they just thought that girls on skates beating each other up looked awesome.

Both Princess Anna Conda and Dirty Britches were at a point in their lives when they should have been fulfilled, over-the-moon with their success. They liked their jobs. They had active social lives. But something was missing. They longed for a creative outlet, something to get them fired up. Dressing like a pinup and bashing the snot out of other girls looked like just what they needed.

They joined the ULC Yahoo! group and started the administrative grunt work that would take them from girls to Rollergirls. There were days when it was just the two of them, hanging on to the dream. "We were excited when the two of us became four," Princess Anna Conda says.

Eventually their league grew to fifty consistent members, skating in a neighborhood parking lot. Then they upgraded to a community center basketball court and finally graduated to the Winwood Skate Center—with a beautiful old-school wooden floor, a disco ball, and neon lights—in downtown Kansas City.

There are times when their fans' outfits and hijinks almost trump the skaters. A group of unofficial cheerleaders who used to be run-of-the-mill ticket holders are now part of the show. Like drag queens jacked up on Jell-O shooters, they make costumes out of foam, and in diva-votion that would make Cher proud, show up with multiple outfit changes for the night, swapping costumes between halves and preening like peacocks. But when their mascara has run and their lipstick has smeared, it's really about the skaters of their four hometown teams:

> Black-Eye Susans: *They may look as fresh as springtime in their sunny yellow uniforms, but these schoolyard bullies have souls as black as their short-shorts. Get ready to hand over your lunch money and hide during recess!*

Dreadnought Dorothys: *These girls take out their enemies with a cyclone of speed and power. You're definitely not in Kansas anymore when cute li'l Dorothy trades in her ruby slippers for brass knuckles and nunchakus.*

Knockouts: *Dressed in their favorite colors—black and blue—these bruisers will blind you with their beauty . . . then knock you into next week with a one-two punch of fast feet and faster fists.*

Victory Vixens: *You think Rosie the Riveter was the bomb, wait'll you get a load of these dames! In blue coveralls and red bandanas, these vamps really know their way around the hangar.*

Some of the sportier girls in our league—Devil Grrl, Buckshot Betsy, Sparkle Plenty, and most especially, Hydra—had high hopes, even in the early stages of the Texas Rollergirls, that one day, we'd play teams from other cities.

I couldn't see it. Were there really enough girls out there willing to defy good sense by lacing up skates and bashing into each other? If the answer to that was yes, wouldn't we kill each other? I knew how brutally we played with our friends. Wouldn't the games be absurdly rough if we didn't know the other girls on the track? It seemed too easy to objectify someone we didn't know and adore—it would be simple to make them the Enemy and tear their heads off.

I love being proven wrong.

In late fall 2004, Arizona Roller Derby, Tucson Roller Derby, and the Texas Rollergirls agreed to play the first-ever series of interleague games. Here in Austin, we established the Texas Rollergirls Red and Texas Rollergirls Blue, two new teams made up of members from all four of our home teams.

The plan for the showdown went like this: traveling versions of the Texas Red and Blue would go to Arizona in early November to play: Blue versus the Tucson Saddletramps, and Red against the Arizona Roller Derby's Tent City Terrors. Then later in the month, all the Arizona chicks would trek to Austin for games at Playland. I was assigned to the Blue team slated to play the Tent City Terrors on our home track.

When the inaugural interleague competitors hit the track in Arizona, the Texas Rollergirls teams rolled right over both the AZ teams on their home turf. But if you talk to the girls who played there, the scores are barely mentioned. Ask about the trip and you'll hear about the sisterhood, the satisfaction of playing the sport against new people, the overall sense of community, and the camaraderie established, first, by bashing into each other on the track and, later, by sharing beers.

TEXAS ROLLERGIRLS RED VS. TENT CITY TERRORS

Saturday, November 6, 2004
Surfside Skateland—Tempe, AZ
FINAL SCORE: Texas Rollergirls Red 101–Arizona Tent City Terrors 61

Texas Rollergirls Red Roster

5 Misty Meaner (Captain)	4x4 Loose Tooth Lulu (Co-captain)
00 Sparkle Plenty	.44 Derringer
4 Hydra	8 Eight Track
10 Trouble	12 Bettie Rage
28 Muffin Tumble	31 Jen Entonic
47 Speedy Marie	*i* Pixie Tourette
XX Cat Tastrophe	13 Anna Mosity (alternate)

Arizona Tent City Terrors Roster

22 Ivanna S. Pankin (Captain)	23 Denise Lightning
67 Sheriff Shutyerpaio	666 Dazy Duke
138 Sick Girl	XXX Suzy Homewrecker
213 Kick Start	70 Lawna Moher
21 Babe Ruthless	99 Trish the Dish
50 Bubbalicious	911 Gamzilla
69 Hippy's Revenge	01 TNTia
4 Jojuanna Beatin	

TEXAS ROLLERGIRLS BLUE VS. TUCSON SADDLETRAMPS

Saturday, November 7, 2004
Bladeworld—Tucson, AZ
FINAL SCORE: Texas Rollergirls Blue 110–Tucson Saddletramps 70

Texas Rollergirls Blue Roster

5" Dagger Deb (Captain)	67 The Wrench (Co-captain)
3 The Crusher	4 Bloody Mary
8 Strawberry	10 Kitty Kitty Bang Bang
21 Buckshot Betsy	22 Slim Kickins
23 Tinkerhell	5 Electra Blu
56 Lucille Brawl	

Tucson Saddletramps Roster

666 Jezze James (Captain)	13 Wyatt Eeka (Co-captain)
0 Clit Eastwood	6 Six Shooter Flo
14 Zoe Bowie	45 Juana Chisum
74 Kamanche	333 Doe Holliday
1881 O. Kay Corral	..30-.30 Bitch Cassidy
XX El Bombadora	

But being part of a skating sisterhood still allows a lot of room for gloating and smack talk. Cat Tastrophe, on the Texas Red team, couldn't resist the urge to provoke the Phoenix skaters—especially when she saw the handmade signs held by Tent City Terrors' fans that dissed our Texas teams. When her Red team scored, she blatantly laughed at the competition; on the jammer line, she whispered threats to her competitor. She fully explored the facets of her catty persona; she's not called Cat Tastrophe for nothing.

Derringer exacted her own revenge. When she and Ivanna S. Pankin got into an on-track scuffle, they were sentenced to arm wrestle each other for an extra point for their team. For a while, Derringer let Ivanna have the upper hand, lulling her into a false sense of security until the denouement, when she slammed Ivanna's hand to the table with so much force, Ivanna's whole body rolled with the impact. Extra point: Red team. Bragging rights: Texas.

But my favorite story about Ivanna S. Pankin was hearing how she had been feeling confident—maybe even cocky—about her team's chances against the Texas Rollergirls . . . and her willingness to admit that the Texas Rollergirls had "schooled them" on Flat Track Derby during our interleague games. The remarkable thing about her reaction was that she seemed pleased to have had her ass handed to her. Guess she and I have that "prove me wrong" thing in common.

Another highlight from the road was enjoyed by my teammate Kitty Kitty Bang Bang. A blocker here at home, she made her debut as a Blue jammer at Bladeworld on November 7. Her first time at the line, she hustled through the pack of Tucson Roller Derby Saddletramps to find herself declared lead jammer. It was a shining moment in what she describes as her "personal journey."

Ms. Bang joined Roller Derby in the aftermath of her divorce, when she was on the threshold of a new life and trying a variety of things for the first time. She cut off her hair. She learned to drive a car. She had the word "Fear" tattooed on her left wrist and "Less" inked on the right, as a reminder to lead with her chin. For the first time in her life, she played a team sport.

I watched Kitty transform herself from hesitant newbie to confident skater. At practices, we encouraged each other during drills. Before games, we psyched each other up with compliments and deep

Liam Frederick

Kitty Kitty Bang Bang preps for her first-ever jam in Tucson, 2004

breathing. There were times Kitty struggled with self-doubt, but she never gave up. Her tenacity paid off: at the 2004 Whammy Awards, she won the trophy for Hotrod Honeys Most Improved Skater, and our fans named her the Most Underrated Skater for our 2005 season.

Her star turn as a jammer in Tucson was just one example of the advantages of challenging unfamiliar opponents and switching up our teams. Finding ourselves on combo teams with former rivals forced us to be open-minded and put past transgressions aside. Playing with new teammates was a lot like going on a first date: everyone was on their best behavior, trying to make a good first impression. Though there were a few awkward moments, it was mostly fun, and there was no specter of long-term commitment.

Back here in Austin, we dubbed our bouts against the Arizona teams "How the West Was Won," made commemorative T-shirts, and promoted the hell out of the game. We also planned a practice scrimmage with the visiting teams and a group dinner—establishing the tradition of making friends with the competition before beating the hell out of them.

The traveling Texas teams had returned from Arizona with the inside scoop on what to expect from the Saddletramps and the Tent City Terrors when we played them here. The prevailing opinion was that they were solid skaters, but were a bit too timid when it came to hitting first and hitting hard. Our Texas Rollergirls defense had overpowered them in both games; if our home teams played authoritatively, we could uphold the Texas winning streak. As members of the home Red and Blue, our reputations were on the line; none of us wanted to suffer the humiliation of a loss in front of our hometown fans on the very track where our sport had been invented.

When we hit the rink, we experienced firsthand that the visiting teams had improved in the three weeks since they'd faced the Red and Blue in Arizona. The scores weren't quite the blowouts of the earlier games, but our home teams got the job done, and there were plenty of fun "firsts." Our Austin fans, who'd been with us since the beginning, got to experience the first interleague play in our home state. One of the Hell Marys' rookies, Nasty Habit, had her first big takeout, sending a rival blocker into the crowd, and Devil Grrl, a veteran skater, took on the role of captain for the first time.

As leader of the Red team, Devil Grrl headed up an intimidating crew of talented players from all four Texas Rollergirls teams. One of the killer lineups she put together showcased blocking machines Vendetta Von Dutch and White Lightnin' with Buckshot Betsy as jammer and Devil Grrl herself at pivot. It was almost unnecessarily mean—but it was a crowd-pleaser and our sold-out audience practically blew the roof off Playland, cheering and chanting, "Tex-as! Tex-as!"

Devil Grrl also convinced Cheap Trixie, usually a Hustler blocker, to hit the jammer line for the first time. Looking adorable, if a little intimidated, in her new Red team uniform, Cheap Trixie fought her way through the pack and was established as lead jammer. On her next lap around the track, she took a whip from White Lightnin' and put points up on the board. The crowd cheered in appreciation. Encouraged, Cheap Trixie approached the pack again, but a Tent City Terrors blocker delivered a solid hit to the outside corner that sent Cheap Trixie into the laps of her cheering fans. For the first time in her derby career, she had the privilege of calling off the jam.

I was a member of the Blue team and was thrilled to find myself playing beside jammer/pivots like Dinah-Mite and Trouble, along with a bunch of my friends from the Hustlers and Hell Marys: Sedonya Face, Misty Meaner, and Freakwood Smack (now a Hell Mary know as Bea Attitude). Just watching how the other players worked together taught me a lot, and I felt my game improving. I also discovered I was a better blocker than I thought, and I fell in love with my Hotrod Honeys all over again. Before playing with the Blue team, I hadn't realized how much I appreciated my own team's "stop being a baby" policy. (There's plenty of bitching among the Hotrod Honeys, but not a lot of whining.)

Anna Mosity and Sedonya Face, captain and co-captain, did a masterful job of devising jam lineups that simultaneously appeased our teammates and helped us dominate the Tent City Terrors. As usual, most of our 79–38 game is a blur in my memory, but I do remember delivering some very satisfactory hits on Ivanna S. Pankin. It's true: you always hurt the ones you love, and I loved her so much I wanted to crush her under my Witch Doctor wheels.

At the end of our game, I received a compliment from Ivanna S. Pankin that puts extra oomph in my strut when I think about it now. Still sweating, flushed, and panting from the game, Ivanna hugged me and said, "You were the scariest one out there for me, girl. I saw you coming, and there was nothing I could do about it. You hit hard!"

HOW THE WEST WAS WON

Sunday, November 21, 2004
Playland Skate Center, Austin, TX
FINAL SCORE: Texas Rollergirls Red 79 vs. Tucson Saddletramps 38

Texas Rollergirls Red Roster

666 Devil Grrl (Captain)	666 White Lightnin' (Co-captain)
111 Annie Social	187 Rosie Cheeks
69 Scarlot Harlot	13 Vendetta Von Dutch
21 Buckshot Betsy	66.6 Tomax Blade
13 Cheap Trixie	XX Cat Tastrophe
07 Lucky Strike	5" Dagger Deb
51 Lady Stardust	74 Pussy Velour
.44 Derringer	

Tucson Saddletramps Roster

666 Jezze James (Captain)	13 Wyatt Eeka (Co-captain)
0 Clit Eastwood	6 Six Shooter Flo
14 Zoe Bowie	45 Juana Chisum
241 Fisti the Kid	333 Doe Holliday
..30-.30 Bitch Cassidy	XX El Bombadora

HOW THE WEST WAS WON

Sunday, November 21, 2004
Playland Skate Center, Austin, TX
FINAL SCORE: Texas Rollergirls Blue 72 vs. Phoenix Tent City
  Terrors 52

Texas Rollergirls Blue Roster

13 Anna Mosity (Captain)	420 Sedonya Face (Co-captain)
19 Reyna Terror	5 Misty Meaner
10 Trouble	11 Melicious
40 oz. Freakwood Smack	50 Tomcat
56 Lucille Brawl	68 Nasty Habit
99 Bunny Rabid	321 Dinah-Mite

Arizona Tent City Terrors Roster

22 Ivanna S. Pankin (Captain)	23 Denise Lightning
67 Sheriff Shutyerpaio	666 Dazy Duke
XXX Suzy Homewrecker	213 Kick Start
70 Lawna Moher	21 Babe Ruthless
99 Trish the Dish	50 Bubbalicious
911 Gamzilla	69 Hippy's Revenge

In 2004, before we'd played interleague games and appeared on *Good Morning America,* before anyone was calling our sport a "phenomenon," before there were more than one hundred leagues around the country, I interviewed Hydra for a magazine article and she told me that her dream was for the ULC to become a nationwide governing organization for our sport, like the NBA or NFL.

In July 2005, her dream came true.

For Immediate Release

ALL-GIRL FLAT TRACK ROLLER DERBY LEAGUES FORM NATIONAL GOVERNING BODY

WOMEN FROM LEAGUES ACROSS THE COUNTRY MEET IN CHICAGO TO ESTABLISH STANDARDS AND TO SCHEDULE INTER-LEAGUE COMPETITION

CHICAGO—August 25, 2005—Fifty-five skaters, representing 20 leagues, met in Chicago in July 2005—the birthplace of traditional American Roller Derby—to form a national governing body for all-girl, Flat Track Roller Derby, in order to create a more cohesive sport with shared rules and requirements for game play.

"Less than one year ago only eight leagues existed in the United States," said Jennifer 'Hydra' Wilson, a skater with the Texas Rollergirls league in Austin, Texas. "Today, approximately 42 leagues have started rolling and are taking their communities by storm. As the magnitude and force of Flat Track Roller Derby continued to mount, we realized we needed to formalize our relationships to establish an association of all of our teams."

Acting as the "WNBA" or "NFL" of the all-girl Flat Track Roller Derby sport, the new governing body formalized a number of requirements and bout (or game) dates in an effort to formally unite leagues across the nation and to elevate the image of member leagues as women who are world-class athletes and business owners focused on the advancement of Flat Track Roller Derby.

"The sport of all-girl, Flat Track Roller Derby was founded as a volunteer, member-run organization that mixes unequaled athleticism and feminine rowdiness," said Kim Sin, founder of the Tucson Roller Derby in Tucson, AZ. "Each league and its members are unique, but we all share common goals: to have fun, to push our physical limits, and to challenge the way people view women. We've come together to create a unified voice and mission to spread the gospel of Flat Track Roller Derby."

Participants in the two-day conference discussed and agreed on the following items:

- Member league requirements and benefits
- Rules for game play
- The first-ever, formalized all-girl Flat Track Roller Derby interleague bouting season September–November, 2005
- The future of the sport and next steps for formalizing the association
- An invitational tournament in early 2006

"We consider the Chicago conference to be the most historic moment in all-girl Flat Track Roller Derby to date," said Denise 'Ivanna S. Pankin' Schubert, formerly of the Arizona Roller Derby and now starting Sin City Rollergirls. "When we brought new life to the sport in 2003, we knew Roller Derby would take over the world—we just didn't realize it would be this soon!"

Members of the newly formed coalition who were in attendance in Chicago included:

Texas Rollergirls—Austin, TX
Dallas Derby Devils—Dallas, TX
Assassination City Roller Derby—San Antonio, TX
Arizona Roller Derby—Phoenix, AZ
Tucson Roller Derby—Tucson, AZ
Mad Rollin' Dolls—Madison, WI
Minnesota Rollergirls—Minneapolis, MN
Atlanta Rollergirls—Atlanta, GA
Kansas City Roller Warriors—Kansas City, MO
Detroit Roller Derby—Detroit, MI
Gotham Girls Roller Derby—New York, NY

Rat City Rollergirls—Seattle, WA

Providence Roller Derby—Providence, RI

Boston Derby Dames—Boston, MA

Carolina Rollergirls—Raleigh, NC

Dixie Derby Girls—Huntsville, AL

Windy City Rollers—Chicago, IL

Rose City Rollers—Portland, OR

Rocky Mountain Rollergirls—Denver, CO

Big Easy Rollergirls—New Orleans, LA

About the Coalition:

The mission of the coalition is to promote and foster the sport of women's Flat Track Roller Derby by facilitating the development of athletic ability, sportswomanship, and goodwill among member leagues. The governing philosophy is, "by the skaters, for the skaters." Women skaters are primary owners, managers, and operators of each member league and of the coalition. All member leagues have a voice in the decision-making process, and agree to comply with the governing body's policies.

The fifty-five girls who represented us at that first ULC meeting willingly purchased their own airline tickets to Chicago and barricaded themselves in the ballroom of the Inn at Lincoln Park for an entire weekend. Yes, they took a break for a pickup Roller Derby game, but the carousing, the imbibing, the devil-may-care attitude that usually swirls around a collection of Rollergirls like a cloud of Chanel No. 5 around Marilyn Monroe was nowhere to be found. Those girls worked. For three full days. When they were finished, they had a beautiful plan that would help the ULC grow up, without losing the DIY, "chicks rule," punk-rock ethos of the roller revolution.

REQUIREMENTS FOR WFTDA MEMBERSHIP

- ♣ League must play seventy-five percent (75%) or more of their public bouts as Flat Track Derby.
- ♣ Teams in league must be comprised of female quad skaters only.
- ♣ Fifty-one percent (51%) or more of league owners must be Flat Track Derby skaters, whether active, injured, or retired.
- ♣ Sixty-seven percent (67%) or more of the league management must be Flat Track Derby skaters, whether active, injured, or retired.

The girls were unyielding in their commitment to formalize the ULC and officially begin interleague play. They dispersed to their hometowns and the e-mail flurry began. In Tucson, planning for the 2006 Dust Devil National Flat Track Championship kicked off. A marketing committee for the ULC was formed to begin spreading the gospel. Most importantly, the rules committee slogged through the regulations of each individual league to find commonalities, iron out differences, and establish the first-ever sanctioned Flat Track Derby rules. By late 2005, they'd done it. The ULC was rechristened the Women's Flat Track Derby Association or WFTDA; we affectionately call it "Woof-Tah." (Although I'm partial to Woof Ta-Da! myself.)

Rollergirls can only be all work and no play for so long. While the WFTDA reps from each league cranked away on their to-do lists, derby fever continued its epidemic sweep across the country. Unofficial interleague competitions exploded. No one cared if the stats of the games didn't affect later rankings; the girls just wanted to get on the track together and see what was what. So the Mad Rollin' Dolls went toe stop–to–toe stop with the Gotham Girls Roller Derby. The Providence Roller Derby took on the Boston Derby Dames. The Minnesota Rollergirls challenged the Carolina Rollergirls. The Sin City Rollergirls welcomed all comers to Las Vegas, knockin' around the track with Arizona Roller Derby and the Boston Derby Dames.

Friendships were forged across state lines, and rivalries—the real reason we enjoy our sport so much—took hold with equal passion. Every legal block, every illegal takedown, every gasp-inducing jammer sneak was noted and stored away for future reference and fuel to stoke the competitive fires of the Dust Devil Championship in February 2006, when twenty all-girl Flat Track Derby teams—and their associated fanatics, friends, families, ne'er-do-wells, weirdos, mascots, coaches, hangers-on, wannabe Rollergirls, retired Rollergirls, writers, filmmakers, photographers, and fishnet fetishists—would invade Tucson, Arizona, for a history-making weekend.

CHAPTER

17

The Texecutioners

I can spot a Rollergirl at a hundred yards. Maybe it's the extra swivel in her strut. Or the definitive combination of Converse sneakers and bulging thighs tucked into cigarette-skinny jeans. Or maybe it was the jacket embroidered with "Windy City Rollers."

I spied my roller sisters across the food court at the Dallas/Fort Worth International Airport when Dave and I were on our way to the Dust Devil.

The sight of the girls—some with skates slung over their shoulders or their helmets strapped to their carry-on bags—overwhelmed me. For the first of many times during that Dust Devil weekend, I got a lump in my throat and my eyes stung. It was an instant, visceral reaction.

In the Austin airport security line earlier that day, I'd been surrounded by cookie-cutter adolescents in black velour track suits, the name of their dance team spelled out in rhinestones across their butts. They all wore the same ponytail, the same fresh-scrubbed cheeks, the same anxious expression painted across their faces. They were Stepford Dancers.

The sight of the Windy City Rollers filled me with an unexpected sense of community. I wondered if that was how real sisters or sorority sisters feel when they run into each other unexpectedly.

The warm fuzzies dissipated, however, when I ran into Marc Stern, also known as the "Chicago Ace." Don't get me wrong. He's a good guy, and he's obviously mad for our sport. A former pro banked track skater, he works for the National Roller Derby Hall of Fame and was also the devoted coach and referee for the Windy City skaters. The problem wasn't Marc. It was that our brief conversation fired up my competitive side.

After the look of acknowledgment that said, "Hey! You're a Flat Track Derby weirdo, too," we explored the typical introductions and small talk. Then Marc looked around and said, "Where's the rest of your team?"

"Oh, I'm not on our All-Star team," I said. "They went to Tucson a few days ago."

"Heh!" he said, laughing. "They got there early to get in some extra practice time, huh?"

I laughed along with him, but I thought, Brother, you have no idea of the hell about to rain down on your skaters.

☠ ♥ ☠

When the Texas Rollergirls began, there was an unspoken agreement: you didn't have to be a star player to have a place on the team and on the track. If you showed up regularly and tried your best, you played. Each team member was allowed to play a roughly equal number of times per game, no matter their skill level. We even shared bout lineups to make sure no one would be too soundly trounced. Before each game, the team captains would exchange lineups to see how their players matched up. For example, if I was slated to jam but was lined up against Dinah-Mite, my captain might put in a money jammer instead so a) I wouldn't be humiliated, and b) we weren't guaranteed a loss.

Eight Track once suggested that we name an All-Star team—just for fun—to play an exhibition game for our fans. Our league almost had another bloody coup! It just didn't sit right with some of us to draw the lines so clearly. Everyone agreed that it took all sixty-plus of us to make the league a reality, and we weren't comfortable with highlighting the girls who were more valuable athletically.

It was all very kumbaya, and we shall overcome. But it wasn't very sporty.

During our 2005 season, we stopped sharing pregame lineups. Unlike other changes we've made over the years, there was no hand-wringing, no angst-ridden, league-wide vote, no beer-fueled speeches at a league meeting. The Hell Marys and the Hotrod Honeys decided not to disclose lineups before our game and suddenly, that was it. No one did it anymore. Welcome to the wide world of sports.

When it came time to select the players who would be on the Texecutioners team that would represent us at the Dust Devil, it seemed like it was time to let go of our sensitivity around naming an All-Star team, too. We all might not have agreed on much, but we definitely all agreed we did not want to lose the Dust Devil. We're the god-mothers of Flat Track. We had to bring the trophy home, and we had to do it with the best team possible.

Which raised philosophical questions: How do we define the best? Who does the defining? And *that* is when the handwringing, angst-ridden, league-wide vote, and beer-fueled speeches at league meetings reappeared.

According to the tournament rules, we could send only thirteen players and two alternates. At the time, the four Texas Rollergirls teams totaled sixty-one. Let me do the math for you: **61 Rollergirls - 15 slots = 46 disappointed Rollergirls.**

We're all owners of the league and despite video evidence to the contrary, if asked, each of us would say we fucking rock on the track. Truth is, there isn't a member of our league that wouldn't do us proud in a tournament. But the rules didn't say, "Teams are limited to fifteen players, unless you're the Texas Rollergirls because we know you all rock and people's feelings will be hurt, so you all can send as many girls as you want."

Before we could debate who should be on the team, we had to debate *how* we would debate who would be on the team. Pages and pages of Microsoft Word documents were posted to our message board. Proposals were merged together. Rewritten. Submitted and retracted. Finally, we had a vote. The league decided to entrust our coaches, The Boss and Quicksilver, along with Buckshot Betsy, with selecting the team, based on a list of criteria that included skating skills and attendance. Their discussions were kept super top secret until phone calls were made to captains to announce the winners of the golden tickets.

Full disclosure: I never honestly expected to be chosen for the Dust Devil team, but I wanted to be. Desperately. I didn't admit it to anyone at the time, not even Dave. When he and I discussed it, we talked about the pressure of the tournament, the extra practices during the off-season, the aggravation and expense of this hobby. But I wanted it. Even though I knew I was a long shot (Top 20 or 25 maybe, but top 15 . . . no way), deep down I hoped. (That's the unflinching optimism that's kept me daydreaming and made me an easy target for bullies my whole life.)

I hoped in vain. When the list was announced, I sniffled a little. I pretended I didn't care and distracted myself by emptying the dishwasher and obsessively cleaning the refrigerator. I had a good cry in the bathroom with the water running so Dave couldn't hear me. Then, openly weeping, I finally admitted to him how I'd hoped this would be the cinematic finale to my piano-nerd-turned-athlete story. Big shuddering breath and increase in volume . . . *"I didn't make THE TRAVEL TEAM."*

After that, I was fine. Because when I looked at the skaters who had made the team, I saw a thing of beauty. They were our best, the women who made our campy hobby a sport. I could imagine them lined up on the track in Tucson, smiling to encourage their competitors, all the while knowing that the friendly gesture only made them seem more intimidating. I could see the other teams' skaters visibly swallow and cross themselves while checking to make sure their mouthguards were securely in place.

Mine wasn't the only name missing from the Texecutioners roster. Dinah-Mite, arguably the best jammer in our league (and, there-fore, the country) had suffered a knee injury during our 2005 champi-onship game. Although she quickly rebounded from her surgery, she wasn't healed by the time the travel team practices began late in the year and couldn't be considered for membership on the team. It's a shame that she was unable to represent us in our first national compe-tition—and that the other teams were denied the opportunity to feel the whoosh of air swirl around them when she blew by.

I eventually adjusted to my good-but-not-All-Star status. Then I got excited. Because I was going to the Dust Devil as a spectator. I could drink beer! I didn't have to train at extra practices during the off-season! I didn't have to bear the burden of bringing the national title home to Austin! I was going on vacation to watch some of my favorite people on the planet have, perhaps, some of their finest moments.

When we pulled into the Bladeworld parking lot for the first bout of the Dust Devil, the place was stupid with Rollergirls. Vans with magnetic signs, trucks with soaped-up windows, cars with "Dust Devil or Bust" filled the lot, and Rollergirls in satin jackets, Dickies work coats, embroidered hoodies, and logo Ts scurried in gangs of three and four, sunglasses on, pink and purple and green and blue and platinum hair glinting in the Arizona morning. It was all the Roller Derby websites come to life. Before the van stopped rolling, we'd flung the door open to climb out.

The first familiar face I saw when I walked onto the Bladeworld rink was Cat Tastrophe. She was radiant, lit up like one of those ceramic dolls covered with tiny holes for Christmas lights to poke through. Her smile when she saw me made my heart jump and ache at the same time. For a split second, I wasn't her teammate, I was a fan, face-to-face with my idol. I felt fluttery and nervous. Then it was all over and the group hug began.

TEXAS ROLLERGIRLS TEXECUTIONERS, 2006 Dust Devil National Flat Track Champions: (back) Rice Rocket #3e8, Barbarella #66, Bloody Mary #4, Lucille Brawl #56, Hydra #4 (Captain), Eight Track #8; (middle) Tinkerhell #23, Cat Tastrophe #XX, Slim Kickins #22, Sparkle Plenty #00 (Co-captain), Derringer #.44, Jen Entonic #13; (front) Trouble #10, Loose Tooth Lulu #4X4, Buckshot Betsy #21

★✪

Ziv Kruger 2006 Dust Devil TucsonRollerDerby.com

Cat Tastrophe #XX

HOTROD HONEYS/TEXAS ROLLERGIRLS
AUSTIN TEXECUTIONERS, 2006 DUST DEVIL NATIONAL FLAT TRACK CHAMPIONS

POSITIONS: *Blocker, Jammer, Pivot, Kitten with a Whip*
FAVORITE QUOTE: *"I wouldn't touch you to scratch you."—Catwoman*

As a kitten growing up in a west Texas border town, Cat cut her claws on the local skateboard scene. During one of her nocturnal prowls, she was almost run down by a speeding Jaguar. Struggling to regain her composure, she heard the click of stiletto heels and was confronted by a fine feline female: Eartha Kitt, the Catwoman! Recognizing a kindred spirit, she took Cat's hand and purred, *"Ma cherie,* a real cat skates on eight wheels, not four!" Transformed, Cat Tastrophe howled, "I'm blowing this litter box!" and with a flick of her tail, found herself in Austin, Texas, with the Hotrod Honeys! Now she passes the time stalking her prey on the track and toying with rival jammers like balls of yarn.

AWARDS: *2005 Texas Rollergirls Jammer of the Year, 2005 Hotrod Honeys MVP, 2005 Hotrod Honeys Best Jammer, 2004 Texas Rollergirls Best Rack, 2004 Texas Rollergirls Camera Hog, 2004 Hotrod Honeys MVP, 2003 Hotrod Honeys Best Jammer*

RIVALS: *Trouble, Honky Tonk Heartbreakers/Texas Rollergirls.* "I'll rough it up with any and all opponents. Any skater who thinks she can get away with cheating is an instant rival."

✪★

The Texecutioners' new uniforms made them look like super-heroes. In an always-keep-'em-guessing move, they'd decided to go Sporty Spice for the tournament and ordered real uniform tops from an athletic supplier. But because they're Rollergirls, they'd gotten creative with scissors, bows, stars, and stitches. Their red, black, and silver sleeveless soccer jerseys—Buckshot Betsy's cropped to show off her ab six-pack, Cat Tastrophe's scooped to display her décolletage—were paired with miniskirts, short-shorts, baseball and football pants, and, of course, fishnets and fanciful knee socks. Their smiles were all outlined in the same glamour-girl red lipstick. Whatever home-team rivalries they had when the Texecutioners formed had clearly been dissolved. They were a team.

> "We acted like a team the whole time. We ate, slept, and dressed with the team in mind. We went everywhere together, passed car keys and hotel keys around in an intricate system, and left no one behind. Moving like a pack the whole trip was my favorite part of the Dust Devil."
>
> —BLOODY MARY, TEXAS ROLLERGIRLS TEXECUTIONERS

The schedule for the Dust Devil tournament—with multiple games scheduled for each team every day—was going to test all the skaters' endurance. Because it was the first national competition, WFTDA didn't have any rankings for the twenty competing leagues. That meant the first day—Friday, February 24—was a Round Robin to determine the top twelve teams and to rank them. To make it as fair as possible, the four most experienced leagues were placed in separate pools.

The Texas Rollergirls were in the Scorpion Pool—scheduled to take on the Atlanta Rollergirls, Gotham Girls Roller Derby, Kansas City Roller Warriors, and Duke City Derby.

During the Round Robin, the teams in each pool would play each other in minibouts (one ten-minute period) so they could be ranked from one to five. Only the top three from each pool (the "top seeds") advanced to Saturday's competition; the bottom two went to the Surly Wench Pub, the unofficial Roller Derby clubhouse downtown, to drown their sorrows.

Here's the all-important kicker: the teams would be ranked ("seeded," in jock talk) not only by their number of wins, but also by point differentials. This setup had two consequences: First, if the Texas Rollergirls took a large, early lead in one of the minibouts, they couldn't "take it easy" on themselves or their competition. Winning the minibout wasn't enough for a high ranking; the Texecutioners had to make the gap in the score as wide as possible to earn the number one seed. And second—and more importantly—each team would play four minibouts on Friday and their placement at the end of the day would determine which team they'd play—and when—on Saturday.

The very first bout of the very first-ever Flat Track Derby national tournament was scheduled to begin at 9:15 a.m. The match-up: Texas Rollergirls vs. Atlanta Rollergirls.

★□

𝔗𝔯𝔬𝔲𝔟𝔩𝔢 #10

HONKY TONK HEARTBREAKERS/TEXAS ROLLERGIRLS
AUSTIN TEXECUTIONERS, 2006 DUST DEVIL NATIONAL FLAT TRACK CHAMPIONSHIP

POSITIONS: *Jammer, Blocker, Pivot, Troublemaker*

Growing up on a farm might not sound glamorous, but Trouble's papa made sure she had the best, including her own private skating rink inside the barn. Trouble's travels and mis-deeds lead her to Chicago, where she was a carhop waitress-on-wheels by day, and a dancing girl in a burlesque revue by night. She loved the fishnets and fringe of her showgirl cos-tume, but hated the rules. (No punching people in the audi-ence! No hip-checking the other dancers!) Her day job made her long to skate in the great wide open—she just couldn't work up enough speed between her customers' cars and the kitchen. So she hopped a bus to Austin and sauntered into the Longbranch Inn for a drink. Across the room, she saw a posse of girls in roller skates and ribbons. One of them, eyeing her red satin fringe, said, "Here comes trouble." They've been fast friends ever since.

AWARDS: *2005 Honky Tonk Heartbreakers Best Jammer, 2004 Texas Rollergirls Best Jammer, 2004 Best Takeout, 2004 Honky Tonk Heartbreakers MVP, 2004 Honky Tonk Heartbreakers Best Jammer, 2003 Honky Tonk Heartbreakers Best Jammer*

RIVALS: *Cat Tastrophe, Hotrod Honeys/Texas Rollergirls; Sheriff Shutyerpaio and Helen Wheels, Tent City Terrors/Arizona Roller Derby*

□★

I don't generally think of myself as a sports fan. I do like to go to ice hockey games and bang on the glass, yelling at the refs and drinking beer. And there is no joy like the joy of telling a Super Bowl player he's a pansy while I shovel popcorn in my mouth during my once-per-year TV football viewing. But until I became a Rollergirl, I wouldn't have considered dressing in team colors and making signs for a sporting event. In the years leading up to the Dust Devil, I'd played in roughly twenty-five Roller Derby bouts, and at the ones in which I didn't play, I always had some league-related job to do. The Dust Devil was my first time as a pure spectator, and I couldn't wait to scream at the action.

The Bladeworld rink is a sports arena—when Tucson Roller Derby started, the rink welcomed them into their hockey and soccer world—so unlike our home turf, it doesn't have roller disco touches. The floor is sport court that, from all reports, is "nice and grippy." Happily, the track was set up with the familiar and infamous Blue Line so fans could get appropriately close to the action. The perimeter of the Bladeworld rink is bordered by a Plexiglas wall, like a hockey arena, and a staircase leads to a second-floor balcony that let me see our game from above, a new vantage point for me.

The surroundings were slightly more athletic than we were used to, but the people—yee-haw and praise the pomade—were our peeps. The motley crew was out in full force, bolstered by gangs of Rollergirls, either in uniform because they would be playing soon, or in their logo Ts and jackets. It was like *West Side Story* and *The Warriors* and *Rumble Fish* mashed up with *Kansas City Bomber* and *Grease.* Beautiful girls abounded, and everywhere I looked I had fashion envy.

When the games started, I was riveted. Someone took a photo of me, rooting for the Texecutioners. It shows an image of myself I've never seen before. My head is thrown back, and my mouth is wide open, my neck flexed with screaming. One arm is wrapped around my middle, and the other hand is clenched, like if I squeezed tight enough the jammer would get through or the blocker would send her competitor into the crowd. I felt like that the entire weekend. I was startled by how much I cared about the sport—and not just the Texas Rollergirls games. All of them. I was caught up. Sure, I've been moved to sniffling by the Olympics, but I've always had a hard time understanding the lyricism and romance applied to baseball or basketball. I get it now. What we saw at the Dust Devil was art and beauty and skill.

Felicia Graham

Melicious in ponytails, cheering

The Texas Rollergirls' first minibout with the Atlanta Rollergirls set the tone for the rest of Texecutioners' day. The final score was 70–1, and Atlanta, bless their derby hearts, didn't score their one point until the last jam.

When the Round Robin was finished, the Texecutioners had won all of their matchups:

Texas Rollergirls 36 vs. Kansas City Roller Warriors 35
Texas Rollergirls 32 vs. Gotham Girls Roller Derby 16
Texas Rollergirls 77 vs. Duke City Derby 6

From some of the scores, you might think the games were dull, one-sided shutouts; you'd be wrong. There wasn't a moment in the arena that wasn't a nail-biter. Because even if the winner of a bout looked like a foregone conclusion, we were seeing skaters play their sport on a competitive level for the first time. When they took the track to face the Texas Rollergirls, the Atlanta team had been playing Flat Track Derby for roughly a year, Kansas City for about fourteen months, and Duke City had been knocking each other around in Albuquerque for less than a year.

"It was amazing to see all the different leagues! I couldn't really get in my head that what we made had turned into a national phenomenon until I saw everyone in their uniforms. It made me cry so many times."

—TINKERHELL, TEXAS ROLLERGIRLS TEXECUTIONERS

The competition on Saturday, the second day of the competition, consisted of eight full-length bouts—each bout was three 20-minute periods. It was set up as a single-elimination tournament, which meant that when a team lost a game, they were out of the competition completely and were, again, off to the Surly Wench to drown their sorrows in fine fermented grains and fried Oreos.

The top four teams from Friday had what's called a "bye": they automatically advanced to round two and were required to play only one game on Saturday. Seeds 5 through 12 played a first round in the morning, and the winners of those games played a second time in the afternoon, against the top four seeds from Friday.

Saturday's competition was the usual fantabulous blur of speeding skaters, cleavage, ruffled butts, and maniacal fans, but a few highlights stand out. During the Rat City Rollergirls versus Sin City (final score: 208–64), Rat City "broke" the scoreboard. It was designed to go up to only 199, so when the Rat City Rollergirls scored 200, the damn thing rolled right back over to zero. The final score on the board at the end of the game *looked* like Rat City 8, Sin City 64.

Next up was Kansas City Roller Warriors versus Providence Roller Derby (final score: 199–71). Yes, they were outscored by 128 points, but Providence was a team of scrappers. The crowd-pleasing moment of that game was when Providence's DaSilva Bullet skated backward in the middle of the pack to dodge a takeout. The crowd went berserk, and she escaped without hitting the floor.

Finally, it was time for the Texas Rollergirls Texecutioners to square off against Carolina Rollergirls (final score: 177–65). Even when the Texecutioners took an early lead, Carolina never gave up, and although both teams' competitive drive was evident, there were a lot of smiles on the track, too. I watched this game with a Texas cheering section, and it was awe-inspiring. Our jammers and blocking pairs were like cheetahs stalking gazelles. Later, when I talked to a few Carolina girls, I told them how impressed I'd been with their upbeat attitudes and the way they played. Militia told me, "It was a privilege to play the Texas Rollergirls. If you're going to get stomped, it's good to get stomped by the best."

The big-enough-to-drive-a-Mack-truck-through point differentials continued in the next two bouts. The Minnesota Rollergirls versus Kansas City Roller Warriors (final score: 120–79) was a barn burner. Snot Rocket, a star jammer from Kansas City, set a tournament record: a seventeen-point jam. (That means she lapped the pack at least four times in two minutes while every blocker on the floor was trying to take her ass out.) Sadly, the other noteworthy event was KC's cofounder Dirty Britches taking a hard fall on her head that necessitated a trip to the ER. She's well-known for her sometimes overtly illegal play and aggressive attitude. (She told *The Pitch*, a Kansas City magazine, "I eat rocks and kick puppies in my spare time.") But there's another reason she's noteworthy among the Rollergirls: she lost her right arm in a childhood accident, making her, at this point, the only one-armed Flat Track Derby skater in the country. It was tough for the crowd to see their unsentimental sentimental favorite go down, and a relief to learn later that she was OK and still smart-mouthing everyone within earshot.

In their second bout of the day, the Mad Rollin' Dolls did themselves proud when they went helmet-to-helmet with Tucson Roller Derby (final score: 82–52), but Tucson ultimately dominated, especially during the second period. In the last half of the game, Tucson scored 32 points to Madison's 8. Thankfully, reminding everyone that Roller Derby is about spectacle as much as sport, two blockers—one from each team—banished to the penalty box by the refs, clasped hands and playfully swung their arms as they took their time getting to the hot seat.

Then it was Arizona Roller Derby—the second-oldest Flat Track league in the nation—versus Rat City Rollergirls. Everyone is in agreement: this was the Dust Devil bout to see. The blogger for Lead-Jammer.com wrote, "It was so exciting that the only scribble in my notebook was 'Holy Fuck.'"

Rat City was on their second game of the day, and I can tell you from firsthand experience, Arizona's Tent City Terrors play with the ferocity of prison inmates taking advantage of their first taste of freedom. But Rat City was firing on all cylinders, too, with standout players Burnett Down, Femme Fatale, Miss Fortune, and D-Bomb refusing to give in to fatigue. The Washington fans were losing their minds with cheering, and the Texas contingent rooted with them for an upset that would put Rat City in contention for the championship. (The Texas Rollergirls–Rat City relationship is a family affair; Austin's Derringer and Seattle's Bonnie Collide are sisters, so we Texans were hungry for the chance to play against Rat City for the title.)

In a turnaround previously unseen in Flat Track Derby, Arizona came back from an eighteen-point deficit to win the game. As the clock ticked down, Arizona's Sheriff Shutyerpaio and Denise Lightning—having lost three of their five jammers to injury or penalties—took turns jamming for their team. The crowd chanted "A-Z!" (clap-clap) "R-D!" (clap-clap) so loudly Sheriff Shutyerpaio couldn't hear the whistle blows to start each jam. Instead, she watched for the ref's abdomen to move with the expulsion of air into the whistle, and took that as her sign that it was time to start sprinting. When the final buzzer blew at the end of the sixty minutes, Arizona had pulled ahead by two. Every spectator was on their feet and every throat was screamed raw. Final score: Arizona Roller Derby 95 vs. Rat City Rollergirls 93.

☠ ♥ ☠

Sunday, February 26, 2006. The first-ever Flat Track Derby National Championship. After forty minibouts, eight full games, countless take-outs, hundreds of penalties, and multiple Rollergirl-into-crowd crashes, the Texas Rollergirls retained their top-seed position.

There were two semifinal games that would decide the contenders for the Flat Track crown: Texas Rollergirls vs. Arizona Roller Derby, and Tucson Roller Derby vs. Minnesota Rollergirls. The vanquished teams would play each other for third place, and the day would culminate in the championship game.

The nonplaying (beer-drinking, smack-talking, sass-walking) Texas Rollergirls gathered together with signs, a cowbell, and our loud mouths to support the Texecutioners. We were joined by Rat City Rollergirls, sporting yellow roses to show their allegiance to their Texas sisters. Our collective energy was off the charts. I was nervous, excited, exhausted, and exhilarated all at once. Looking at the scores now, our tension level needn't have been as high as it was; the Texecutioners took a twenty-point lead in the first period of their semifinal, then extended it to a twenty-eight-point gap in the second. But I can assure you, we didn't take the win for granted. Ever. As we'd seen with Arizona's amazing comeback on Saturday, fortunes can change quickly on the Roller Derby track, and we gnawed our nails with every thrown elbow and step out of bounds. The final score was 114 to 81. Texas advanced to the championship.

The Tucson-Minnesota semifinal followed roughly the same pattern. Tucson took the lead—58 to 24—in the first period and dominated throughout the game. Final score: Tucson 136, Minnesota 75. That meant Minnesota would play Arizona Roller Derby Tent City Terrors for third place.

Over the course of the Arizona versus Minnesota game, I developed a devastating Rollergirl crush on Sheriff Shutyerpaio. For the second time during the Dust Devil, circumstances conspired to make her one of only two jammers for her team.

To give you some perspective on what that means . . . imagine the fitness magazine you read in the grocery store checkout line. In between a recipe for low-fat blueberry muffins and "Six Weeks to Beach-Ready Abs" is an article about interval training. It recommends that you add short bursts of high-intensity aerobics to your regular routine; "Try adding a few thirty-second bursts of jogging to your evening walk around the neighborhood."

Sheriff Shutyerpaio playing the jammer position in every other jam for an entire game is like you running at a full-out sprint for two minutes, then resting for two minutes, then sprinting for two minutes, and so on. Repeat continuously for almost an hour, and amp up the challenge by adding four other girls who want to kill you to the mix. How'd you like to do that as your workout tomorrow morning? Through it all, Sheriff Shutyerpaio never showed signs of physical or mental fatigue. She smiled. She encouraged her team. When she skated, she cut through the pack like a woman on a mission. Final score: Arizona Roller Derby 115, Minnesota Rollergirls 88. With that, Arizona Roller Derby secured their rank as the number three league in the nation.

★□

Loina McWhorter/lainamewhorterphotography.com

Helen Wheels #67

HOME TEAM: *Bruisers/Arizona Roller Derby*
TRAVEL TEAM: *Sheriff Shutyerpaio #67, Tent City Terrors/Arizona Roller Derby*
POSITIONS: *Jammer, Blocker, Pivot, The Law*
FAVORITE QUOTE: *"Move or BLEED!"*
LIKES: *skating anywhere, anytime; watermelon; bulldogs; traveling; meeting new/visiting cool derby girls; clean, freshly lubed bearings*
DISLIKES: *broke-down, bald wheels; mean-hearted people; trying to find good skating facilities*

Abandoned by her Native American tribe at a roller skating rink on the shores of Gitchigumi, this devilish diva's charm ensured her fate would not be gloomy. In a somber family tradition, the rink owners cemented Helen's place in their family by strapping a pair of skates on her feet, but her happy times came to an abrupt end when her true nature revealed itself. She tried to scalp unsuspecting session skaters! Cast out by her adopted family and townsfolk, wandering lost in the desert, wayward Helen was again taken in, this time by a team of nurses—the Bruisers—who gave her a true home . . . Arizona Roller Derby.

AWARDS: *2004–2005 Triple Threat (Best Jammer/Pivot/Blocker), 2004–2005 Best Endurance, 2004–2005 Most Dedicated (in attendance), 2004–2005 Best Fight, 2004–2005 Best Knock-down/Layout Block, 2004–2005 Best Bruiser Jammer, 2004–2005 Best Bruiser Pivot, 2003–2004 Best Rookie, 2003–2004 Best Knock-down/Layout Block (Helen Wheels nailed her opponent so hard, the victim peed herself).*

□★

It was time for the final showdown: the Texas Rollergirls versus the Tucson Saddletramps. We'd played them in a sort of warm-up game at Playland in December 2005, and the score had been Texas 81, Tucson 45. In that game, Tucson had come out swinging and taken an early lead, but our team tightened up its packs, focused on killer hits, and slowly pulled away to build an insurmountable lead.

The Dust Devil was a long weekend of emotional and physical exertion for our Texecutioners. They looked fit and menacing; I hoped they'd be able to sustain their energy. The only thing between Texas Rollergirls and a historic title was sixty minutes, ticked off two at a time.

I'd heard that the Texecutioners had been resting quite a bit (The Boss reportedly did bed checks each night), and none of them had drunk beers for at least two weeks (for Texans, that's like a kid giving up candy for Lent). I'd written out one of my all-nutrients-no-fun eating plans for them, and the rumor was that they followed it. (Bloody Mary's exact words to me were, "As soon as the last game is over I'm eating whatever I want, Melicious, and I'm drinking a damn beer.")

I stood on a bench to watch the action, surrounded by my nearest and dearest: Dave, Dirty Deeds, Electra Blu, Muffin Tumble, Belle Starr, Bloody Mary's husband, Brandon. We clutched hands. We clinked plastic beer cups. I'll be damned if I can remember any specific plays, but I have sense memories that flash like the colors in a kaleidoscope. Tinkerhell gave me a sly wink from the pivot line when I screamed her name in encouragement. Eight Track walloped a Saddletramp out of bounds and into the legs of the announcers' table. Barbarella, like a character from *The Matrix,* defied gravity as she bobbed and weaved and ducked, hugging the boundary line with one foot. Cat Tastrophe, true to her name, remained on her feet against all odds, the red ribbons on her uniform streaming behind her.

To the showboats, I offer a heartfelt thank-you for remembering that flaunting is as much a part of our sport as falling. When Lucille Brawl found herself stuck behind a Saddletramp, she pantomimed pinching the booty that blocked her, flirting with the crowd and riling them up. Although a gentlewoman's agreement was in place throughout the weekend—no fighting!—Bloody Mary took a flying leap at her real-life friend Sloppy Flo during what should have been the last jam of the game, and tackled her to the floor in a crowd-pleasing homage to the spirit of Ann Calvello.

The score stood at Texas 129, Tucson 96, with fourteen seconds remaining on the clock. What's a team to do when the clock must tick down? Big girl jam! Eight Track pulled the star cover over her helmet and for that fourteen seconds, she moved faster than I've seen before or since. The buzzer sounded. Pandemonium ensued. The Texas Rollergirls Texecutioners were the first Flat Track Champions.

★□

Michael R. Osborne

𝕭𝖑𝖔𝖔𝖉𝖞 𝕸𝖆𝖗𝖞 #4

HELL MARYS/TEXAS ROLLERGIRLS
AUSTIN TEXECUTIONERS, 2006 DUST DEVIL NATIONAL FLAT TRACK CHAMPIONS

POSITIONS: *Jammer, Blocker, Zealot*
BLOOD TYPE: *AB+*
FULL NAME: *Mary Grace Margaret Catherine O'Brien*
WHAT MAKES HER BLOOD BOIL: *Hail Marys, cheap vodka, anything pink*

Until she met the Hell Marys, this Mary was a blue-blooded prep school princess, with little to worry about in life except where Daddy would hemorrhage money next. After an incident with Father Florencio and the communion wine at mass one Sunday, Sister Helen Fury recommended a transfer to Our Lady of Perpetual Forgiveness so that Mary might receive greater spiritual guidance. The Hell Marys didn't take an immediate liking to her, and bloodshed inevitably ensued when Mary rolled up in her birthday present—a brandnew red Alfa Romeo. But the girls found themselves in detention together and the bad blood was quickly resolved. Now Mary would move heaven and earth for any one of her Hell Marys sisters.

AWARDS: *2005 Texas Rollergirls MVP, 2005 Hell Marys MVP, 2005 Hell Marys Best Jammer, 2005 Statisticians' Award for Most Penalties*

□★

If you ask them now, many of the Texecutioners deny shedding tears at the awards ceremony. But Rollergirls lie. My favorite photo of them is a group shot, with each of them doing exactly what they *would* do in that situation. Eight Track is crying, her hand pressed to her face in a futile attempt to stop the tears. Rice Rocket, Jen Entonic, and Cat Tastrophe (voted Texas Rollergirls 2005 Camera Hog), stand together, smiling directly into the camera, pride and contentment on their faces. Lucille Brawl's head is thrown back in laughter and next to her, Slim Kickins, Loose Tooth Lulu, Barbarella, and Derringer have their arms raised overhead in victory. Off to the side and in the back, Hydra, Buckshot Betsy, Sparkle Plenty, and Bloody Mary look thoughtful and, maybe, tired.

Ziv Kruger 2006 Dust Devil TucsonRollerDerby.com

"I don't think I had ever been so tired as I was at midnight on day one, waiting to hear if we'd gotten top seed. I remember lying on the locker room floor between games trying to gain some energy. Those tears I cried during the award ceremony were not just from happiness and pride, they were from fatigue and pain, too."

—CAT TASTROPHE, TEXAS ROLLERGIRLS TEXECUTIONERS

When each member of the team had been awarded a personal Dust Devil trophy, Kim Sin took the microphone to announce the MVP of the game: the jammer exterminator, Eight Track. It was a proud moment, not just for our monster blocker, but for our sport. The recognition of a defensive player as MVP was a major roll forward for the game, an acknowledgment that, just as football players would forever be sacked without their Big D, our fast-dodging jammers would run into walls without their blockers.

★□

Eight Track #8

2005–2006 HOTROD HONEYS/TEXAS ROLLERGIRLS

2002–2004 HUSTLERS/TEXAS ROLLERGIRLS

AUSTIN TEXECUTIONERS, 2006 DUST DEVIL NATIONAL FLAT TRACK CHAMPIONS

POSITIONS: *Blocker, Pivot, Jammer Killer*

FAVORITE QUOTE: *"Hey, Eight Track! Do you think you could put Buckshot Betsy right into my lap tonight?"—Texas Rollergirls fan*

EIGHT TRACK FACTOID: *After her retirement at the end of the 2006 season, Eight Track hung up her skates to attend a college of mortuary science.*

Born in Plano, Texas, this nomadic navy brat was known for skating through base housing, smashing mailboxes and headlights with a hockey stick. As punishment, she was banished to live with her kin in rural Arkansas (where Bibles were thumpin', cousins was humpin', and banjos could be heard in the distance). She escaped to Austin to exercise her expertise in inflicting pain, but finding trouble in a peace-loving town like Austin ain't easy. She partied with the Hustlers for a while, but this rabble-rouser wasn't meant to be settled. So she headed for the wrong side of the tracks and joined a gang of punk-rocking, switchblade-flipping skater babes: the Hotrod Honeys.

AWARDS: *2006 MVP, Dust Devil National Flat Track Derby Championship, 2005 Texas Rollergirls Best Blocker, 2005 Texas Rollergirls Most Feared, 2005 Statisticians' Award for Best Blocker, 2005 Hotrod Honeys Best Blocker, 2004 Hustlers Best Blocker, 2003 Texas Rollergirls Best Blocker, 2003 Hustlers Best Blocker*

Rivals: *Buckshot Betsy & Sparkle Plenty, Honky Tonk Heartbreakers/Texas Rollergirls; Sheriff Shutyerpaio/Helen Wheels, Tent City Terrors/Arizona Roller Derby; Doe Holliday, Tucson Saddletramps/Tucson Roller Derby*

□★

After the championship bout, hedonism reigned at the Club Congress, the nightclub and bar tucked into the lobby of the Tucson hotel where all the Rollergirls had taken up residence. Scores of skaters, blowing off steam after the stress of three days of concentrated play, were ready to bare skin and truths to all onlookers. The hotel lobby looked like a *Where's Waldo?* of Rollergirls, a blur of color and motion and unadulterated acting out. Girls sang and danced, pretended to throw punches, vamped for photos, did tequila shots, and hugged and kissed each other and not-so-innocent bystanders.

There's a Rollergirl code of ethics that dictates no tales of afterparties be told, and I won't break that code here (especially because I would, in the course of telling tales, incriminate myself). But suffice it to say, Rollergirls know how to celebrate and we did . . . all night long.

During the Dust Devil tournament, all eyes were on the track. But what was going on around the competition was equally as impressive. The Dust Devil was the brainstorm of Kim Sin, founder of Tucson Roller Derby; the tournament was her last hoorah before retiring from the league. The planning and execution were lead by Sloppy Flo, Tucson's 2005 MVP and her team's top jammer in the Dust Devil Championship bout (47 points in fifteen jams).

"It was really humbling to go to Tucson to represent Texas Rollergirls, and to see that Flat Track Roller Derby is so much bigger than Texas now. It's taken on a life of its own, and the sport will continue long after I retire from it."

—DERRINGER, TEXAS ROLLERGIRLS TEXECUTIONERS

In support of Sloppy Flo, league members, friends, and family of the Tucson Roller Derby did everything to make the Dust Devil a reality: securing a venue and registering the twenty teams, scheduling the games and planning social activities for visiting skaters, marketing the event and managing the sold-out crowds, booking bands for the championship game and ensuring the snack bar staff never ran out of beer.

From across the country, other leagues pitched in to make sure the Dust Devil had all the community spirit the occasion required. The announcers' table was a Who's Who of show-offs and loudmouths—including our own Texas Rollergirls crew—with play-by-play and color commentators from various leagues trading turns on the mic to call the action. On the track, referees from Tucson and Seattle and other derby towns rubbed elbows with Quicksilver from Austin to keep the unruly Rollergirls in line. The skaters were the stars of the show, but the Flat Track Derby community—rallied by the hostess with the mostess, Tucson Roller Derby—helped throw the world's first Flat Track Derby tournament.

The crew lived and died by the clock, and over the course of almost twenty hours of Roller Derby games, they stayed (mostly) on schedule.

Then they did something even more amazing.

When the ledgers were closed and the money had been counted, the girls of the Tucson Roller Derby returned the entry fees they'd received from the competitors. Then those girls—second in the nation, first in our hearts—took 10 percent of the net profits from the Dust Devil, divided by nineteen (excluding themselves because they hadn't needed to travel to compete in the tournament), and sent a check to every participating league.

By the skaters, for the skaters.

RESOURCES

WOMEN'S FLAT TRACK DERBY ASSOCIATION FOUNDING MEMBERS

Women's Flat Track Derby Association
www.wftda.org

Alamo City Rollergirls—San Antonio, Texas
www.alamocityrollergirls.com

Arizona Roller Derby—Phoenix, Arizona
www.azrollerderby.com

Assassination City Roller Derby—Dallas, Texas
www.assassinationcityderby.com

Atlanta Rollergirls—Atlanta, Georgia
www.atlantarollergirls.com

B.A.D. Girls—Bay Area, California
www.bayareaderbygirls.com

Big Easy Rollergirls—New Orleans, Louisiana
www.bigeasyrollergirls.com

Boston Derby Dames—Boston, Massachusetts
www.bostonderbydames.com

Carolina Rollergirls—Raleigh, North Carolina
www.carolinarollergirls.com

Dallas Derby Devils—Dallas, Texas
www.dallasderbydevils.com

Detroit Derby Girls—Detroit, Michigan
www.detroitrollerderby.com

Dixie Derby Girls—Huntsville, Alabama
www.dixiederbygirls.com

Duke City Derby—Albuquerque, New Mexico
www.dukecityderby.com

East Texas Bombers—Tyler, Texas
www.myspace.com/easttexasbombers

Gotham Girls Roller Derby—New York, New York
www.gothamgirlsrollerderby.com

Grand Raggidy Roller Girls—Grand Rapids, Michigan
www.gr-rollergirls.com

Houston Roller Derby—Houston, Texas
www.houstonrollerderby.com

Kansas City Roller Warriors—Kansas City, Missouri
www.kcrollerwarriors.com

Mad Rollin' Dolls—Madison, Wisconsin
www.madrollindolls.com

Minnesota Rollergirls—Minneapolis, Minnesota
www.mnrollergirls.com

Ohio Rollergirls—Columbus, Ohio
www.ohiorollergirls.com

Philly Rollergirls—Philadelphia, Pennsylvania
www.phillyrollergirls.com

Pikes Peak Derby Dames—Colorado Springs, Colorado
www.pikespeakderbydames.com

Providence Roller Derby—Providence, Rhode Island
www.providencerollerderby.com

Rat City Rollergirls—Seattle, Washington
www.ratcityrollergirls.com

Rocky Mountain Rollergirls—Denver, Colorado
www.rockymountainrollergirls.com

Rose City Rollers—Portland, Oregon
www.rosecityrollers.com

Sin City Rollergirls—Las Vegas, Nevada
www.sincityrollergirls.com

Texas Rollergirls—Austin, Texas
www.txrollergirls.com

Tucson Roller Derby—Tucson, Arizona
www.tucsonrollerderby.com

Windy City Rollers—Chicago, Illinois
www.windycityrollers.com

ROLLER SKATING & ROLLER DERBY SITES

How Stuff Works/Roller Derby
www.entertainment.howstuffworks.com/roller-derby.htm
A how-to for our sport, featuring the Atlanta Rollergirls.

National Museum of Roller Skating
www.rollerskatingmuseum.com
Official site for the museum in Lincoln, Nebraska.

RollerGirls—www.groups.yahoo.com/group/roller_girls
A Yahoo! group for skaters, rookies, widowers, and other Flat Track Derby
fans; includes a link to the Rollergirl Name Registry.

Skate Log—www.skatelog.com
Articles and news about quad and inline skating.

U.S. Rollergirls—www.usrollergirls.com
A comprehensive site of all Roller Derby leagues around the world, including team info and message boards.

Wayne's Derby World—www.waynesderbyworld.blogspot.com
A frequently updated blog from a committed Roller Derby fan.

Wikipedia/Roller Derby—www.en.wikipedia.org/wiki/roller_derby
A detailed look at the sport, including an ever-growing list of start-up and
established Flat Track leagues.

GEAR

Tell 'em Melicious sent you!

Pads

Pro Designed
www.prodesigned.com
Custom pads made by Wild Bill. Personal service, awesome pads, reasonable prices.

Skates

Sin City Skates
www.sincityskates.com
Owned by Ivanna S. Pankin and Trish the Dish of Sin City Rollergirls. Excellent personal service and fair prices.

Skate Mall
www.skatemall.com

Low Price Skates
www.lowpriceskates.com

ACKNOWLEDGMENTS

To the photographers who generously granted me permission to use their photos, thank you for making Rollergirls look so good while being so bad: Rob Butler (RJB PHOTO), Maraya Chasney (www.c-hphoto.com), Celesta Danger, Rebecca Davis (www.rebeccadavis photography.com), Liam Frederick, Felicia Graham, Amy Halligan, Michael Harmon, Timothy Hughes (www.timothyhughes.com), Ziv Kruger (soundcouncil@yahoo.com), Marc Majcher, Laina McWhorter (www.lainamcwhorterphotography.com), Michael Osborne, Deborah Shelton (www.photoplasm.com), and Larry Stern. Also, my deep gratitude to Beau Been and Scarlot Harlot for their rapid response to my photography-related distress calls.

I'd like to acknowledge the writers who captured Rollergirls' exploits in words so engaging I wished I'd written them myself: Ken Coppage, author of *From Roller Derby to Rollerjam;* Jason Socha, blogger for LeadJammer.com. To Chris Gray (friend to the Texas Rollergirls and my Social D liaison) and the kind folks at the *Austin Chronicle,* and to Jack Broom of *The Seattle Times,* thank you for allowing me to reprint your words.

Kisses and slugs to all of the Texas Rollergirls and their widowers for your support and enthusiasm in sharing your tales from the track with me. To my badass Hotrod Honeys, I'm so proud to wear the black and pink. Faster, faster! Kill! Kill! Kill!

A special thank-you to Derringer, Hydra, Lucille Brawl, Kitty Kitty Bang Bang, Bettie Rage, Vendetta Von Dutch, and The Wrench for reliving Texas Rollergirls history with me; to Buckshot Betsy, Dagger Deb, Punk Rock Phil, Sparkle Plenty, and Trouble for your Honky Tonk Heartbreakers anecdotes; to Julio E. Glasses, Jim "Kool-Aid" Jones, Whiskey L'Amour, Chip Queso, and Hot Wheels for the skinny on your announcer family; to Helen Wheels for your friendly, timely responses to my many questions about the Arizona Roller Derby; to Kim Sin for your unrelenting confidence in me and for sharing details of Tucson Roller Derby's early days; and to Crackerjack, Princess Anna Conda, Head Trauma, Ivanna S. Pankin, and Militia for telling me the stories of your rookie derby days.

To the Texas Rollergirls Vegas travel team, I knew you could do it! Congratulations on your win in Sin City—thank you for supporting your MIA teammate and letting me keep the jacket.

Women of WFTDA and rookies everywhere: my helmet is off to you. Thank you for the daily inspiration to be the best Rollergirl I can be.

To the Texas Rollergirls support crew, sponsors, and Playland staff, my gratitude for helping us entertain our hometown with Rock 'n' Rollerderby.

A big kiss of thanks to all of the women and men who armed me with the photos and Roller Derby personal "bios" for your trading cards; and to Costa, Roller Derby's number one fan, for loving our sport as much as we do. To all the Rollergirls across the U.S. of A. who answered my call for info and gave me a peek into your lives, thank you for having faith in a roller sister you've never met.

Dirty Deeds, thank you for daydreaming and plotting with me; I'll take that latte whenever you're ready to join me for our big adventure. Bloody Mary and Brandon, your excitement and support boosted my confidence. Crazy Duke, your myspace.com love notes kept me going; thank you. My beloved DeadMotleySexMaidens—Peter Elliott, Chepo Pena, Adam Tyner, and Lisa Wickware—I raise an ice-cold beer in gratitude to you; y'all rock my world.

Love and bruises to Meredith Hays, the world's greatest agent, for kicking my ass and encouraging me to live up to my Rollergirl ideals. You're the tops, Merry Death. To Judith Ehrlich, Amanda Patten, Betsy Haglage, and Lauren Spiegel, thank you for your help and guidance.

To my pals in the trenches—Tim, Carl, Stacey, and Cyndie—and to sweet Charlotte, thanks for making me feel like a superstar. To Rich, Alex, Cheryl, and Peter, thank you for your kind words, for reading rough drafts, and for making me laugh when I could have cried. To Dick Ferrante, I miss our walks by the Bay and conversations about books; thank you for being my storytelling muse.

Thank you to Diane Sawyer and the *Good Morning America* cast and crew for your willingness to give Roller Derby a try; and to Bob Dotson and Laurie Singer of NBC's *Today* show for putting me at ease and making me feel like a celebrity.

To my favorite tough guy, Mike Ness, thanks for providing the soundtrack for my life.

Mom and Dad, I love you. The words "thank you" are too small to convey the depth of my gratitude for your unconditional love and generosity.

Most especially, I need to thank Dave for being D the B, for holding my hand from one crazy adventure to another, and for believing—even when I don't—that I can do anything my heart desires.